BEYOND THEIR SEX

Learned Women of the European Past

BEYOND THEIR SEX

Learned Women of the European Past

Edited by
Patricia H. Labalme

New York University Press
New York *and* London
1984

First paperbound edition 1984

Copyright © 1980 by New York University

Library of Congress Cataloging in Publication Data
Main entry under title:

Beyond their sex

Includes bibliographical references and index.
1. Women—Europe—History. 2. Education of women—
Europe—History. 3. Europe—Intellectual life. I.
Labalme, Patricia H.
HQ1148.B49   305.4'094   79-56638
ISBN 0-8147-4998-4
ISBN 0-8147-5007-4 pbk.

Manufactured in the United States of America

Contents

Contents

List of Illustrations

PLATE 1. A vision of Hildegard of Bingen.

PLATE 2. Christine de Pisan writing her manuscript.

A LA ILLVSTRISS·ETEX
ᴄEL⁝M·M⁝LEONⓇAⅮRᴬ
GONᴬⱤ·DVⅆⅅ·FERRᴬ⁝DL
MOⅅ⁝DReGERE⁝ELⱤE
GⱤE⁝ANT⁝ⓒRⱤZANᵒ⸴

Plate 3. Eleonora of Aragon, Duchess of Ferrara.

PLATE 4. Eleonora of Aragon's personal staff.

Studious She is and all. Alone,
Most visitants, when She has none,
Her Library on which She looks
It is her Head her Thoughts her Books.
Scorninge dead Ashes without fire
For her owne Flames doe her Inspire.

PLATE 5. Margaret Lucas, Duchess of Newcastle at her desk.

PLATE 6. Elena Lucrezia Cornaro Piscopia with symbols of literature and science. The identification reads: "Elena Cornaro Piscopia Dottorata publicamente nello studio di Padova" and the legend is: "Alli allori d'Euganea unica fosti" (among the laurels of Padua, you were unique).

Après avoir acquis le Secret et la Gloire
De rendre utiles des Romans,
Elle va semer d'agremens
Les grandes veritez que renferme l'Histoire.

PLATE 7. Marguerite de Lussan, writer of novels and popular
histories.

PLATE 8. Catharine Sawbridge Macaulay as Clio.

A. L. G. NECKER

BARONNE DE STAËL HOLSTEIN

PLATE 9. Madame de Staël.

List of Contributors

ROLAND H. BAINTON, Titus Street Professor Emeritus of Ecclesiastical History at Yale University, author of three volumes entitled *Women of the Reformation* and other works on the Reformation period.

NATALIE ZEMON DAVIS, Professor of History at Princeton University, author of *Society and Culture in Early Modern France* and other works on sixteenth-century European society.

JOAN M. FERRANTE, Professor of Comparative Literature at Columbia University, author of *Woman as Image in Medieval Literature* and other works on Dante and Medieval poetry.

WERNER L. GUNDERSHEIMER, Professor and former Chairman of the Department of History at the University of Pennsylvania, author of *Ferrara: The Style of a Renaissance Despotism* and other works on Italy and France in the Renaissance.

MARGARET L. KING, Associate Professor of History at Brooklyn College, City University of New York, author of "Caldiera and the Barbaros on Marriage and the Family" in *The Journal of Medieval and Renaissance Studies* and other articles in the two fields of women humanists and Venetian humanism in the early Renaissance.

PAUL OSKAR KRISTELLER, F.J.E. Woodbridge Professor Emeritus of Philosophy at Columbia University, author of *Studies in Renaissance Thought and Letters* and numerous other works on Renaissance philosophy and humanism.

PATRICIA H. LABALME, Lecturer in the General Studies Program at New York University, has taught history at Wellesley, Barnard, and Hunter Colleges and is the author of *Bernardo Giustiniani: a Venetian of the Quattrocento* as well as articles on Venetian society and culture in the Renaissance period.

CHAPTER 1

Introduction

Patricia H. Labalme

The seven essays in this collection were inspired by tercentenary celebrations for the first doctorate in philosophy awarded to a woman in 1678, the Venetian Elena Cornaro. Most were originally delivered as papers in commemorative conferences held at Swarthmore and Vassar Colleges, two of over one hundred similar meetings in the United States and abroad. It was clear from such observances that the day of the learned woman had finally, if tardily, arrived. For of the learned women discussed in this volume, very few besides Elena Cornaro earned such academic recognition. Yet all were acknowledged as gifted intellectually and trained far beyond the usual vocational skills of their sex; all were recognized as poets, scholars, historians, administrators, or discriminating patronesses. In some cases, these learned women were venerated; in others, reviled for their intellectual achievement. Unusually endowed, they led uncommon lives that nevertheless yield, in juxtaposition, connecting themes and a common contour.

How might a woman acquire her education? Joan Ferrante describes the primary routes: tutoring at home; schooling in convents; and occasionally, participation along with boys in a local school,

1

although the church tended to frown on such commingling. Primary education was easier to secure than higher education where, it was feared, a male teacher might threaten the chastity of a female student. The tale of Abelard and Heloise was cautionary. Their love affair, her child, their secret marriage, his castration at the instigation of her vengeful uncle, and their retirement to separate monastic existences amply illustrated the dangers and possible consequences of such a pedagogical relationship. Not only was the instructor a threat, but the content of instruction, that classical literature upon which all education was based, contained tales of illicit love, explicit sexual description, and bawdy humor. Accordingly, it was long considered a potentially corruptive force. Nonetheless, some women were educated, and many, from noble families, to an advanced level.

For a highly educated woman, her family's position and purposefulness were decisive. Indeed, all the women discussed in this book came from courtly or urban upper classes, and only their elevated status and particular environment made possible the cultivation of their talents. In every case, the family was responsible. Many of the learned women of the past were instructed directly by their learned fathers. Among these were Christine de Pisan in the fourteenth century and Catharine Sawbridge Macaulay in the eighteenth century, discussed by Natalie Davis, and several ladies of the fifteenth-century Italian Renaissance who appear in Margaret King's essay, Alessandra Scala, Laura Cereta, and Caterina Caldiera; all benefited from paternal pedagogues. Sometimes this educated daughter replaced a missing son, as did the medieval fictional heroines discussed by Joan Ferrante, Melior and la Pucele, whose fathers considered these daughters their only heirs. Occasionally, a family itself had a tradition for learning that it urged upon its female members. Margaret King finds this true of the Veronese Nogarola family who specialized in learned women, and Werner Gundersheimer identified elements of this tradition among the Este women of Ferrara. Women within a family might influence one another; professional teachers, however, were all male. A woman might learn, but outside the convent she could not teach. The prohibition was St. Paul's: "a woman must be a learner, listening quietly and with due submission. I do not permit a woman to be a teacher, nor must a woman domineer over a man; she should be quiet" (1 Tim. 2:11-13).

That is why, when universities developed as corporations licensing the professions and teaching, women were naturally excluded from them. For centuries they were barred from university degrees in the arts or philosophy, in law, medicine, and most of all theology. Paul Kristeller describes one woman, Alessandra Scala, who may have attended university lectures and discusses two possibly mythical ladies who lectured in law and medicine (Novella at the University of Bologna and Trotula at the University of Salerno). More verifiable were a number of fourteenth-century women who received royal licenses to treat specified diseases but knew no Latin and therefore had no university education. A few of these even gave public lectures, but only one woman practitioner of the fifteenth century, Costanza Calenda, appears to have been fully qualified by a medical degree. Elena Cornaro's degree was in philosophy, and not until the eighteenth century did other women achieve doctoral degrees and, at Bologna, teaching chairs. (Not until the twentieth century was there a female doctor of theology.) Such illustrious exceptions, as Paul Kristeller writes, "confirm the rule that women were excluded from university studies and degrees, and from the careers of university teaching and of the academic professions." It came to be an educational world quite different from the less academically structured one of the twelfth century, where brilliant women were enthusiastically received. The world of the university was beyond the reach of women.

There was a world, however, always within the reach of women, the world of eternal truth. Piety might be a highroad to religious wisdom. Damaris followed Paul down from the Acropolis; Marcella and Laeta corresponded with St. Jerome; a voice from heaven, it was claimed, taught Hildegard of Bingen. All Christian piety in women was commendable. It could take the form of meditations, of spiritual poetry, of a mysticism such as Roland Bainton perceives in the *Prisons* of Marguerite de Navarre who was "rapt into a realm where learning itself may be relegated to the realm of vanity." It might produce visions as scientifically complex as Hildegard of Bingen's, or pungent letters of practical advice from that same lady to a wide religious audience in the twelfth century. It might exercise itself in translations, and there were numerous female translators of pious works in the Renaissance and the Reformation. Devotional concerns knew no class, and many a woman from the lower echelons was learned in her Bible, knowing much of it by heart. Spiritual biography and autobiography, conventual and ecclesiastical history attracted many of the first women historians, and Natalie Davis traces their careers in her essay on women as practitioners of the historical genre. Some women such as Catherine of Siena, whose only profession was piety, took active political roles. Some who had inherited political roles, such as Eleonora of Aragon, Marguerite de Navarre, and Elizabeth of England, found in religion a framework, as Werner Gundersheimer puts it, for the creative exercise of their talents. Queen Elizabeth's *Devotions* is a collection of her own prayers in English, Latin, Greek, Italian, and French. The learned Venetian Elena Cornaro had among her chief literary efforts a translation from Spanish into Italian of a sixteenth-century devotional text and a collection of poems, her own and others, lauding a popular Lenten preacher. Religious endeavor both encouraged and limited the literary productivity of learned women. But none wrote on theology: that is for the Doctors, said St. Teresa.

Chastity was another form of spiritual expression, and many learned ladies, including Elena Cornaro, practiced it in defiance of the more worldly ambitions of their families. Chastity was a defense against the encumbrances of marriage. It offered psychic freedom. It served as a barrier against the cruel criticism often leveled at learned women. Isotta Nogarola was accused of incest and promiscuity. An eloquent woman was reputedly unchaste; a learned lady threatened male pride. The book-lined cell of Margaret King's title symbolized the retreat, at some cost, of many learned women from a hostile world.

For women who were learned had gone beyond the expectations for their sex. These expectations were, in the Italian idiom, *maritar o monacar,* marriage or the convent. Advanced learning was necessary for neither. Intellectual activity, that highest human function, was not appropriate for women. The Aristotelian notion of a woman as a defective man lingered on, reinforced by Thomistic theology in which woman's finality (unlike man's) was her sexuality, her bodily generative function. As late as the seventeenth century, a woman's natural humors—cold and moist—were considered un-propitious for cerebral activity. A woman who excelled intellec-tually disregarded the boundaries of her sex and mental powers, as Cassandra Fedele put it. She became an intellectual transvestite. Christine de Pisan, one of the earliest women to write an historical work, was praised as a "virilis femina" and said of herself, "now I am truly a man." Such a transformation was prescriptive for any woman of intellectual ambition. She must set aside her woman-hood, with its assumed weaknesses, its vanities, its narrow concerns. She must embrace a sexual ambiguity. She must become, like the classical *virago* in a new form, an armed maiden, an Amazon of the mind, and although she might deny every aggressive intention, she was often viewed with scorn and alarm.

That alarm had some justification. Many learned women es-chewed marriage, with its burdens of childbearing and household management. This was to defy normality, to interrupt, horizontally, that system of marital and dynastic connection so crucial to the power structure of past societies, and vertically, the continuity of the clan. The value assigned such family continuity is nowhere better illustrated than in the popular celebrations that greeted the first male heir born to Eleonora of Aragon, duchess of Ferrara. Eleonora was so highly placed that she could both fulfill her marital and dynastic obligations and encourage learning at the court of Ferrara. But she, personally, was no scholar. More typical was the choice Alessandra Scala proposed to Cassandra Fedele: "Shall I marry, or devote my life to study?" Both married, and both gave up their studies. Even where a woman intended to continue her work, society might not condone it. Catharine Sawbridge Macaulay's rep-utation as a recognized historian was so precarious that her second marriage to a man half her age "totally extinguished all curiosity about her opinions."

Learned men hate learned women, wrote Madame de Staël. Un-learned women had no use for those of their sex who had separated themselves from the female world and female nature. "The donkeys tear me with their teeth," said one Renaissance woman, "the oxen stab me with their horns." Elena Cornaro was accused of folly; Margaret Lucas (a seventeenth-century woman of letters) was dubbed "Mad Madge." The figure of the sorceress, so often associated in medieval literature with a brilliant heroine, is still adumbrated in later accusations of mental instability. The attribution of magic powers, as Joan Ferrante suggests, could rationalize the vulnerability men felt, and if not magic or madness, then malice was charged. Literature written by women was considered plagiarized. Opponents of Christine de Pisan claimed that clerks had forged her work.

As best they could, learned women defended themselves from such attacks. They participated in the literature of the "Querelle des Femmes." They wrote treatises that defined Adam's culpability as greater than Eve's. They lashed out against what one Venetian nun called the "paternal tyranny" that placed unwilling daughters in convents. They insisted, as did a late-sixteenth-century poetess, that better education would make women as esteemed as men. Some even asserted the superiority of their sex, joining in this campaign certain male writers, the earliest of whom appears in Eleonora of Aragon's entourage. But these male defenders were more interested in the literary battle than in any reconstruction of society, and there were too few learned women to form an effectively defensive brigade. They were too often isolated from one another. They lacked a mutual society and made no concerted effort. Their briefs went largely unheard, their programs unheeded.

What difference, then, did learning make in these women's lives? To start with, they were a special group. Born into families of elevated status, they were often recognized early in their lives as precocious, if not prodigious. Encouraged, tutored, trained to perform like circus ponies, they were treasured and often exploited— for social or political purposes—by their ambitious male promoters. At some point in their young adult lives, most had to opt for marriage, which might end scholarly pursuits, or for the isolation of a convent or domestic book-lined cell. Some, such as Margaret Peutinger, managed both careers. Most were like Ginevra Nogarola, who gave up her studies when she gave up her "manus immaculata," that immaculate hand with which she had copied ancient texts. Those who continued their intellectual pursuits often produced meager results. Others were more prolific, but apologetic. Margaret Lucas, writing biography, chose a modest and "particular history . . . the most secure, because it goes not out of its own circle, but turns on its axis, and for the most part keeps within the circumference of truth." Catharine Sawbridge Macaulay trusted that her "candor and industry" would offset "the defects of a female historian." Their confidence was so fragile, and that frailty often found somatic expression in chronic illness. Elena Cornaro nearly fainted when she had to speak in public, and she died relatively young and suitably consumptive.

Yet within the restraints imposed by their societies, and in spite of self-doubt and sometimes illness, learned women possessed privileges, power, and certain freedoms. Hildegard of Bingen ran an abbey and vigorously corresponded with popes, emperors, and kings. Eleonora of Aragon administered, and ably, a duchy. Margaret Peutinger could correct Erasmus on a biblical text. Elena Cornaro could at once free herself from the constraints and artificialities of female luxury and accept academic accolades. Surely all these women, like Marie de France, especially those who lacked a public forum, could experience within themselves the liberating function of their imaginations, could enjoy the exercise of their remarkable minds. "Great things by reason of my sexe, I may not doe," wrote Anne Locke; but she also knew "that which I may, I ought to doe," and so with a sense of personal fulfillment, she translated a text of Calvin's from the French. Aware of the problem posed by their unusual capacities, most learned women did what they could do.

The essays that follow range in tone from a passionate identification of thwarted ambitions to a cheerful survey of feminine achievements. They are the work of four women and three men. Joan Ferrante opens with a consideration of the education of women in the Middle Ages and proceeds to examine the experience of three women in particular: Heloise, Hildegard of Bingen, and Marie de France. Werner Gundersheimer then portrays a learned woman as public figure and patroness: Eleonora of Aragon, whose court yielded one of the earliest feminist treatises. Less prominent politically but reflecting many of the experiences of their medieval predecessors are some learned women of the Italian Renaissance, participants in the fairly new humanist movement, discussed by Margaret King. The role of women in humanism is then examined more broadly by Paul Kristeller, who relates that role to others

played by learned women within and beyond the university. Involved in the world of action as well as that of learning are the
women Roland Bainton considers, deeply engaged, alone or alongside their husbands, in the Reformation. My essay focusses on a
particular society through an intimate exploration of the life of
Elena Cornaro, whose academic success occasioned comment in
her own day as again in our own. Finally, in contrast to Elena
Cornaro, who would have preferred solitude to the publicity her
father imposed upon her, several women historians of the early
modern world, discussed by Natalie Davis, forged from their domestic experience histories that showed them eager and worthy to
join the public fray of literary and historical debate.

   Broad as these essays are in mood, time, and place, varied as is
their focus, they deal, perforce, with a limited group of women,
selected by the interests and predilections of the contributing
scholars. Not included are learned women of Eastern Europe such
as Anna Comnena or learned women artists or many others born
later, earlier, or outside the boundaries chosen by the individual
contributors. Those included serve as examples of the potentialities
and problems of learned women in past centuries. They have been
analyzed on the bases of their lives and their works, but not treated
as psychological cases, nor as pitiable misfits. Articulate as they
were, they were also in most cases discreet about their feelings and
frustrations. Few deplored their limitations or struck a feminist
stance. Their situations may appear ambiguous; mutatis mutandis,
so is the situation of many a learned woman today. If we perceive
that they were forced into pretersexuality by narrow views of womanhood; if, in their extraordinary lives, we discover contradictions,
they nevertheless bravely lived out those contradictions and were
more often than not hailed as heroines for that accomplishment.
Let us accord them no less respect.

CHAPTER 2

The Education of Women in the Middle Ages in Theory, Fact, and Fantasy

Joan M. Ferrante

There is no question that many women of the nobility were educated during the Middle Ages,. some to a high degree. We have records of them in the correspondence of famous men, in historical accounts of contemporary chronicles, and in fictional portraits of contemporary romance, as well as in their own writings. What we do not have is a comprehensive study of the education available to women; [1] we must piece together allusions in letters and lives and romances with passages from monastic rules, and supplement them with the writings of the women whose work is extant, in order to deduce what they must have been taught and where.

Like boys, most girls acquired their education in monastic schools, but some were tutored at home, particularly in royal courts: Charlemagne, who took great interest in education, had his daughters taught along with his sons. "He proposed that his children should be instructed so that the daughters as well as the sons would be educated first in the liberal studies, which he himself had taken pains over," [2] and Alcuin was their teacher. Charlemagne's sister Gisela and his daughter Rectruda later corresponded with Alcuin about the joys of reading holy works, and he sent them his commentary on the Gospel of John, the most difficult of the Gospels, as he notes, with compliments to their learning: "Most noble in the holiness of the Christian religion and most devout in the zeal for wisdom . . . I praise you for the highest devotion in that most holy desire for learning."[3] There are indications in the earliest vernacular romances that princesses and other aristocrats were often tutored at court by the resident chaplain. By the twelfth century, it was also possible, if not usual, for others to be tutored at home; Heloise, the niece of a canon, was taught in her uncle's home by one of the most famous teachers of the time, Abelard.

In many instances, a woman's education did not go beyond reading the Psalter and signing her name, but even at that it was more than most laymen could do.[4] Throughout the Middle Ages, there are examples of laywomen who were highly educated in relation to their societies and to their families. Among the Christianized Germanic peoples in the early Middle Ages, the women of royal families were usually better educated than the men. In some cases, education was apparently considered effeminate. When Theodoric's daughter, Amalaswintha, whose intellectual accomplishments were praised by Cassiodorus, attempted to have her son educated, his people, the East Goths, objected because letters inhibited manliness.[5]

But learned men appreciated the achievements of educated (and powerful) women: Adalperga, daughter of the last Lombard king, Desiderius (eighth century), was commended for her wisdom and learning by Paulus Diaconus, who wrote his Roman History for her because she had objected to one he had sent her by Eutropius.[6] The Carolingian empress Judith was praised by Walafrid Strabo and Ermoldus Nigellus, and Rabanus Maurus wrote a commentary on Judith and Esther for her.[7] Irmintrude, the wife of Charles the Bald, spent her time praying or reading books, according to John Scotus Eriugena.[8] Adela, the daughter of William the Conqueror, was celebrated as a woman of culture, her ability to read attested to by Hildebert of Lavardin, her delight in Books by Baudri of Dol; Hugh of Fleury, who dedicated his ecclesiastical history to her rather than to illiterate princes, calls her "learned in letters" (litteris erudita).[9] In a letter to Alix of Chartres, daughter of Eleanor of Aquitaine, Adam de Perseigne remarks how pleased he is to be able to write to her in Latin; [10] whether her sister, Marie de Champagne, "one of the outstanding literary patrons of her day," could read Latin is not certain, but the name of her tutor, Alix de Mareuil, is recorded in a charter.[11]

Various anecdotes in lives and chronicles attest to the learning of still other royal women: the well-known story of Aelfred's mother offering a book she could read as an inducement to her children to learn to read, which Aelfred won by secretly memorizing the text, is related in Asser's *De rebus gestis Aelfredi*.[12] Ekkehard, in the *Casus Sancti Galli*, tells of Empress Adelheid, wife of Otto I, finding her son laughing over a book; when she asked why, he gave her the book to read herself because, Ekkehard explains, she was "exceedingly literate" *(litteratissima)*.[13] Hedwig, niece of Otto I, is said to have passed her days after the death of her husband reading Latin poets with Ekkehard II of Saint Gall.[14] The biographer of St. Margaret, wife of Malcolm III of Scotland, says that she discussed even the most subtle questions with the learned men of her circle and that her husband fondled her books because they were so dear to her, even though he could not read them.[15]

These women were educated either at home or in convents. Some public or nonmonastic schools existed, but we have only scattered information about them. We know of them partly because they were forbidden from time to time. A bishop of Soissons in the ninth century prohibits parish priests' teaching boys and girls together in their schools,[16] and a fourteenth-century French ordinance proscribes masters or mistresses taking students of the opposite sex.[17] From these prohibitions, one assumes both that it was acceptable for girls to attend school outside convents and also that there were coeducational schools. Froissart, in the middle of the fourteenth century, tells of sharing a bench with girls at school and giving them little gifts to win their favor.[18] Between the ninth and fourteenth centuries, we know of some others. Lothar established state schools in Italy in the ninth century,[19] and a chronicle reports that the daughters of Manegold of Lutenbach ran a lay school in the eleventh; [20] schoolmistresses are listed in public records in Paris, one in 1292, twenty-one in 1380.[21] It is likely that there were more such schools, particularly from the thirteenth century on, but it is unlikely that they offered girls much more than basic letters. Indeed, there is a thirteenth-century satiric poem which advises male students to learn at least the canonical hours and the Psalter, if they cannot master all of grammar, so they can fall back on teaching girls if necessary.[22] Convent schools, on the other hand, at least the better ones, taught the trivium, Holy Scripture, the Fathers, and music, and some gave the rudiments of medical care. Religious houses trained not only their own novitiates but the sons or daughters of the nobility and, in the high Middle Ages, of the wealthy bourgeoisie as well. The practice was so widespread and education so desirable by the late twelfth century that families who could not afford to send their daughters to orthodox convents in southern France were sending them to heretic houses, a fact which led to the founding of a new Dominican monastery in 1206.[23]

Despite the tradition, which began with Paul, of discouraging the education of women, religious schools produced virtually all the great intellectual women of the Middle Ages. Paul had said: "But I suffer not a woman to teach, nor to usurp authority over the man, but to be in silence" (1 Tim. 2:12). If they could not teach publicly, there was little reason for them to go beyond the study of letters to rhetoric, let alone philosophy. This injunction would be cited often in succeeding centuries; Thomas Aquinas distinguishes between private and public teaching, however, allowing women to do the former but not the latter (see *Summa Theologica*, II-II, q. 177, a. 2; and III, q. 55, a. 1). But even Paul did not disdain to teach religion to women, and some of the major early Fathers of the church, particularly Origen and Jerome, gave a good deal of time and attention to the education of women on holy matters. Jerome was capable of fierce attacks on women, not only on the morally loose, but also on those religious fanatics who went mad in their cold, wet cells, deluded themselves into thinking they understood Scripture, and then dared to teach it,[24] but he also praised and encouraged the learning of those he admired: Marcella's incredible ardor for the scriptures, her meditations on God's law day and night, her successful and public battles against heresy at a time when priests and monks were succumbing to it (127.4). When people complained to Jerome that he was wasting his time on the weaker sex, he answered: "If men asked me questions about Scripture, I would not be speaking to women," [25] implying that women were more zealous students of religion.

Jerome took the education of women, from the earliest age, quite seriously. He tells Laeta how to teach her child, Paula, to read and write: give her letters on boxwood or ivory to play with; put a guiding hand over hers when she learns to trace them in wax; reward her for joining syllables; let her have companions so the competition will stimulate her to learn; let her always have a good teacher, a man of erudition, not a silly woman, so she will not have to unlearn anything later (107.4, 5); let her learn Greek and learned Latin early so her tongue will not be corrupted by vulgar speech (107.9). He warns against letting her hear anything spoken except what pertains to God, or listen to any music except psalms (107.4). He sets forth an impressive reading list from Scripture and the early Fathers—with the proper training she will even be able to read the Song of Songs without danger (107.11)—and finally, he offers himself as her teacher and nurse, saying he will carry her on his shoulders and form her stuttering words, more glorious than the philosopher who taught the king of Macedon, referring to Aristotle, because he will be training a bride for Christ (107.12).

This is perhaps the first plan laid out for the education of girls by a major Christian figure; after Jerome, others included passages about education in their rules for nuns, though not in the same detail. Caesarius of Arles, in the sixth century, says that girls should be taken in who already know their letters and that none should be taken in simply to be educated (§7); that they should all learn their letters (§18); that one of the sisters should read aloud until terce, while the others worked (§20); and that they should always think about Scripture even when there was no reading (§22).[26] Abelard, in the twelfth century, goes further in his encouragement of study among the nuns of the Paraclete, the monastery he helped to found and which he left under Heloise's guidance. Citing the precedent of Jerome, he tells them that they must study, that Scripture is the mirror of the soul, but without sufficient knowledge one cannot see what it reveals.[27] One must understand the words in order to be able to instruct others, to recognize errors that arise from different translations. He urges them to learn the three languages of Bible study, Latin, Greek, and Hebrew, and assures them that no one is better fit to guide them in such studies than their abbess, Heloise, who is expert in all three, something which can be said of few men in this period; what we have lost among men, let us recover in women, he urges.[28] In the rule he gives the nuns at Heloise's request, he tells them to read or be read to and instructed between all the offices of the day until sext; [29] at no time is the convent to be without reading. The nonintellectual offices in the house are to be carried out by the unlettered, leaving those better suited to study more freedom to engage in it. What Abelard is proposing is an intellectual elite, pursuing its studies in an ivory tower, with their other needs supplied by the less gifted.

Another program for the education of women should be mentioned, although it was never put into effect. Pierre Dubois suggested a scheme to win over the Holy Land for Christianity by sending young men and women, carefully trained, to teach, care for, and marry pagan princes and dignitaries. He sent his program first to Edward I of England, then to Philip IV of France, and neither tried it, but it tells us something about the educational system he knew.[30] The children were to be chosen for a natural disposition to study at age four or five, and sent to school; they were all to be instructed in Latin grammar and logic, in the language of the region they were to be sent to, and in the basic texts and articles of the faith. The boys who were to become priests would be trained in theology; the girls with an aptitude for it, in basic natural science and then in medicine or surgery, practice as well as theory. Their knowledge of religion would help them guide their pagan husbands and children to the faith; their expertise in medicine would draw pagan women to them for instruction. What is interesting about this plan, apart from the medical orientation, which I shall discuss later, is the basic training in Latin grammar and logic for both sexes, which is put forth as something fairly standard; although the author feels that science has to be made plainer to women because of the weakness of their sex, he seems to have no doubts about their ability to learn Latin. This is presumably because the church continued to train women in Latin in the better convents, despite the general decline in the thirteenth century.

Monastic schools had a long tradition of learned women, beginning with the first monasteries in the West, and many famous early teachers such as Boniface and Alcuin included women among their disciples. In the early centuries, when double monasteries flourished, many were run by abbesses famous for their learning: [31] Anstrude of Laon, Gertrude of Nivelle, who was reputed to have sent agents to Rome to buy books, and to have taught the allegorical senses of Scripture; [32] Bertille of Chelles, whose reputation supposedly attracted students of both sexes from Britain and who was asked to send a colony of monks and nuns to set up similar houses in Britain; [33] Hilda of Hartlepool, who, according to Bede (*Ecclesiastical History*, 4.23 and 4.24), was consulted by kings and princes and visited regularly by religious men who took pains to instruct her because of her wisdom; not only was she the abbess of Hartlepool, but she also founded and supervised a monastery at Streanaeshalch; she was so zealous in encouraging the study of Scripture that her monastery produced five bishops of singular merit, as well as the poet Caedmon.

Double monasteries were particularly strong in the seventh century, when English royal princesses were sent to France to study at them,[34] but they were more and more restricted in the eighth century, until they were finally forbidden in 787.[35] They reappear in the twelfth century, though never to the same extent. The best known from this period is probably Fontevrault, founded by Robert d'Abrissel, who left it under the supervision of an abbess when he died.[36] In 1177, the motherhouse sent twenty-four nuns and a prioress to establish a house at Amesbury; since French was the language of the upper class in England, many royal princesses were sent to school there.[37] Gilbert of Sempringham, who had been educated in France, set up a kind of double monastery, where he encouraged the education of women.[38]

By the twelfth century, many regular women's convents had acquired reputations for learning and for the production of manuscripts, although that practice had begun much earlier. In the convent founded by Caesarius of Arles, nuns were apparently set to copying religious books in the sixth century: "between psalms and fasts, vigils and readings, let the virgins of Christ copy holy books beautifully"; [39] and there were isolated instances of such activities at Chelles in the late eighth century [40] and at Maaseyk in the ninth.[41] In the twelfth century, the art of book copying and illuminating was beginning to flourish in convents, as it would for more than two centuries. From this period, several nun-scribes are known by name: Diemud of Wessobrunn, c. 1057-1130, according to the annals of her monastery, wrote many volumes with her own hand in a beautiful and legible script, both for divine service and for the public library of the monastery; she left a list of them in one of her missals, and they include several missals with various readings and offices, gospels, epistles, Bibles in two and three volumes, commentaries by Gregory, Origen, Augustine, histories by Cassiodorus and Eusebius, lives of saints, Augustine's *Confessions* and fifty of his sermons, Jerome's *De Hebraicis quaestionibus,* and an alphabetical gloss.[42] Leukardis of Mallesdorf, a nun of Scottish or Irish origin, who apparently knew Greek, Latin, and German, transcribed manuscripts which were admired by the monk-scribe Laiupold.[43] Two other women are known not as scribes but as writers and overseers if not designers of famous manuscripts: Herrad of Landsberg, abbess of Hohenburg from 1167 to 1195, whose *Hortus deliciarum,* an encyclopedic work apparently written for the education of her nuns, is now lost, but is known to us from the study of Engelhardt; [44] in the *Hortus,* Herrad cites Eusebius, Jerome, Isidore, Bede, and Peter Lombard, and shows a respect for pagan learning as well: the miniatures depict the nine muses, the seven liberal arts, and Socrates and Plato below the figure of Philosophy. The illuminated manuscript was presumably done under Herrad's supervision, although the final product may have been done elsewhere, even after her death.[45] Hildegard of Bingen, whose work will be discussed later, also probably supervised an illuminated copy of one of her books of visions, *Scivias,* though again the version that survived was probably not done in her convent.[46]

Hildegard was known for her letters as well as for her religious and scientific writings; she corresponded with many of the great men of her period—popes, kings, noblemen, bishops. Indeed, through the extant correspondence of famous men, we can trace a series of women learned enough to write in Latin, to cite pagan and Christian authorities, and even to comment on the style of their correspondents. Among Anselm's letters, over three dozen are addressed to women, many to Countess Ida or Queen Mathilda, the wife of Henry I. Some of the queen's letters are also preserved, including one in which she tells Anselm how important his writing is to her, how she embraces what he sends her and continually rereads it (PL 158: 138, no. 96), and another in which she comments on his style, comparing it with Cicero's for gravity, Quintilian's for sharpness, Paul's for doctrine, Jerome's for diligence, Gregory's for effort, Augustine's for explanation, and the Gospels for the sweetness of eloquence (156, no. 119). One assumes that she had some knowledge of the authors she cites. Peter Damian corresponded with Agnes of Poitou.[47] Peter the Venerable corresponded with several women, among them Heloise (see below, p. 19). Bernard of Clairvaux exchanged letters with a number of noble or royal laywomen as well as with nuns.[48] Thomas of Canterbury sent a letter to his "dear daughter" Idonea, asking her to take the pope's letters he had sent to her and bring them to the archbishop of York, in the presence of other bishops or at least of other witnesses, and to transcribe them beforehand, retaining the originals so that the latter could not be suppressed later (PL 190: 670-72, no. 196). This letter reveals not only Idonea's capacity to read and write Latin but Thomas's confidence in her ability to carry off a ticklish political mission. There are numerous other women whose learning is attested by the letters or poems addressed to them.[49] And, of course, there are the women whose own literary works have survived: Hroswitha's Latin plays, the Provençal poems of the women troubadours, the French *lais* of Marie de France, the learned works of Hildegard of Bingen, the many German and English mystical writings of nuns.[50]

The dominance of universities in education in the thirteenth century brought with it a decline in the education of women; although some monasteries continued to teach Latin and to run scriptoria, as they had before, the education of men was moving in a different direction. It was no longer simply the study of the trivium, from which one might move into philosophy and theology, or the quadrivium, if one had access to good teachers, but a much more formal training in specialized areas of law, medicine, and theology, aimed at preparing men for careers in government, university teaching, the professions, or the church. Professionals received degrees by examination and were usually not allowed to practice without a license or official sanction. Since women could not attend university, by and large they were excluded from these fields; thus, the existence of universities creates a much larger gap between the levels of education available to men and women than had been the case before.

Only in medicine were there exceptions, and even there only in certain cases. Women had been connected with healing and caring for the sick from the early Middle Ages, often as a religious vocation.[51] Nursing and the medicinal uses of plants were the subject of study in convents. In the thirteenth century, there are records of laywomen practicing medicine in France. Hersend attended Louis IX, who awarded her a life pension; [52] others are mentioned in the 1292 Paris census, eight doctors and twelve barbers or practical surgeons, but they were probably not licensed.[53] In 1322, Jacoba Felicie was tried in Paris for illegal practice, although many patients testified to her skill and success.[54] In Italy, however, there are records of women being officially licensed, at least from the fourteenth century, and suggestions that the tradition of women as respected practitioners of medicine was much older. Francisca, wife of Matteo de Romana, was licensed in Calabria in 1321.[55] Venturella Crisinato of Salerno was given the right to practice surgery in 1322 in consequence of public examinations.[56] Dorotea Bocchi taught medicine and moral philosophy at Bologna in 1390; [57] Costanza Calenda lectured on medicine in Naples in the fourteenth century; [58] and Allesandra Giliani (+1326) dissected human bodies and prepared the cadavers for demonstration, filling the blood vessels with liquid to harden them, and then painting them so they could be seen clearly, for the classes of Mundinus at Bologna.[59] Trotula, the twelfth-century woman who was supposed to have taught at Salerno and to have written medical texts, is apparently a fiction,[60] but her legend was quite popular. Rutebeuf (+1280) alludes to her in his *Diz de l'Erberie*, in which a doctor claims to be in service with a "madame Crote of Salerno . . . the cleverest lady in the four parts of the world." [61] Chaucer's Wife of Bath also cites her as one of the authorities in her husband's book: "in which eek ther was Tertulan,/ Crisippus, Trotula, and Helowys" (Prologue to her Tale, 11. 676-77). Earlier writers, although they do not mention Trotula specifically, do support the general tradition of medical women in Salerno. Orderic Vitalis, in the early twelfth century, describes a man "so skilled in medicine that in the city of Salerno, which is the ancient seat of the best medical schools, no one could equal him, except one very learned woman";[62] and Marie de France, in the late twelfth century, sends the hero of one of her *lais* to a famous woman doctor at Salerno, a rich woman who knows all about the art of physic and medicine *(Deus Amanz,* 11. 95-100). Thus, from the beginning of Salerno's importance as a center of medical study, there is a tradition of women doctors in the city, not nuns or nurses, but women educated in the arts of medicine.

Medicine and literature, both religious and secular letters, are the intellectual fields in which women made some sort of name for themselves in the Middle Ages. I would like now to look at three outstanding examples of historical women from the twelfth century, a period of tremendous intellectual activity, and a period in which the training of women did not differ so markedly from that of men as it later would. Of the three, two were nuns: one, Heloise, whose education included private lessons with a celebrated philosopher, is now known mainly by reputation, since only a few of her letters are extant; the other, Hildegard, left behind a considerable body of writings which touched on science and philosophy, as well as descriptions of mystical visions and a large and widespread correspondence. Both Heloise and Hildegard wrote in Latin. The third woman, Marie de France, was a laywoman of noble birth, who has left three works, all in French, all intended for a secular audience. Among them, they illustrate the main spheres of achievement of intellectual women during this period.

Heloise was renowned among her contemporaries for her learning. Her knowledge of the three biblical languages was praised not only by her former teacher and lover, Abelard, whose view may possibly be prejudiced, but also by a more neutral observer, Peter the Venerable. Peter speaks equally warmly of her learning and corroborates her knowledge of Hebrew: "the name Debora, as your erudition knows, means 'bee' in Hebrew"; just as Heloise is a Debora in leading her people to fight for God, so she is a bee in spreading the honey she has gathered, the "secret sweetness of sacred letters" *(sacrarum litterarum secreta dulcedine)* to her sisters by public instruction. Peter says he was aware of Heloise's reputation for learning when he was quite young and before she became a nun. Even then, she devoted all her efforts to the knowledge of letters and secular learning, while most of the world, most men, were indifferent to it: "you were not yet known for religion, but the fame of your honorable and praiseworthy studies reached me. I heard at that time that you were a woman who devoted yourself to literary knowledge and the study of secular learning." She outdid all women and almost all men and then, as a truly philosophical woman, turned from secular studies and chose "the gospel over logic, the apostle over physics, Christ over Plato, the cloister over the academy." Peter himself takes delight in communicating with her because of her "famous erudition" and would protract it if he could; he wishes Cluny could enjoy her presence and be enriched by her gifts: "I myself would have preferred those riches of religion and learning to the greatest treasures of any kings." [63]

The extent of Heloise's learning is reflected in her own letters, in which she cites both the Old and the New Testament frequently, but also the Fathers of the church and classical authors, Cicero, Seneca, Ovid, Lucan, Persius, Macrobius.[64] Peter's reference to her study of Plato and of logic suggests that she went much further in her studies than most women usually did; her own series of theological questions which she put to Abelard, the forty-two *Problemata*, and her arguments against their marriage, show that she had not simply read and studied but had mastered the material and the method and could argue as a philosopher. The *Problemata* include questions on divine law, justice, mercy, and contradictions among the Gospels, which reveal both a careful study of the texts and a willingness to confront difficult issues.

Heloise must have had an exceptional mind as well as good early training. Abelard says he was attracted to her primarily by her reputation for learning, the reputation Peter spoke of, and she did advanced studies with the foremost philosopher of her time. Her education otherwise followed a normal pattern in that she was taught at the convent of Argenteuil when young and tutored at home, but it was unusual inasmuch as she was simply the niece of a canon, who educated her far beyond the norm for her class, and hired the foremost teacher to tutor her. That Abelard claims to have manipulated himself into the position does not detract from the canon's willingness to hire him. And however much Abelard took advantage of the situation to seduce his student, he nonetheless taught her a good deal. However distracted she may have been by Abelard's advances—and his description in the *Historia calamitatum* suggests that they often intruded on the lessons [65]—Heloise did learn, and her overwhelming reputation for wisdom and learning as an abbess are probably due as much to his training as to her brilliance and dedication.

In her strength of will and the force of her feelings, however, Heloise may have been more than Abelard's equal. Her desire to avoid marriage rather than ruin his career—not simply in the worldly sense of ecclesiastical advancement, but in the very practical sense of the obstacles family life poses to study and writing—and her determination to keep the marriage secret after it had been forced on her, choosing shame for herself and her uncle rather than disrupt Abelard's career, reveal her courage and her devotion, to learning as well as to her lover. The words she uttered with sobs and tears as she rushed to take the veil, against the wishes of her friends and clearly against her own inclinations, suggest a heroic and perhaps also a theatrical streak; they are Cornelia's words before her death in Lucan's *De bello civili* (VIII, 94 ff.): "O great husband, o marriage unworthy . . . why was I guilty of marrying you if I was to bring you sorrow? Now accept the penalty . . . which I will gladly pay," [66] a dramatic choice, but hardly suitable to her religious vocation. Heloise' love for Abelard never falters; she can say, years after their affair, that if the emperor of the world wished to honor her with marriage and endow her with the whole world, she would hold it a greater honor to be known as Abelard's whore than as Augustus' empress.[67]

Nonetheless, with a stoic sense of duty and endurance, Heloise fulfilled the obligations of an abbess with a skill and devotion that won her the respect of the great religious leaders of her time—Peter the Venerable; Bernard of Clairvaux, who was one of Abelard's most energetic enemies; and a series of popes, who attest to the excellence of her administration. Peter says: "indeed you are a disciple of truth, but also, in that office as it pertains to those entrusted to you, a teacher of humility. The teaching of humility and of the whole heavenly discipline was committed to you by God; therefore, not only for yourself, but for the flock entrusted to you, you take care, and because of all of them, you will receive greater favor. Certainly the palm will be given to you for all of them." [68] Heloise concerned herself with the daily life of the convent, pressing Abelard for a suitable rule for her nuns because Benedict's rule presented problems for women, and with its intellectual life, putting to him the theological questions which troubled them in their studies. She prefaces the questions with the reminder that Abelard had exhorted her and the nuns to study Scripture, implying that it was his responsibility to help them in their efforts. Although Abelard left the main responsibility for educating the nuns in Heloise's hands,[69] he also wrote a number of works for them, presumably at her request. Thus, even if Heloise did not leave any major work of her own, she was responsible for much that Abelard did, certainly the works for the Paraclete: the series of Hymns and Sequences, a Psalterium, Sermons, the Commentary on the Hexaemeron.[70]

Hildegard of Bingen is a very different figure, in personality and in the pattern of her life, but she is like Heloise in her international reputation and contacts, her learning, and her position as abbess of her convent. Hildegard was a German nun, whose mystic visions encompass much of the scientific knowledge of her time, along with considerable religious doctrine. She was also a prolific correspondent who exchanged letters with popes, emperors, kings, counts, archbishops, abbots, abbesses, and simple monks and priests. She has the distinction of being the only woman who has a volume of the *Patriologia Latina* entirely to herself (197), making her, in a way, a "Father" of the church; she is also considered a saint by some, although she was never formally canonized.[71] Born in 1098 in southwest Germany, probably of petty nobility, she was walled up at the age of eight with a recluse aunt; their apartment was eventually opened up and expanded, and finally, as Hildegard's reputation grew, turned into a regular Benedictine convent. In 1147 she founded a new convent at Rupertsberg near Bingen, where she remained until her death in 1179. She knew Latin, Scripture, the liturgy, some biblical exegesis, music—a number of songs are attributed to her—and something of natural science and the more philosophic study of the cosmos.[72] Her visions were read and praised by popes; a papal commission to investigate her miracles and visions gave them a favorable report in 1147. Bernard of Clairvaux commends her "interior erudition" and her "anointment to teach about all things" (PL 182: 572, no. 366). Her science was respected enough to be studied by Paracelsus' teacher in the sixteenth century; [73] and a twentieth-century historian of science treats her as one of the more original medical writers of the Latin West in the twelfth century.[74]

In her works, Hildegard discusses the spheres of the heavens in terms of the elements, the universe as a series of concentric spheres; the zones of the atmosphere; the seasons as caused by the winds; the movement of heavenly bodies; the structure and inner workings of the human body; the nature of metals, stones, plants, trees, and animals. As a mystic, she claimed that she had no human sources for her material, that a voice from heaven told her to speak and write what she had seen, but there are suggestions in her works of the influence of current Neoplatonic thought, particularly of the Chartrians; Guillaume de Conches; and Bernard Silvester, whose *Cosmographia* she may have known before she wrote the second of her visions; and she may have had some contact with Arab science through the Latin translations becoming available in the latter half of the twelfth century.[75] Although the format is quite different—Hildegard's lessons are given in a series of visions which are interpreted by a heavenly voice for their religious or scientific significance—the content is similar to what is found in contemporary biblical exegesis and in the philosophical and scientific works of the Chartrians. (See Plate 1.) In two of her three major visions, *Scivias*, begun in 1141, and the *Liber divinorum operum simplicis hominis*, begun in 1163,[76] Hildegard describes her visions pictorially,[77] and then interprets them. The visions are either symbolic—mountains with windows in them, winged figures of great light, the firmament as a huge egg—or narrative—the rebellion of the angels and the fall of man. The interpretations are either religious—the mountain represents the strength and stability of the kingdom of God; the universe declares the omnipotent God, incomprehensible in his majesty, inestimable in his mysteries—or scientific—telling how the body is formed in the uterus, how the rings of the firmament are shaped—or philosophical, the causes of man's actions. In the *Scivias*, Hildegard presents the universe with the earth as a sphere at the center of concentric zones, whose outermost zones are spherical, ultimately egg shaped; in the *Liber*, she shifts to the more conventional view of concentric spheres, but she posits different causes for the independent movements of the planets and a more complex series of zones. The *Liber* also contains a long section on the creation, using the Genesis text but interpreting it to include current scientific views of the cosmos, as was done in the twelfth-century Hexaemeral commentaries of Abelard, and Thierry of Chartres, and in the writings of Guillaume de Conches and Bernard Silvester, who attempted to reconcile the creation according to Genesis with Plato's views in the *Timaeus*.

Hildegard's visions were something of a "best-seller"; everyone who was anyone wanted a copy, and people talked about them without having read them. Her prophetic gifts were admired by popes and emperors. Even John of Salisbury acknowledges and consults them. In a letter to Girardus la Pucelle in 1167, he asks Girardus to go through his copy of the "visions and oracles of that holy and famous Hildegard . . . whom Pope Eugene embraced with the affection of special charity" and let him (John) know whether they reveal anything about the end of the current schism, because "she foretold that there would be no peace in the time of Pope Eugene, except at the end," and apparently she was right (PL 199: 212-20, no. 199). The divine source of her words gave Hildegard a boldness in dealing with the important men of her time that is occasionally overwhelming. When Pope Anastasius writes to her saying how much he has heard about her, how highly his predecessor thought of her, and asking her to send him her writings (PL 197: 150), she answers with a stirring attack and exhortation that must have surprised him: "O man, who has wearied of restraining the magniloquence of pride among the men placed in your bosom . . . why do you not recall those who are shipwrecked, who cannot rise from their troubles without help? Why do you not cut the root of evil which suffocates the good and useful plants? You neglect Justice, the daughter of the king . . . who was committed to your care. You permit her to lie prostrate on the earth, her diadem smashed, her tunic torn." [78] Hildegard's treatment of the emperor Frederic Bar-

barossa is similar; she tells him to beware how he holds the staff of office lest the highest king, that is, the one to whom he too is subject, throw him down and destroy him because of the blindness of his eyes, which do not see rightly (187).

The authenticity of some of the letters has been questioned. [79] It would not have been unusual for false letters to be inserted among the real ones, particularly when famous names are involved, and there is no question that in some manuscripts letters are combined, in others the addresses are changed. But we do know that Hildegard corresponded with many of the people named, and the question of authenticity in individual cases cannot be resolved until we have a good critical edition. I have therefore chosen examples which are characteristic of her style and her attitudes and which give a sense of her, whatever the final decision about the separate pieces.

The bulk of the correspondence is with less important figures, though the list includes archbishops and abbots, many of whom address Hildegard as *magistra*. Apparently her visions and prophecies gave her a reputation for extraordinary wisdom; she was the "Dear Abby" of the twelfth century, to whom everyone came or wrote for advice or comfort. One abbot writes that he has read her book on the sacraments of the divine mysteries and, believing the Spirit of Truth to speak through her, humbly asks her to tell him if his desire is in accord with God's will; he is the abbot of R. and has just been elected abbot of S.—"God knows how little I wanted either"—would it be prudent and salutary to give up this burden? Hildegard's answer, in this as in other similar cases, is no; a pastor cannot pick and choose, he has a duty and God has chosen him (285-86). An abbess writes that she wants to renounce her position and wall herself up in the solitude of a cell. Hildegard tells her that her mind is clouded by the evil around her, that the peace and rest she seeks is not what God intended, that she must continue to use the light she has been given to lead others to pasture (321-22).

Elizabeth of Schönau, a visionary herself who later became a saint, writes with a distressing problem: rumors are circulating about her, and prophetic writings are appearing under her name which she claims to have nothing to do with. She has been having visions, but she has kept them hidden because she did not want to

appear arrogant or as the author of novelties, "ut arrogantiam evit-
arem, et ne auctrix novitatum viderer" (215)—hardly a tactful remark to make to someone known for her visions and not at all shy
of revealing them—until the angel who brings them angrily accused
her of hiding the gold, God's word, which she was given to pass on
to others; then the angel angrily beat her with a whip. That con-
vinced her to reveal them to her abbot, who made them public, but
when the predictions did not come true, she was ridiculed. The
next time she saw the angel, she asked for an explanation, and he
told her that her prophecies of disaster had moved people to amend
their ways, so that God had spared them. Unfortunately, people
continued to make fun of her so she turned to Hildegard for conso-
lation. Hildegard told her that man is a small, earthen vessel, made
by God to do his work; all creatures but man follow God's com-
mands. Those who sing God's mysteries are like a trumpet, which
can give forth a sound only if someone blows into it. She ended
with a confession and a prayer: "I too lie in the cowardice of fear,
sometimes making a small sound on the trumpet by means of the
living light; whence God help me, that I may remain in his service"
(216-18).

Some abbots write to Hildegard about their congregations' private problems; one asks if she can help a noblewoman whose children have died and who is now sterile. Hildegard promises to pray
for her and her husband (292-93). Another tells about a noblewoman who has been possessed for some years by an evil spirit; he
and his monks have tried for three months without success to dispel
it; despairing that their own sins are the obstacle, he turns to Hildegard. She recommends an elaborate procedure of exorcism, which
he tries, but it works only temporarily. When the demon returns
and distresses the woman even more, the abbot gives up and an-
nounces that he is sending the woman herself to Hildegard (278-80).
Unfortunately, we do not know how the story ended.

Hildegard had problems of her own in her administration, some
of which are described in the letters. Toward the end of her life, a
young man who had been excommunicated was buried in the cem-
etery adjoining her convent, and the ecclesiastical authorities of the
region demanded that the body be removed. She refused to comply
on the grounds that he had received the last rites. Even when her

convent was placed under interdict, she held firm, and after considerable correspondence and negotiation, the ban was lifted (281 ff.). She was, in other words, capable of practical action, as well as of theoretic advice.

We know a good deal about the two abbesses, Heloise and Hildegard, where they grew up, where they lived their adult lives, who their friends were, what they accomplished. The third of my historical women, Marie de France, is almost a total mystery, except for her work.[80] She was probably noble, so we assume from her education and her interests, and connected in some way with the court of Henry II and Eleanor; since she often gives a word in English as well as French, she was presumably writing for the Norman court. She knew Latin, from which she translated the *Purgatory of St. Patrick*, a vision of an otherworld journey, and English, from which she translated the Aesopic Fables, and she may have known some Welsh.[81] We date her works somewhere between 1160 and 1215. We know her name because she gives it to us at the beginning of the *lais* and rather forcefully at the end of the fables and of the Purgatory, by which time she was presumably known:

> I shall name myself so it will be remembered:
> Marie is my name, I am from France.
> It may be that many clerks
> will take my labor on themselves.
> I don't want any of them to claim it.
> Epilogue to the Fables, 11. 3-7 [82]

She was apparently a popular writer; there are translations or other versions of the *lais* clearly dependent on hers in Old Norse (nine in a thirteenth-century manuscript), Middle English, Middle High German, Italian, French, and even in Latin (the *Laustic* appears in Alexander of Neckham's *De naturis rerum*, thirteenth century).

Marie has a strong sense of her own powers and a moral obligation to her audience:

> Whoever has received knowledge
> and eloquence in speech from God,

should not be silent or conceal it,
but demonstrate it willingly.
    Prologue to the *Lais*, ll. 1-4 [83]

Those who know letters should give their attention to the books
and words of philosophers, who wrote down moral precepts so that
others might improve themselves, she tells us in the Prologue to the
Fables (ll. 1-11). She never allows us to forget her role as author,
reminding us continually at the beginning or end of a *lai*, or both,
that she is the one who put it into the form we are hearing. In two
of the *lais*, she has the main character, a man in *Chievrefeuil*, a
woman in *Chaitivel*, compose a *lai* about the situation she describes; in other words, she writes a lai about the making of a *lai*,
the ultimate gesture of the self-conscious artist. The *lais*, which are
the most interesting of her works and the most original, are short
narrative poems, from 118 to 1184 lines, often build around a central symbol. Marie deals with love in all of them, from different
perspectives; in some she condemns love that is selfish or posses-
sive, in others she shows that if one is prepared to suffer and sacri-
fice for it, love can give what the world cannot or will not—it can
free us, in spirit at least, from the constraints of the world, chivalry
for men, marriage for women. Her heroes and heroines are often
outcasts or exiles, rejected by their family or their society, who find
a new world in love which sometimes enables them to return to the
"real" world and cope with it. Marie's concern is with the problems of people, men and women both, who are not happy in their
lives, and the attempt to find a workable solution. She is apparently
not satisfied with the contemporary romance treatment which deals
primarily with men finding themselves through a combination of
chivalric adventures and love, whose problems are usually solved,
when they are, in an ideal but rather abstract way. What she suggests, and this is unusual, is that one can free oneself in the mind,
by will and imagination, from the world outside, rise above it in
some way, but not necessarily change or leave it; what one changes
is one's own perspective.

The hero or heroine who needs love—a knight rejected by his
court, like Lanval, a woman imprisoned by an old and jealous husband, as in *Yonec*—wills it and it comes. Locked in a tower with no

company but her husband's old and suspicious sister, the wife in *Yonec* daydreams:

I have often heard
that one could once find
adventures in this land
that brought relief to the unhappy.
Knights might find young girls
to their desire, noble and lovely,
and ladies find lovers
so handsome, courtly, brave, and valiant,
that they could not be blamed,
and no one else would ever see them.
If that might be or ever was,
if that has ever happened to anyone,
God, who has power over everything,
grant me my wish in this.

(11. 91-104)

When she finishes, a great bird flies in to her room and turns into a knight as she stares at it, as if her look drew out its human form. He tells her he has loved her a long time but that he could not have left his land or come to her until she asked for him. He comes whenever she wills it and supplies all that her life lacks, and she would presumably be happy to go on forever with this arrangement, but that is impossible. Her joy, the one thing she cannot hide, alerts her husband; he spies, sets a trap of sharp blades in the window, and fatally wounds the bird. Suddenly, the wife is able to leave the tower, leaping out the window to follow her wounded lover; in other words, she can escape if she wants to, but she needed love to give her the will and the courage to free herself. She follows the lover back to his land, where he dies, and then returns to her husband, armed with a ring to make him forget all that has happened; from this time on he no longer has the power to imprison her, because *she* has changed.

I do not know whether it took a woman to present a solution that was neither religious nor bound up with success in the world—those of her heroes who achieve worldly glory learn that love is of higher

value—but the fact is that a woman did. Perhaps because secular
life rarely gave a woman an external focus for her ambitions, a
public forum in which to act, Marie looked inward and discovered
the liberating function of the imagination for herself and for her
heroes and heroines. Hildegard and Heloise were both abbesses,
both administrators with various kinds of responsibility and, paradoxically, with wide contacts in the world, but apart from the religious life, there were few roles for women to play outside the
home unless fate cast them temporarily as regents for their husbands or children, a possibility not open to many. Perhaps the same
sort of frustration that Marie deals with in her *lais*—the feeling of
imprisonment in a situation that does not allow one to act—is felt
by the better-educated heroines of contemporary romances. Unable
to act directly or publicly, they turn their knowledge to the practice of magic and try to control the fates of others that way.

In the final section, I shall discuss attitudes toward highly educated women as they are revealed in twelfth-century romances.
Magic powers were often attributed to women in literature, and in
life, as a way, I suspect, of rationalizing the vulnerability men felt.
That is, rather than admit the weakness of lust in himself, he focused on the power that attracted him; if the power were magic, he
was not responsible for giving in to it. But in the romances I shall
talk about, the emphasis shifts from magic to intellect; the women
are not strange creatures with inexplicable supernatural powers but
are highly intelligent and highly trained. It is their education which
enables them to do unusual things.

There are many women with medical skills in medieval romance,
working with herbs, drugs, and plasters, to heal the sick and
wounded, but occasionally they employ drugs to control the mind.
The heroine's nurse in Chrétien's *Cliges* is a *mestre,* a sage, who
knows a good deal of necromancy. She comes from Thessaly, where
"devil's work is done." She makes one potion to give the heroine's
husband so he will dream he is sleeping with his wife and wake
feeling satisfied, but leave her a virgin, and another potion to make
the heroine appear to be dead. To support the pretense, the nurse
procures the urine of a dying woman and submits it to the court
physicians, who agree that the heroine is beyond help; the plan is
temporarily jeopardized by the appearance of a medical team from

Salerno who see that she is still alive and suspect treachery; they try every kind of torture to arouse her and would presumably succeed in killing her if it were not for a mob of women who break into the palace and kill them. There must be a comment here on the learned doctors' willingness to destroy the patient in order to prove their diagnosis. In any case, despite the best efforts of the doctors, the heroine does not die, and the nurse is able, with ointments and plasters, to restore her battered body. There may be a trace here of the traditional division between theory, the province of the Salerno doctors, and practice, the nurse's healing powers.

The same combination of powers to heal the body and to influence the mind is found in Queen Isolt, the mother of Tristan's love. In the more sophisticated versions of the story, by Thomas and Gottfried,[84] she is a skilled physician who understands herbs and medications and the treatment of wounds better than anyone else, and cures Tristan of two poison wounds, but she also makes potions. It is, in fact, her love potion, destined for Isolt and her husband, Mark, that Tristan and Isolt drink by mistake, an instance of excessive cleverness backfiring; this problem is characteristic not only of such women but also of the male figures in the Tristan romances, where characters attempt to control fate, but instead become its victims, in contrast to Marie's *lais*, where characters learn to live with their fate.

In earlier versions of the Tristan story, for example, Eilhart's poem, Isolt herself has the magic healing powers, but the authors of more sophisticated late-twelfth-century romances prefer to keep their heroines free of that taint, so they make her mother the physician-magician. The daughter is, instead, educated in the arts: she reads and writes; she composes poetry; she knows various languages, including French and Latin, although she is Irish; and she sings and plays several instruments. Through her music, she has the power to hold men's thoughts, but she does not abuse that power. In the French-Scandinavian version, she is taught everything by Tristan, and she demonstrates her wisdom with public responses and opinions to the wise men of the court;[85] in the German poem, she has already been taught languages and music by a priest, but is brought to a higher level in all her accomplishments by Tristan's tutoring.[86] The echoes of the Abelard-Heloise story, love growing out of the lessons, are obvious. Isolt's intellectual achievements make her the fit companion, and the only one, for the hero. The high point of the love, in these versions of the story, is achieved in exile, when the two lovers live alone in a cave in the wilderness and spend their time talking, telling stories, and playing music, as well as making love, and sharing an intellectual or artistic life on a level their social peers cannot attain.

Ironically, perhaps, it is the brilliant hero, Tristan, who is envied and feared for his unusual powers; it is he who is suspected of being a sorcerer. Like Abelard, his abilities attract hostility, while those of Heloise and Isolt seem to evoke only admiration. In the two other romances I shall mention, *Le Bel Inconnu* and *Partenopeu de Blois*, the woman has the magic powers, but as the result of her extraordinary education, and they operate only to bring the hero to her. Once the love is consummated, she seems to have no more control over events than the hero does, an indication perhaps of the superior powers of love.

In *Partenopeu*, the heroine, Melior, who is in many ways the central character of the romance, has been taught the seven liberal arts, which she learned first and completely, all of medicine (herbs; cold and heat; the causes, nature, and cures of all diseases), then divinity, the old law and the new; by the time she was fifteen, she had surpassed all her teachers—and she had had more than two hundred of them—and then she went on to necromancy and enchantment.[87] Although her powers are greater than anyone else's, what she does with them in the privacy of her or her father's chambers is to call up apparitions—wild beasts, armed knights by the thousands, fighting—and make people invisible to each other. One cannot help thinking that the poet is describing the powers of the creative artist here, the one person who can actually make worlds appear and disappear at will, particularly since Melior also tells stories to her lover to entertain him.

One factor in Melior's education is of particular interest: she was taught so much because her father thought she was his only heir, the only child he would have. This is too often the case with the exceptionally educated women in these works to be coincidental: the heroine of *Bel Inconnu* is also her father's only heir; Isolt is an only child, as Heloise was, at least in her uncle's home; one of the few specific mentions of a literate woman in Chrétien's work is the young girl reading a romance to her parents in *Yvain*, who take great pleasure in seeing and hearing her because she is their only child.[88] This is an interesting corroboration of modern findings about successful professional women.[89] The point seems to be that these medieval women, like many of their moderns counterparts, were educated like men because they filled the place of sons for their fathers.

Melior's powers bring the hero to her, but demands of family and country call him away; indeed all the forces of his world operate against the love. His mother, not surprisingly, is disturbed that Melior refused to let her lover see her in the light; suspecting the devil's work, she conspires with the king and the bishop of Paris to keep the two apart. She even gives her son a potion to make him forget Melior and marry a nice French princess, but this is a minor kind of magic which is only temporarily effective; she is not in Melior's league. She does succeed in separating them, at the cost of driving her son into a severe depression. The solution is provided not by the magician-lover but by her sister,[90] who uses simple common sense, native cleverness, and compassion to restore the hero and reconcile the heroine. The heroine is made to suffer at length for her perhaps excessive desire to control the situation and to conceal her own feelings, both of which may be the result of her highly refined intellect, but she is allowed to win in the end, and we are encouraged to sympathize with her.

In the remaining romance, the *Bel Inconnu*, we are also meant to sympathize with the heroine, but she does not get the hero. Once again, we have a woman trained in the seven arts, "arithmetic, geometry, necromancy, astronomy, and the others," [91] because she is her father's only child and he loves her so (cf. 11. 1933-39). She also learns to divine the future. Like Melior, however, she reveals the extent of her education to the hero only after they have made love and when he is about to leave her in any case; both heroines seem to fear that men are put off by too much learning in a woman. The heroine of *Bel Inconnu,* known only as La Pucele, also draws the hero to her; she has the power to oversee his adventures, to cause her voice to come to him at a great distance, to test him with strange nightmares. Going to her room one night, he suddenly

thinks he is on a thin plank over raging torrents; grabbing hold of
something, he shouts for help and then wakes to find himself cling-
ing to a bird's perch in front of her door, to his great embarrass-
ment.

La Pucele can do all this, and she can foretell what will happen,
but she cannot control the outcome of the action she initiates. She
lures the hero to her with adventures she knows he cannot resist:
the first is to rescue her from a situation she had created, knights
forced to stay with her, killing all comers, until they are defeated.
This is a standard romance episode but seen here from the woman's
perspective—what do you do if you don't like your champion? Her
problem is that if a knight can hold on for seven years, she is
obliged to marry him; the present one has lasted five years and she
does not like him, so she must find someone to defeat him. In the
other adventure, the hero rescues a woman who has been turned
into a dragon by an enchanter when he touched her with a book (1.
3341). This is perhaps the most direct example of the danger of
education for women. Unfortunately for the heroine, this second
woman falls in love with the hero and, although she lacks la
Pucele's powers, she is clever enough to know what attracts him—
chivalry—and with Arthur's help, she lures him back to her to fight
in a tourney. That is where the romance ends. Here it is clear that
the heroine has outwitted herself, but this is not necessarily an
indictment of educated women; the poet, Renaut de Beaujeu, en-
closes the whole story in the frame of a plea to his lady, and what
he says to her at the end is that if she will be nice to him, he will let
the hero return to his love; if not, he will leave him to languish
forever. In other words, the poet's lady, the audience, that is, is
expected to root for the brilliant heroine.

That is not, I think, unusual for this period. The enthusiasm for
education in the twelfth century is real, not just because it has
practical applications in religious life and society, but because it is
perceived as a good in itself. Knowledge can provide wonderful
powers, sometimes magical. The highly educated and intelligent of
both sexes are generally admired, although, like Abelard and Tristan, they may also be envied or feared. In such an atmosphere, the
educated woman, Heloise, Hildegard, can command the respect

and attention of the male establishment, and the educated heroine, Isolt, Melior, la Pucele, can elicit the sympathy of the audience. In this period, at least, we are meant to root for the brilliant heroine.

Notes

1. Charles Jourdain wrote an article, "Mémoires sur l'éducation des femmes au Moyen Age," in 1874 (published in *Mémoires de l'Institut national de France,* Académie des Inscriptions et Belle-Lettres 28 [1874]: 77-133), which is still the best comprehensive source on the subject. Works on the education of men or the monastic life of women touch on aspects of the education of women, but I have found nothing else that deals with it directly. Eileen Power's chapter on education in *Medieval English Nunneries* (New York, 1964), pp. 237-84, concentrates on the fourteenth and fifteenth centuries. Furthermore, both Power and Nicholas Orme *(English Schools in the Middle Ages* [London, 1973], pp. 52-55) make it clear that the education of women in England was vastly inferior to education on the continent, at least after the Anglo-Saxon period, the only time when English nuns, according to Power (p. 237), were conspicuous for their learning. In their studies of literacy among the laity, both Herbert Grundmann ("Litteratus-illiteratus," *Archiv für Kulturgeschichte* 40 [1958]: 1-65) and James W. Thompson *(The Literacy of the Laity in the Middle Ages* [Berkeley, 1939]) refer frequently to women who were unusually well educated in relation to their societies, particularly in the royal families of Christianized Germanic peoples in the early Middle Ages, but they do not, for the most part, tell us how they were educated.

2. "Liberos suos ita censuit instituendos ut tam filii quam filiae primo liberalibus studiis, quibus et ipse operam dabat, erudirentur" *(Einharti Vita Caroli Magni,* ed. Philipp Jaffé, *Bibliotheca Rerum Germanicarum,* 4: 526).

3. "Nobilissimis in Christianae religionis sanctitate et in sapientiae studiis devotissimis . . . quantum in sanctissimo sapientiae studio optimam in vobis laudo devotionem" (Migne, *Patriologia Latina,* hereafter cited in text as PL, 100: 740). The women's letters can be found in the same volume, pp. 738-40.

4. Grundmann, pp. 9, 14; Thompson, pp. 87-88.

5. Grundmann, p. 30; Thompson, pp. 13-14.

6. Thompson, p. 15.

7. Ibid., p. 30.

8. Ibid., p. 32.

9. Ibid. p. 168 (citing *Monumenta Germaniae Historica* SS 9.353).

10. See John F. Benton, "The Court of Champagne as a Literary Center," *Speculum* 36 (1961): 583.

11. Ibid., p. 586; comment on Marie, p. 587.

12. See Grundmann, pp. 35-36.

13. Thompson, p. 83.

14. Ibid., p. 88.

15. Ibid., p. 171.

16. Jourdain, p. 89.

17. *Chartularium universitatis Parisiensis*, 1357, cited by Lynn Thorndike, *University Records and Life in the Middle Ages* (New York, 1944), pp. 239-40, §17. "Every master or mistress shall keep within his allotted bounds, not exceeding in number or sex of pupils or even in quality of books." §23. "A woman should teach only girls." In Wherwell, England, the archibishop forbade boys being educated by nuns in 1284 (see Power, p. 573, citing an Episcopal Register).

18. "Et quant on me mist à l'escole,/ où les ignorans on escole,/ il y avoit des pucellettes/ qui de mon temps erent jonettes;/ et je, qui estoie puceaus,/ je les servoie d'espinceaus,/ ou d'une pomme, ou d'une poire,/ ou d'un seul anelet de voire;/ et me sambloit, au voir enquerre,/ grant proece à leur grasce acquerre." "L'Espinette amoreuse," *Oeuvres de Froissart*, ed. August Scheler (Brussels, 1870), I: 88, ll. 35-44.

19. Philippe Delhaye, "L'Organisation Scolaire au XIIe Siècle," *Traditio* 5 (1947): 211-68. Delhaye notes that there were municipal schools in Italy by the thirteenth century, but we do not know what existed between (p. 213).

20. *Chronicon Richardi Pictaviensis*, cited by Jourdain, p. 93, and Thompson, p. 135.

21. Jourdain, p. 127.

22. "Horas et psalterium discas valde bene / scolas si necesse est puellarum tene," cited by Thompson, p. 115.

23. John H. Mundy, *Europe in the High Middle Ages* (New York, 1973), p. 209; Micheline de Fontette, *Les Religieuses à l'age classique du droit canon* (Paris, 1967), p. 90, gives the date as 1207.

24. *Sancti Eusebii Hieronymi Epistulae*, ed. Isidorus Hilberg, *Corpus Scriptorum Ecclesiasticorum Latinorum*, 56, 3 (1918), no. 130.17. Henceforth the numbers of the letters will be given in the text.

25. Letter to Principia, 65; this letter is cited by Abelard in the Epistola ad virgines Paraclitenses de studio litterarum, *Petri Abaelardi Opera*, ed. Victor Cousin (Paris, 1849), 1: 229.

26. S. Caesarii, *Regula Sanctarum Virginum,* ed. Germanus Morin, *Florilegium Patristicum,* 34 (Bonn, 1933). Leon Maitre, *Les Ecoles Episcopales et Monastiques de l'Occident* (Paris, 1866), p. 260, cites the order of the Council of Cloveshove, that abbots and abbesses must provide diligently for incessant study in their "families."

27. Heloise throws this back at Abelard when she sends him the theological problems to solve (Cousin, p. 238).

28. Ibid., pp. 234 and 236. Mary M. McLaughlin, "Peter Abelard and the Dignity of Women," *Pierre Abélard—Pierre le Vénérable,* Colloques Intenationaux du Centre National de la Recherche Scientifique, 546 (Paris, 1975): 330-31, thinks Abelard is exaggerating her mastery of the scriptural languages. On contemporary interest in Hebrew studies, see D. E. Luscombe, *The School of Peter Abelard* (Cambridge, England, 1970), pp. 236-37.

29. For the text of the rule, see T. P. McLaughlin, "Abelard's Rule for Religious Women," *Medieval Studies* 18 (1956): 241-92. The authenticity of the rule has been disputed recently by John F. Benton, "Fraud, fiction and borrowing in the correspondence of Abelard and Héloise," *Pierre Abélard—Pierre le Vénérable,* pp. 469-506, but the question is not yet resolved. Another twelfth-century rule for nuns, Aelred of Rievaulx's *De Institutione Inclusarum,* ed. C. H. Talbot in *Aelredi Opera, Corpus Christianorum,* Continuatio Mediaevalis, 1 (Turnholt, 1971), says that nuns should divide their time between psalms, reading, prayer, and work of the hands, §9.

30. *De recuperatione terrae sanctae,* 1309, cited by L. Thorndike, pp. 138-49. That Latin education continued in convent schools we can assume from the rule of Montargis, 1250 (see Raymond Creytens, "Les Constitutions Primitives des Soeurs Dominicaines de Montargis," *Archivum Fratrum Praedicatorum,* 17 [1947]: 41-84, esp. §23), and from the fact that all seventy-four Dominican houses for women in 1300 had libraries (see Matthaus Bernards, *Speculum Virginum* [Köln/Graz, 1955], 1). Vincent of Beauvais, however, writing on the instruction of noble children in the midthirteenth century, when he comes to the girls, is primarily concerned with their moral education *(De Eruditione Filiorum Nobilium,* ed. Arpad Steiner [Cambridge, Mass., 1938], chaps. 42-51).

31. In general, double monasteries in England were ruled by an abbess; in France it might be an abbot or an abbess. See Mary Bateson, "Origin and Early History of Double Monasteries," *Transactions of the Royal Historical Society,* n.s. 13 (1899): 164.

32. Bateson, p. 158, and the *Histoire littéraire de la France,* 3 (1735): 444, citing Mabillon, *Acta Sanctorum.*

33. *Histoire Littéraire*, p. 445.

34. Bateson, p. 155; Thompson, p. 117.

35. At the Second Council of Nice, Bateson, p. 163.

36. Fontette, chap. 3.

37. Lina Eckenstein, *Women under Monasticism* (Cambridge, England, 1896), p. 205.

38. Ferdinand Hilpisch, *Die Doppelklöster, Entstehung und Organisation* (Münster, 1928), pp. 71 ff.

39. "Inter psalmos atque jejunia, vigilias quoque et lectiones, libros divinos pulchre scriptitent virgines Christi" *(Vita Caesarii*, 1. 33, cited by W. Wattenbach, *Das Schriftwesen im Mittelalter*, 4th ed. [Graz, 1958], p. 445). Cf. George H. Putnam, *Books and Their Makers during the Middle Ages* (New York, 1962; repr. of 1896-97 ed.), 1: 53.

40. Annemarie W. Carr, "Women Artists in the Middle Ages," *The Feminist Art Journal* 5, 1 (1976): 5-6.

41. *Vita Harlindis et Reinilae*, cited by Wattenbach, p. 445; the writers of the life found it amazing that nuns should be writing and painting when strong men found it an oppressive task. Putnam says the transcription of manuscripts was the "principal and most constant occupation of the learned Benedictine nuns" and that "some of the most beautiful specimens of calligraphy" from the Middle Ages are their work (pp. 52-53).

42. Putnam, pp. 79-81. Carr notes that several Diemuds have been discovered (p. 6).

43. Wattenbach, p. 445. Gutta of Schwarzenthau, c. 1175, is mentioned by Wattenbach, p. 445, and Eckenstein, p. 237.

44. C. M. Engelhardt, *Herrad von Landsberg und ihr Werk* (Stuttgart, 1818).

45. Carr, p. 8 and fnn. 20-24.

46. Carr, p. 7 and fn. 18; Charles Singer, *From Magic to Science* (New York, 1958), p. 205. In the thirteenth century, several convents collected and transcribed mystical writings or recorded the visions of their fellow nuns (Eckenstein, pp. 328 ff.).

47. Thompson, p. 89.

48. Maria d'Elia Angiolillo, "L'Epistolario femminile di S. Bernardo," *Analecta Sacri Ordinis Cisterciensis*, 15 (1959): 23-55.

49. See Jourdain, pp. 89-92; Maître, pp. 258-63; *Histoire littéraire*, pp. 9, 131; Grundmann, p. 31.

50. Contemporary fiction also presents many learned women; though the extent of their learning may be exaggerated, their existence is significant. Several will be discussed below (pp. 30 ff.); Jourdain mentions a number of French romances and chronicles in which extraordinary learn-

ing is ascribed to certain women, particularly in languages and astronomy (pp. 113-15).

51. Kate Hurd-Mead, *A History of Women in Medicine* (Haddam, 1938), chap. 2.

52. Muriel J. Hughes, *Women Healers in Medieval Life and Literature* (New York, 1943), p. 89.

53. Hughes, p. 83.

54. Hughes, pp. 89-90; Hughes lists the variety of names that exist in Middle French for women in medicine: *fisiciennes, miresses, chirurgiennes, barbières, médecines, guarisseuses, norrices, sage-femmes, vielles femmes* (p. 86).

55. Paul O. Kristeller, "The School of Salerno," *Studies in Renaissance Thought and Letters* (Rome, 1956): 505n.; Salvatore de Renzi, *Storia documentata della Scuola Medica di Salerno,* 2d ed. (Naples, 1857), p. 531, notes that the university of Salerno attested to her fitness and doctrine and that the king's physicians and surgeons examined her.

56. de Renzi, p. 520.

57. See Serafino Mazzetti, *Repertorio di tutti i professori antichi e moderni della famosa università di Bologna* (Bologna, 1848), p. 59, item 513. The daughter of a professor of moral philosophy and practical medicine, herself *laureata* in philosophy, Dorotea Bocchi taught her father's students publicly with great success, after his death.

58. Hughes, p. 62.

59. Hughes, p. 74.

60. Kristeller, p. 505.

61. Madame Crotê de Salerne . . . la plus sage dame qui soit enz quartre parties du monde *(Rustebuefs Gedichte,* ed. A. Kressner [Wolfenbüttel, 1885], pp. 115-29, ll. 6 ff.).

62. *The Ecclesiastical History of Orderic Vitalis,* ed. and trans. Marjorie Chibnall (Oxford, 1969), 2: 76-77 ("Physicae quoque scientiam tam copiose habuit, ut in urbe Psalernitana ubi maxime medicorum scolae ab antiquo tempore habentur neminem in medicinali arte praeter quandam sapientem matronam sibi parem inveniret," III, ii, 70).

63. The quotations from Peter in this passage are based on the Latin text in *The Letters of Peter the Venerable,* ed. Giles Constable (Cambridge, Mass., 1967), 1: "hoc nomen Debora, ut tua novit eruditio, lingua Hebraica apem designat" (305); "nomen non quidem adhuc religionis tuae, sed honestorum tamen et laudabilium studiorum tuorum, michi fama innotuit. Audiebam tunc temporis, mulierem . . . litteratoriae scientiae . . . et studio licet saecularis sapientiae, summam operam dare" (303); "mulieres omnes evicisti, et pene viros universos superasti . . . pro logica

aevangelium, pro phisica apostolum, pro Platone Christum, pro academia claustrum tota iam et vere philosophica mulier elegisti" (304); "praetulissem opes religionis ac scientiae maximis quorumlibet regum thesauris" (306).

64. The authenticity of most of Heloise's extant letters (all but those to Peter the Venerable and to Abelard requesting his answers to the *Problemata*) has been questioned. Most scholars now accept the authenticity of Abelard's letters, with some qualifications, see Jacques Monfrin, "Le problème de l'authenticité de la correspondance d'Abélard e d'Héloise," *Pierre Abélard—Pierre le Vénérable*, pp. 409-24, for a résumé. Mary McLaughlin thinks the letters of both are authentic but probably edited in a collaborative effort. The letters in question have recently been edited by J. T. Muckle; the *Historia calamitatum* in Medieval Studies 12 (1950): 162-213, and Heloise's letter in *Medieval Studies* 15 (1953): 47-94. They will be hereafter cited as Muckle (1950) and Muckle (1953).

65. Muckle (1950), pp. 183-84.

66. Ibid., p. 191.

67. Muckle (1953), p. 71.

68. "Es quidem discipula veritatis, sed es etiam ipso officio, quantum ad tibi commissas pertinet, magistra humilitatis. Humilitatis plane, et totius caelestis disciplinae tibi a deo magisterium impositum est, unde non solum tui, sed et commissi gregis curam habere, et pro universis, majorem universis debes mercedem recipere. Manet tibi certe palma pro omnibus" (304-5).

69. M. McLaughlin, p. 331, n. 146.

70. Luscombe, p. 18.

71. *The Catholic Encyclopedia* (New York, 1913), 7: 352.

72. On the music, see Marianna Schrader and A. Führkötter, *Die Echtheit des Schrifttums der heiligen Hildegard von Bingen* (Köln/Graz, 1956), p. 21. The notion that Hildegard was illiterate, which is based on her saying she dictated to a monk, is not to be taken seriously. She exaggerates her own inadequacy in order to exalt the divine source of her material, but the content of her visions is sufficient indication of her learning, and even the divine injunctions tell her specifically to write *(Scivias*, PL 197: 383: "Dic et scribe quae vides et audis"), as she does (*Liber*, 742: "manus tandem ad scribendum tremebunda converti").

73. Singer, p. 223.

74. G. Sarton, *Introduction to the History of Science* (Baltimore, 1927), 2:310.

75. Singer, pp. 200-39, esp. p. 235.

76. Hildegard dates her works and herself at the beginning of them. The

third visionary work, *Liber vitae meritorum,* is mainly a moral work, which I have not seen. For a study of it, see Angela Rozumek, *Die sittliche Weltanschauung der heiligen Hildegard von Bingen* (Bayern, 1934).

77. Illuminated manuscripts exist of both, *Scivias* in a twelfth-century version which may have been supervised by Hildegard, Wiesbaden MS, the *Liber* in a thirteenth-century work.

78. "O homo, qui . . . lassus es ad refrenandum magniloquia superbiae, in hominibus in sinum tuum positis, cur non revocas naufragos qui de magnis casibus suis surgere non possunt nisi per adjutorium? Et quare non abscindis radicem mali, quae suffocat bonas et utiles herbas, dulcem gustu, et suavem odorem habentes? Filiam regis, scilicet justitiam . . . et quae tibi commissa fuerat, negligis. Tu enim permittis hanc filiam regis super terram prosterni, quia diadema et decor tunicae ejus scinditur" (151).

79. Schmeidler rejects several of the pope's letters among others (Bernhard Schmeidler, "Bemerkungen zum Corpus der Briefe der Hl. Hildegard von Bingen," *Corona Quernea, Festgabe für Karl Strecker* (Leipzig, 1941), pp. 335-66; Schräder and Führkötter analyze the various manuscripts and accept the majority of the extant letters. Since there has been no critical edition and no new edition since Migne, the question remains for scholars to resolve.

80. For the fullest recent study of both, see Emanuel J. Mickel, Jr., *Marie de France* (New York, 1974).

81. She cites a few Breton words in the *lais,* but she never claims that she got her stories directly from a Breton source.

82. Me numerai pur remembrance:
Marie ai nun, si sui de France.
Put cel estre que clerc plusur
Prendreient sur eus mun labur,
Ne voil que nul sur li le die;

(Fables, selected and edited by A. Ewert and R. C. Johnston [Oxford, 1966]; repr. of 1942 ed.).

83. Ki Deus ad duné escience
E de parler bon'eloquence
Ne s'en deit taisir ne celer,
Ainz se deit volunters mustrer.

(Lais, ed. A. Ewert [Oxford, 1969, repr. of 1st ed., 1944). The translation is taken from *The Lais of Marie de France,* trans. R. W. Hanning and J. M. Ferrante (New York, 1978).

84. The part on Isolt's education is no longer extant in Thomas's version, but we have a good idea of it from the Scandinavian translation by Brother Robert *(Tristrams Saga ok Isondar,* ed. Eugen Kölbing [Heilbronn, 1878]).

Gottfried von Strassburg, *Tristan und Isold,* ed. Friedrich Ranke, 4th ed. (Berlin, 1959), also goes into some detail on the subject.

85. Brother Robert, chap. 30.

86. Gottfried, ll. 7715 ff. and 8000 ff.

87. *Partenopeu de Blois,* ed. Joseph Gildea, 2 vols. (Villanova, 1967), ll. 4573 ff.

88. Chrétien de Troyes, *Yvain,* ed. T. B. W. Reid (Manchester, 1952); repr. of 1942 ed.), ll. 5365-73. The heroine of the same romance, Laudine, reads psalms in an illuminated Psalter, l. 1414.

89. See Carolyn Heilbrun, *Reinventing Womanhood* (New York, 1979), for discussion and bibliography on this subject.

90. The sister is presumably an afterthought, either of the father or of the author; she is an integral part of the story, but the heroine's unusual education is explicable, apparently, only in terms of her having been an only child.

91. Renaut de Beaujeu, *Le Bel Inconnu,* ed. G. Perrie Williams (Paris, 1967), ll. 4939-41 and 1933-39.

CHAPTER 3

Women, Learning, and Power: Eleonora of Aragon and the Court of Ferrara

Werner L. Gundersheimer

On July 3, 1473, Eleonora of Aragon entered Ferrara in triumphal procession.[1] Twenty years later, at the age of forty-three, she left in the simplest way available to a Renaissance princess; robed as a penitent, and accompanied by six hundred silent mourners, she was taken to her favorite convent, Corpus Domini. In accordance with her instructions, no bells tolled as her body was lowered into a crypt near the altar of the nuns' modest chapel.[2] The deadly pneumococcus had done what twenty years of anxiety and hard work, including seven pregnancies, had not succeeded in doing to this diminutive daughter of King Ferdinand of Naples.[3] Though my primary concern is to offer some reflections on the two decades of Eleonora's career framed by these momentous events, it is worth considering each of them as well. In many ways, they may help us to perceive the meaning of her life and work at the court of Ferrara. These ritualistic observances tell us something not only about the special importance of this particular dynastic marriage.[4] When Eleonora came to Ferrara to marry Duke Ercole I, she came,

43

not so much as a unique human being, but more as a walking symbol of *normality*, of *continuity*, and of *enhanced status*.

I

Eleonora's own traits as an individual were at least in the beginning secondary to her official, threefold role as a public figure. As a product of a similar kind of rigidly ranked, courtly society, Eleonora probably understood this. From all indications, she was well prepared for the role she was expected to play.[5]

First of all, the very presence of a woman at the head of Ferrarese society—a "first lady"—represented a return to a form of social *normality* that had not existed in any stable way since 1441, when Ricciarda da Saluzzo, widow of Niccolò III, left Ferrara, probably upon the instructions of her step-son, the new Marquess, Leonello d'Este. As the mother of his legitimate half brothers Ercole and Sigismondo, she became persona non grata when Leonello took control.[6] Leonello's marriages, like his reign, were brief. The first, to Margherita Gonzaga, daughter of the marquess of Mantua, ended with her death before Leonello came to power. The second, to Maria of Aragon, daughter of King Alfonso the Magnanimous, ended after only five years in 1449, when she too died after a long illness.

From 1450 to 1472, Ferrara was ruled by Borso d'Este, Leonello's half brother. Borso was a bachelor, and there is some reason to believe that he may have been a homosexual. He had no recorded children, a rare phenomenon even for unmarried noblemen in fifteenth-century Italy. The explanation for this, at least on one level, is simple—"non usava con le donne," reports the chronicler Hondedio da Vitale.[7] His most intimate friend and beneficiary was his *referendarius*, Ludovico Casella, a commoner upon whom Borso conferred the highest honors, including a state funeral in which the weeping duke led the funeral procession in person. An anonymous chronicler reports this with astonishment, "for the House of Este has never gone with the body of any subject." He adds: "I cannot tell you the grief which the aforementioned Signore had, for he loved him more than any brother that he had."[8] And one might add that he had a fair number. Casella, though married twice, was also childless. He named Borso as executor of his will. Whether or not this extraordinary friendship included a sexual dimension, it is clear that Borso made no attempt to provide for his subjects a normal familial role model. When Ercole succeeded him, in 1471, the new duke was already thirty-six and still unmarried. He had produced a daughter out of wedlock, but this can only have been cold comfort to those who hoped their signore would be a *paterfamilias* as well as a *pater patriae*. Eleonora's arrival thus represented, in a way that few other Renaissance marriage entrances did, the beginnings of a return to a condition of social and even sexual *normality*.

The new dynastic match also promised *continuity*, defined as a return to a regular form of succession to signorial authority. Normally, this was expected to pass from father to son. The complicated marital and extramarital alliances of Niccolò III and the peculiarities of his sons had disrupted this standard procedure, so that three of Niccolò's sons had now ruled in series.[9] Moreover, both Borso and Ercole could have been regarded in strict legal terms as usurpers, in that they prevented the succession of Niccolò, the legitimate son of Leonello and his first wife, Margherita Gonzaga. Since there were still other sons of Niccolò III waiting in the wings if anything happened to Ercole, and since Niccolò the son of Leonello still claimed the duchy from his headquarters in exile in Mantua, the prospect of a marriage that might produce a new generation of potential rulers and reestablish a traditional pattern of succession had an obvious appeal.

An additional consequence of the baccalaureal regime of Borso d'Este was that Ferrara had to forgo the *enhanced status* that Italian dynasties and states derived from advantageous marriage alliances. The ramifications of this were not only social but political, diplomatic, and military. Leonello's match with Maria of Aragon had provided an initial, if transitory, Neapolitan connection. Then came the fallow years of Borso. Now, as a result of the negotiations concluded at Naples by Ercole's emissaries and King Ferdinand, a new liaison with one of Italy's greatest ruling houses would be forged. The diplomatic posture of Ferrara, especially with respect to the papacy and Venice, would be strengthened, and the new duchess would be provided with a handsome dowry.[10] With luck, since she was young but not too young, she might be fertile, providing an abundance of marriageable offspring with which to build an even more prestigious network of dynastic connections. The promise of these real and potential benefits would not have been lost on any reasonably sophisticated Ferrarese observer, as Eleonora made her progress toward the Este city in the late spring of 1473. It was certainly not lost on the rulers of the cities through which she passed on her journey north, for they received her with pompous displays of deference. The Florentines, who valued money as much as anyone, spent 10,000 florins to entertain her. The triumphal celebrations in Rome, Florence, and elsewhere also served to enhance the self-perception of the family and court into which she had been consigned.[11]

II

A walking symbol Eleonora may have been, but it did not take long for her new subjects to size her up as a person. Certainly no beauty, she was very much her own person, and made no immediate effort to conform to the fashions of the Ferrarese nobility. One description presents her much as she appears in the miniature portrait in the Morgan Library, which Berenson attributed (optimistically) to Tura.[12] (See Plate 3.) None of the surviving portraits even faintly suggests that she was a woman of unusual ability and attainments, though her qualities emerge in the documentary sources upon which any serious study of the first duchess of Ferrara must be based.[13]

What mattered at the time was that she was there, a feminine presence from a royal family. If her rank as a princess conferred prestige on Ferrara and the added legitimacy of enhanced social worth on the Estensi, it also gave her an unusually strong hand in dealing with her spouse and her new subjects. As the daughter of the king of Naples, Eleonora had and would continue to maintain a power base of her own. How far this entered into the calculations, or even the awareness, of Ercole and his advisors when they arranged the match can probably never be known. But it seems to have made no impression on the Ferrarese chroniclers, nor on the jubilant throngs that turned out to greet her.

Even the announcement of the impending match had produced an unprecedented outpouring of popular sentiment. It came in November 1472, half a year before the event itself. One witness reports that "by this news all the subjects of Duke Ercole took comfort, celebrating and rejoicing for three days straight." [14] All the shops and businesses shut down, and the commune sponsored a series of public bonfires, which became the sites of boisterous displays of excitement, "with the people burning more things for joy, with so many noises of bells, firecrackers, explosions, and songs and cries that it was a very great wonder." Moreover, this happened not only in the capital but throughout Ercole's domains, "on account of the great happiness of his subjects." [15]

The historian is not to blame if his sources occasionally sound like narrators in second-rate film versions of grade B historical novels. He must, however, accept the responsibility of carefully examining these sources for possible bias. In the case of the "anonymous chronicler" quoted above, we have a document composed over many decades by several hands. This is a bourgeois, not a courtly, chronicle; the authors do not hesitate to reveal sources and forms of popular discontent when it surfaces, even when it is directed at the Estensi themselves. There is accordingly no reason to doubt this account. Indeed, other observers confirm its accuracy. Ugo Caleffini, whose dry, notarial voice in an unpublished chronicle of the years 1471 to 1494 offers so many detailed observations of Ferrarese life, provides substantially the same information.[16]

Compared with this apparently spontaneous outburst of enthusiasm, the actual wedding celebrations have a staged and artificial character. The sense of occasion has been ritualized into the pageantry of official receptions, religious ceremonies, elegant balls, and jousts. Even so, more spontaneous energies break through. From Regenta to Ferrara, there was dancing in the streets of every village. During the official celebrations, which lasted eight days and included ambassadors (with large retinues) from all the leading Italian cities, an effort was made not to exclude the general population of Ferrara. In what appears to the modern reader as token acknowledgment of their presence, they responded with cries of "Duca, duca." Caleffini notes that acclaim: "ognihomo ad una voce." He also appends to his description of the festivities a list of the "presents" given to Eleonora by the various guilds of Ferrara. Altogether, they raised a healthy sum.[17]

III

Once the euphoria had worn off, the new duchess was expected to fulfill more basic kinds of obligations. Paramount among these was, to put it bluntly, reproduction. No ruling member of the Este house had produced an heir, or even an heiress, in the past four decades. Ercole's claim to the duchy was not unassailable as long as Leonello's legitimate son lived, waiting in the wings in Mantua. As soon as Ercole could produce a legitimate successor, his own position would be immeasurably strengthened. Accordingly, he and the duchess undertook a vigorous program of procreation, which bore its first fruits on the night of May 17, 1474, when Eleonora gave birth to a daughter, whom in good Spanish fashion she named Isabella. On June 29 of the following year, Beatrice was born.

The proximity of these two births is notable for a social historian, for it indicates that Eleonora was being impregnated at the fastest possible rate. It is highly unlikely that she nursed Isabella, and the spacings of her subsequent pregnancies indicate the continuous use of wet nurses for the ducal offspring.[18] The chronology is as follows:

Isabella	May 17, 1474
Beatrice	June 29, 1475
Alfonso	July 21, 1476
Ferrante	September 19, 1477
Ippolito	March 19, 1479
Sigismondo	September 18, 1480
Alberto	October 16, 1481

This pattern of virtually annual deliveries seems to have been interrupted only by the advent of the Venetian war in 1482, which marks Eleonora's emergence as a power in the administration of the state. By then, she had produced a quantity of sons adequate for most contingencies, and her services were more urgently needed for other matters.[19]

Aside from the spacing of these births, and the equally interesting fact that they were so abruptly and permanently curtailed after
1481, it is instructive to observe their impact in the city. The arrival of Isabella evoked a tumultuous celebration—bonfires all
around the city and popular clamor.[20] Thirteen months later, when
Beatrice was born, "no one celebrated, because it was wished that
she might have been a male." [21] Indeed, the event receives only
extremely terse mention in the chronicles. Obviously, the birth of
Isabella was celebrated as evidence of Eleonora's fecundity. With
that question settled, what mattered was that she perpetuate the
male line.

This conclusion emerges clearly in reports on the birth of Alfonso, which was treated as a national holiday. Churchbells rang,
stores were closed for three days, and prisoners were released. Caleffini intimates that these and other events were not exactly
planned by the duke or the commune. The *popolo* appears to have
taken over:

All of a sudden all the people were in arms on the piazza; and
they ran to the prison, where they freed twenty-two prisoners;
and took them out to liberty. And then all the windscreens of
the shops surrounding the piazza, and the chests, and the wood
found on the ground and all over the place wherever it might
have been; all the booths of the notaries that were at the head
of the staircase of the city hall and elsewhere, all were burned;
along with all the windows and all the tables of the podesta of
Ferrara, and with all of the armatures of the bell-tower of the
bishop's church of Ferrara—in celebration. Lights burned on
all the towers all that night. On the piazza, in the direction of
San Romano, there were three huge fires, and three others on
the other side.

The *popolo*, in its *alegreza*, also ran to the university and burned
up the doors and benches of the scholars. Damage was widespread
throughout the city. Worst of all, Caleffini noted, was that the
record books of some of the notaries were destroyed in this incendi-

ary celebration, which has all of the elements of a riot. No wonder
we learn that "the duke then had a bit of a fever." [22] As for the
duchess, the surviving accounts cite her role only in passing.

The significance of the birth of a legitimate heir emerges very
clearly in another form. Just a few weeks after Alfonso's birth—he
had not even been baptized—Niccolò, the son of Leonello and
therefore the only other legitimate pretender to the duchy, made a
vain and desperate attempt to seize power in a violent coup.[23]
Though there is no direct evidence regarding his timing, it is rea-
sonable to conjecture that the birth of Alfonso presented him with
an ultimatum.

Meanwhile, Ercole and Eleonora lost no time in their effort to
assure a large flock of siblings. Ferrante's arrival was greeted in
more restrained fashion. He was born in Naples, where Eleonora
had gone for the wedding of her father, Ferrante or Ferdinand, to
his second wife. The news of her delivery did not reach Ferrara for
about a week, and neither Ercole nor his brother Sigismondo was
present at the time. Nonetheless, Caleffini reports, the news produced "uno pocho de feste de campane." [24] When Eleonora returned from Naples in November, the infant Ferrante stayed there,
as did Beatrice, by now two years of age. Alfonso, who had barely
attained his first birthday, had already been legally betrothed
to Anna Sforza, daughter of the recently assassinated Galeazzo
Maria.[25]

Ippolito, who was to attain fame as the patron of Ariosto and
notoriety as the instigator of one of the great crimes of passion of
the sixteenth century, was born in Ferrara.[26] Little notice was
taken of an event that by now had become routine, although one
chronicler reports some fireworks and the ringing of bells.[27] Even
these restrained observances are not reported for the births of Sigismondo and Alberto, which followed in rapid succession. Eleonora
had produced a child in every calendar year from 1474 to 1481,
except for 1478. In that year, Ercole fathered Giulio d'Este, the
only illegitimate child that he recognized during his years as duke.

IV

So far it would appear that for Eleonora, the Freudian shibboleths hold true—anatomy really was a kind of destiny. The outward aspects at least of her biological history conform very nicely to what Erik Erikson has described as the role of women in patriarchal societies: "she has let herself be confined and immobilized, enslaved and infantilized, prostituted and exploited, deriving from it at best what in psychopathology we call 'secondary gains' of devious dominance." [28] But there is other evidence to suggest that Eleonora, while making all the requisite sacrifices at the altar of motherhood, held a significantly broader view of a woman's potential role in society, even a society as dominated by men as the Este court was and for many years had been. Indeed, she created around her own person a group of writers and thinkers who fully accepted the idea of female excellence, and even superiority. As we briefly consider the range of her activities in politics and culture, the reasons for the loyalties and enthusiasms she aroused should become apparent.

Eleonora approached the obligations of her life from a twofold base of support: secular and religious. On the one hand, she maintained a team of functionaries to handle her correspondence, manage her financial affairs, organize her household, and coordinate her activities with those of the duke, with whom she maintained what might be called an affectionate formality. On the other hand, she was constantly in touch with, and derived great comfort from, the supernatural. Prayer was a daily part of her regimen, but her devoutness went beyond the ritualized piety expected of wellborn women in the fifteenth century. For her, it would appear, religion was not merely a covert form of "enslavement and infantilization," but rather provided a framework for the creative exercise of her talents.

An entry in Caleffini's chronicle enables us to gauge precisely the size and salary of Eleonora's personal staff in 1476, long before her most active period in Ferrarese political affairs.[29] (See Plate 4.) Her own personal expense account was 700 *lire marchesine* per month,

an enormous sum. Ranking courtiers and diplomats received between 20 and 80, and many retainers were paid as little as 3. Much
of this apparently went to charitable gifts. Eleonora was well
known for her generosity to poor girls in need of a dowry, and to
religious houses and the urban poor. Her administrative staff num-
bered seven, all men. Heading the list for 1476 was a Florentine,
Iacopo Acciaiuoli, listed as a "compagno." He was followed by
three Ferrarese functionaries: a seneschal, a chamberlain, and a
chancellor. The staff is completed by three other Ferrarese "gentlemen." This group is augmented by a category of ten gentlemen and
citizens, most of them Ferrarese but including one Neapolitan and
one Milanese. They are listed as *scudieri*, or squires, so they may
have been companions at arms, possibly with some executive responsibility. Their stipends ranged from 22 to 30 *lire marchesine*
per month, which is exactly the same as the salaries paid the
scudieri of the duke. In addition, there are thirty-four other salaried
workers, such as grooms, tailors, musicians, pantrymen, and a number of maidservants. All of this of course was exclusive of the ladies
in waiting with whom the duchess often spent her leisure time.

The very existence of such a sizable full-time staff presupposes a
high level of activity. In fact, during her childbearing years Eleonora continued to live an active life. Even during her pregnancies,
she traveled considerable distances, notwithstanding the rigors and
discomforts involved. She visited some of the Este territories outside Ferrara in September 1474; went to Modena in the seventh
month of her pregnancy in May 1476, returning in time to deliver
Alfonso; earlier in the same year, she had visited Venice in response
to an invitation from the signoria. In 1477, early in another pregnancy, she journeyed to Naples for a long stay, and in 1480 went off
to Mantua for a summer holiday; and so on. During all these travels, she dispatched her keen perceptions back to Ferrara. Her letters from Milan to Ercole during the wedding festivities for
Beatrice d'Este in 1491 reveal an observer finely attuned to social
nuance and acutely aware of her own actions and gestures.[30]

During her periods of residency in Ferrara, Eleonora also maintained a vigorous pace. Although occasionally drawn to such rural
pursuits as hunting, she spent far less time than Ercole at the various Estean retreats in the countryside.[31] As a result, it was she who

often served as the final arbiter of political and diplomatic decisions. Many of her letters seek retroactive approval from the duke for some action she had to take during his frequent expeditions on military campaigns or, more commonly, pleasure trips outside the city. For long periods, it was Eleonora, not Ercole, who knew and coped with the details of day-to-day events.[32] When Eleonora died, her reputation for competence, and Ercole's for a studied indifference to duty, were so extreme that her father is reported to have said, "Now the strongest bastion against the French is expunged."[33] If Ferdinand actually said this, it was a prescient remark; within a year the troops of Charles VIII were at the gates of Naples. Caleffini makes the contrast even stronger. After a detailed description of the duchess' religious and charitable activities, he writes: "She listened to the people, heard their pleas, and was accepted by the Ferrarese people. And the duke devoted himself to having a good time and playing [cards] and riding around the park."[34]

Clearly, for all her courtly responsibilities, the sacred also filled a major part of Eleonora's days. Early in 1492 Caleffini observed that "Our Duchess for certain is completely holy. Now she has dismissed from her household all drinkers, buffoons, and riff-raff. She takes communion often. Every day she stands in the oratory to pray, and almost every day she is with the sisters in the convents. And she does so many charitable acts that no one could ever count, believe, or know them, and that is most certain."[35] This suggests an activist's sort of piety, quite consistent with the moral revitalization which Eleonora and Ercole urged on the Ferrarese with dubious results.[36] Baptista Mantuanus confirms this general picture, indicating that Eleonora's political role was also well known outside the Este domains.[37]

Letters of condolence sent to Isabella d'Este, and even Ercole's epistle to the young Cardinal Hippolyto provide support for a view of Eleonora as an active, public-spirited woman who approached her secular duties from a base of profound spirituality.[38] Nonetheless, we find her as a spectator at jousts and theatrical performances, dances and dinner parties. More commonly, however, her activities tend to typify a *type serieuse*—visiting a ducal secretary on his deathbed; paying a call at the *ospedale;* serving as a witness for a betrothal or a wedding; attending a religious play, a Lenten sermon, or a learned debate on a point of doctrine.[39]

Given this general pattern of activity, and her Neapolitan-Hispanic background, one readily understands the relatively minor impact of humanist learning in her intellectual formation. Eleonora's personal library is known to us, in the form of an inventory published by Bertoni.[40] The titles indicate a preponderance of devotional works, such as breviaries, books of hours, Psalters, offices of the Blessed Virgin, lives of the saints. Though there were some exceptions, like the *De laudibus mulierum* by the Ferrarese notary Bartolommeo Goggio, and such works as Pliny's *Natural Histories* in translation, Caesar's *Commentaries,* and several French books of unknown but presumably literary substance,[41] secular and classical learning was left to the larger and more catholic interests of her husband and her eldest daughter. In a sense, Isabella's intellectual formation was to Eleonora's as that of Pantagruel was to be to Gargantua's half a century later: the new generation were beneficiaries of a more secular, more classical, and more ethically centered educational program. Although the social and political roles of mother and daughter are not dissimilar, there is a generational gap in intellectual emancipation and cultural broadening. And unlike Isabella, Eleonora was in no sense a grand acquisitor. Less imperious and demanding, far less willful and self-seeking, Eleonora was content to exercise the power that devolved upon her, rather than seeking aggrandizement. Much of her ambition seems to have been projected onto her children, and both she and they reveal this in diverse ways.[42]

To the extent that Eleonora was at all receptive to humanist culture, it was the moral and didactic aspect of the classical revival that she favored. As a young woman in Naples, she had already been the dedicatee of a vernacular work on governing well, subsequently re-presented to her as a wedding gift in Latin translation by Baptista Guarino.[43] Later, she accepted from Bartolommeo Goggio a learned treatise advancing the view that women are superior to men.[44] Toward the end of her life, the scholarly Carmelite Jacopo Foresti da Bergamo published in Ferrara another work on the exemplary qualities of women, in which Eleonora figured prominently.[45]

It is not surprising that a woman who could function as regent of a major state, lead its government in wartime, administer a sizable private estate, maintain a lively and literate correspondence, and serve as a pillar of public charity and morality—and all the while raise and advance the careers of a sizable family—had a circle of devoted admirers. Given the added circumstance of a husband who lacked something of her self-discipline and dedication to work, it even becomes possible to envision a setting in which the notion of female superiority could be seriously advanced in the Italian Quattrocento.

V

But here perhaps it would be wise to step back and approach this situation from a slightly different perspective, by asking what it means for women's history that we should be able to identify such learned and powerful women in the relatively distant past. Clearly Eleonora was exceptional, even among the royalty of her own time. She owed her prominence not only to her own talent and industry but also to the accidents of birth, an arranged marriage, a sturdy constitution, a particularly receptive public, and an astute and competent, but somewhat lazy husband. Her success, then, is largely a function of exceptional circumstances, which to an extent overturned the structural obstacles to a woman's achievement of some learning and considerable authority.

To understand the extent to which this is so, one might ask how many other women in Ferrara were able to benefit manifestly from her achievement. The answer is not encouraging to those who would like to find a profeminist trend in Renaissance society. For in its way, Eleonora's case confirms the conclusions Margaret Leah King has reached in her study of scholarly women in the Quattrocento. No other Ferrarese women of Eleonora's generation were able to defy the laws of male supremacy in an analogous, let alone comparable way. This holds true even of Eleonora's immediate circle. All of the sensitive staff positions in her household were filled by men. When she acted as regent, she directed the all-male staff attached to her husband. The works dedicated to her were all written by men; the treatises, poems, and orations that memoralized her were by men; and her surviving correspondence with nonrelatives is with men. Eleonora may have functioned effectively in a man's world, but she carried no other women on her coattails.

Except for one. Isabella d'Este alone, of all the women in Ferrarese courtly circles, emerged as a power in the worlds of politics and learning. The reasons for her ascendency, as in her mother's case, were partly personal, and partly structural. Like Eleonora, Isabella married down, though not as dramatically so as her mother. The Gonzaga were an ancient and distinguished family, but they lacked some of the antiquity, and the territorial sway, of the Estensi, and lagged a few steps behind in the race for noble titles. Isabella was thus an attractive "catch" for the Gonzaga, in purely dynastic terms. The fact that they had given shelter and logistical support to Niccolo di Leonello d'Este, who had tried in 1476 to overthrow her father, makes the match even more comparable to that of Ercole and Eleonora, for Ercole had long been at odds with her father, King Ferdinand, before his Neapolitan connection was made.

Isabella thus came to her marriage as a kind of "natural symbol" of reconciliation and acceptance; she too was able from the beginning to deal with her new family from a position of strength. Like Ercole, her husband, Francesco, was often in the field, providing scope for her administrative talents to emerge, and time for her to cultivate other interests. Her enthusiasms in the visual arts seem more closely related to her father's example; her patronage of painters and men of letters shows the same intense pursuit of beauty, magnificence, and self-aggrandizement. Isabella's advisors and assistants, too, were men, and no other women at Mantua reveal comparable learning or influence during her lifetime.

If one had to isolate a single factor to explain the attainments of a handful of extraordinary women who achieved worldly rather than merely religious success in the Renaissance, that factor would have to be social rank. It was life at the very pinnacle of a given society that might enable a woman to cultivate interests that lay beyond the narrow world of *Kinder, Küche, Kirche*. The women surrounding Eleonora and Isabella, almost all of them noble but still subordinate, amply demonstrate that mere wealth and high social status were not enough. They are literally ladies in waiting; well-groomed, well-bred people, many of whom, given more favorable circumstances, might have functioned well beyond the limits of such an ancillary role. But the limits were there. These women stood below the summit, and this affected their horizons.

The fact that Eleonora and her counterparts in other Italian cities did not produce a mass movement should not be taken to mean that their attainments were insignificant in the history of women. The conditions that enabled them—and only them—to transcend normal restrictions also made it possible for them to foster, however briefly, a new sort of intellectual climate. In the circle of Eleonora, and later of Isabella, it became possible for some to articulate an extremely positive view of women's potentialities. That the writings in which these views were expressed seem to have had no immediate, large-scale influence merely echoes the transitory impact of the women who inspired them. It was to take far more sweeping changes in ideology and socioeconomic development to produce a major reassessment of the destiny of "the second sex." But in the northern Italian courts of the late Quattrocento, in many ways, there are signs of a new awareness slowly being fanned into life. In the careers of women like Eleonora, this awareness could find a firm contemporary social base.

Notes

1. The principal contemporary descriptions are those of Ugo Caleffini and the anonymous chronicler. For the latter, see G. Pardi, ed., *Diario Ferrarese dall'anno 1409 sino al 1502 di autori incerti*, in *Rerum Italicarum Scriptores*, rev. ed., ed. G. Carducci, V. Fiorini, P. Fedele (Bologna, 1900-2), 24, pt. 7 (Bologna, 1928): 88-89, hereafter cited as DF. Caleffini's chronicle has never been published, although it is the single most important documentary source for the social and political history of Ferrara from 1471 to 1493. Citations refer to the new, stamped numbers in the original manuscript, Biblioteca Apostolica Vaticana, MS Chigiana I, I, 4, *Chronica facte et scripte per Ugo Caleffino . . .*, hereafter cited as Caleffini. G. Pardi published a truncated and selected paraphrase of this chronicle, which is more readily consulted: *Diario di Ugo Caleffini (1471-1494)*, R. Deputazione di Storia Patria per L'Emilia e la Romagna, Sezione di Ferrara,

Serie: Monumenti, 2 vols. (Ferrara, 1938, 1940). Both of these sources note the elaborate preparations made by the city for Eleonora's entry: decorative arches, allegorical *tableaux,* and other symbols of triumph.

2. *DF,* p. 132, "fu sepulta al Corpo de Christo senza sonare campane et con una regola de frati sola . . ."; cf. Caleffini, p. 298, and the entry on p. 229 of the invaluable chronicle of the notary Bernardino Zambotti, *Diario Ferrarese dall'anno 1476 sino al 1504,* ed. G. Pardi, published as an appendix to the anonymous chronicle (see n. 1, above); cited hereafter as Zambotti.

3. Eleonora's letters to Ercole, beginning in mid-September, document a rapid decline in her health. The first symptoms are restlessness and fever, apparently accompanied by acute spasmodic cough. On September 13 she writes that the past night brought "inquietudine assai; et è successo il parocismo et seguita secundo intenderà v.ra. ex.tia per littere de li medici che serano qui alligate." This letter and others in the series are quoted *in extenso* by L. Chiappini, *Eleonora d'Aragona, prima Duchessa di Ferrara* (Rovigo, 1956), p. 90. Chiappini's little book is the only monographic study of Eleonora. Its main achievement is the presentation of previously unpublished letters, or excerpts from letters, drawn from the series Carteggio dei Principi: Casa, of the Archivio Segreto Estense in the Archivio di Stato in Modena. Chiappini generally omits the archival citations. A full-scale biographical study of Eleonora, based on archival sources, is urgently needed. I have not been able to find the medical reports to which she refers in the letter quoted above.

Her reference to a "paroxysm" combined with "restlessness" and reports of fever mentioned in other letters quoted by Chiappini have led me to interpret the term, not as a fever convulsion, but as a spasm of coughing. Evidence of pulmonary difficulties emerges in some remarks by Caleffini, who on October 8 (fol. 298) reports that the duchess is near death as a result of "male de coste et fluxo." Pain in the ribs and flux, or copious discharge of bloody fluids, considered together with fever and "paroxysm," would seem to point in the direction of pneumonia, though the diagnosis cannot be verified. The same terms are used in Ercole's letter to his son Hippolito, announcing Eleonora's death (p. 96): "male dele coste dopoi chel hebbe piu giorni alcuni febre."

4. There is a rich scholarly literature on the symbolics of power as expressed in public spectacle in early modern Europe, little of it influenced by anthropological studies, which have helped to shape the conceptual framework for what follows here. Of particular interest are R. Strong, *Splendor at Court: Renaissance Spectacle and the Theatre of Power* (Boston, 1973); S. Anglo, *Spectacle, Pageantry, and Early Tudor Policy* (Oxford,

1969); D. M. Bergeron, *English Civic Pageantry, 1558-1642* (London, 1971); *The Courts of Europe: Politics: Patronage and Royalty, 1400-1800*, ed. A. G. Dickens (New York, 1977). For citations of the relevant comparative and cross-cultural analysis, see esp. the notes in a suggestive article by C. Geertz, "Centers, Kings and Charisma: Reflections on the Symbolics of Power," in *Culture and Its Creators*, ed. J. Ben-David and T. N. Clark (Chicago, 1977). On dynastic continuity, see E. H. Kantorowicz, *The King's Two Bodies* (Princeton, 1957), pp. 317-36.

5. For the intellectual climate of the Neapolitan court, we still fall back on E. Gothein, *Die Culturentwicklung Sud-Italiens in Einzeldarstellung* (Breslau, 1886), the second half of which was translated by T. Persico as *Il Rinascimento nell'Italia meridionale* (Florence, 1915). Diomede Carafa, one of the most venerated and influential courtiers of the Aragonese monarchs, dedicated to Eleonora his most important treatise on government, dealing with public administration; the preservation of authority; economic and political problems; and the duties of a ruler in advancing agriculture, commerce, and domestic harmony (see n. 43, below). On Carafa, there is mainly T. Persico, *Diomede Carafa, uomo di stato e scrittore del secolo XV* (Naples, 1899); and, most recently, the bio-bibliographical article by F. Petrucci in *Dizionario Biografico degli Italiani*, 19 (Rome, 1976): 524-30.

6. *DF*, p. 27; she left Ferrara on October 24, 1443, "per stare," taking all of her personal possessions with her. She returned to Ferrara on June 9, 1472, and died there two years later.

7. Unpublished chronicle in the Biblioteca Comunale di Ferrara, MS C1 I, 757; cited by G. Pardi, "Borso d'Este," *Studi Storici*, ed. A. Crivellucci, vols. 15-16 (Pisa, 1906-7). Professor Lewis Lockwood brought this phrase to my attention and was the first to notice its pointed implications, though he cautiously suggests that Borso "remained a bachelor, thus preventing civil war at his death." See "Music at Ferrara in the Period of Ercole I d'Este," *Studi Musicali* 1,1 (1972): 111. There is new evidence to suggest that homosexuality was a serious problem in Ferrara in the 1470s. The Pierpont Morgan Library possesses a copy of the 1476 redaction of the statutes of Ferrara, *Statuta civitatis ferrariae* (Ferrara: Severinus Ferrariensis). Book IV, *De variis delictorum penis*, deals with criminal punition. On fol. 110v, opposite a rubric mandating the death penalty for unnatural sex acts, a contemporary hand has noted "Hoc statutum hodie vaccat ne tota gens pereat." Caleffini, fol. 40v, indicates in 1475 the alarming fact that few men are marrying in Ferrara: "pochissimi e pochissimi maritazi se fano in Ferrara: et songli tante zovene da marito che è cossa stupendissima. Et la ragione e che sono tante putane casalenghe in Fer-

rara, che la brigata non circa di tore moglie." Whether his explanation of domestic prostitution, or the prevalence of male homosexuality explains the superfluity of marriageable girls is not clear. For some useful hypotheses on these kinds of problems, see D. Herlihy, "Some Psychological and Social Roots of Violence in the Tuscan Cities," in *Violence and Civil Disorder in Italian Cities, 1200-1500*, ed. L. Martines (Berkeley & Los Angeles, 1972), pp. 129-54, esp. p. 146, on sex ratios.

8. *DF*, pp. 58-59.

9. This, too, is of course a kind of continuity, as I have argued in *Ferrara: The Style of a Renaissance Despotism* (Princeton, 1973), pp. 173-75; but it is not the sort of continuity upon which dynastic regimes can depend indefinitely. Only succession from parent to child—from generation to generation—can assure some degree of permanency. Cf. Kantorowicz, n. 4, above.

10. This and other aspects of the marriage have been covered by L. Olivi, "Delle Nozze di Ercole I con Eleonora d'Aragona," *Memorie della R. Accademia di Scienze, Letter ed Arti di Modena*, ser. 2, 5 (Modena, 1887): 34 ff.

11. Aspects of Eleonora's ceremonial journey have been studied by Olivi and by C. Corvisieri, "Il trionfo romano di Eleonora d'Aragona nel giugno del 1473," *Archivio della Società Romana di Storia Patria* 1 (1878): 475-91; and Chiappini, *Eleonora d'Aragona*, pp. 13-17.

12. Chiappini, p. 16, offers this judgment: "Ottima fu l'impressione suscitata da Eleonora *nonostante fosse piccoletta e piuttosto bruttina*" (italics mine). Caleffini simply notes that her hair is dark and worn down in the Neapolitan style, while the anonymous diarist (pp. 88-89), while using adjectives like "nobille" and "illustrissimo" to describe Eleonora, avoids "bella" and its superlatives, though he uses them eight times in describing other aspects of the festivities, including the appearance of "tute le belle done da Ferrara." The most candid description of the new duchess is that of Hondedio da Vitale (MS cit. in n. 7, entry of August 22, 1489): "questa Dona era de statura bassa e picola, grassa e grosa, lo volto largo, lo colo curto, più bruno che biancha, la bocha picola, lo ochio negro e picolo, ecc." This was written toward the end of her life, but she was only thirty-nine.

13. See especially the letters quoted throughout Chiappini, *Eleonora d'Aragona*, esp. pp. 52-58.

14. *DF*, p. 82: "per questo se confortava tutti li subditi del prefacto duca Hercole a farne tre giorni continui festa et faluo. . . . Et tre giorni continui durce questo; et come fu facto in Ferrara, fu facto per tutte le cittadi,

castelle et logi di epso signore duca Hercole, per alegreza grande che hebeno li suoi subditi."

15. *DF,* p. 82: The terms used by the Ferrarese chroniclers to describe what went on during these festive periods are sometimes difficult to translate. I have rendered *schiopeti* as firecrackers, but without any confidence that the English term gives any real sense of what was going on; perhaps gunfire would be better. Similarly, I give *bombarde* as explosions, but it is impossible even to guess what sorts of explosions these were.

16. Caleffini, fol. 11v. This account is so close to that of the anonymous chronicler that it seems they may have a common origin, although normally there is substantial stylistic and substantive variation between the two accounts.

17. Caleffini, fol. 19 yr. Twenty-eight guilds are listed, with a total contribution of 2,644 *lire marchesane,* 11 *soldi.* The larger gifts were:

Notari e procuratori	£400
Bancheri de ferrara	£280
Muraduri	£200
Doctori de leze	£168
Doctori de medexine	£160

It is understandable that the learned professions stood at the upper end of this list, given Ferrarese income structures; what is surprising is such a large gift from the builders. The building trades in fifteenth-century Ferrara deserve particular study, such as has recently been directed to their Florentine counterparts by R. Goldthwaite, "The Florentine Palace as Domestic Architecture," *American Historical Review* 77 (1972); 977-1012, and a forthcoming book. It is also worth noting that most of these major guilds made their contributions in what might be called hard currency— florins or ducats—which are given along with their equivalent value in Ferrarese coin.

18. The intervals between births and new pregnancies during the period in which Eleonora was bearing children averaged less than six months. The most recent discussion of upper-class childbearing and child-rearing practices in early modern Europe is L. Stone, *The Family, Sex, and Marriage in England, 1500-1800* (New York, 1977), pp. 42-65. But see also P. Laslett, ed., *Household and Family in Past Time* (Cambridge, 1972), for several useful studies.

19. Eleonora ceased childbearing at the very beginning of the war of Venice and Ferrara, in which she became deeply involved. During critical

periods of the struggle, Ercole was incapacitated by the recurrence of a serious injury to his foot. While Venetian troops were besieging Ferrara, he lay virtually in a coma, while Eleonora managed Ferrara's resistance and maintained the credibility of the regime. This period represented her coming of age as a ruler to whom even the duke looked for advice, support, and continuous hard work. My *Ferrara*, pp. 215-16, does not stress this development sufficiently; it emerges more clearly in E. G. Gardner, *Dukes and Poets in Ferrara* (London, 1904), chap. 6, "The War of Ferrara," pp. 165-211.

20. *DF*, p. 90, mentions the event in passing, but Caleffini, fol. 25, notes some public disturbances by way of celebration.

21. *DF*, p. 90: "Nacete una fiola al duca Hercole, chiamata Beatrice, figliola di madonna Leonora sua moglie, et non si fece allegreza, perchè volea ch'el fusse maschio." Caleffini merely records the birth.

22. Caleffini, fol. 62, gives the best account, concluding with the words "Et anche in molto altri lochi feceno danno grande; ma pezo (peggio) di notari a chi furno brusi li libri, instrumenti, et processi per dicta alegreza. Et nota chel duca tunc havea uno pocho de febra." This is an excellent example of a celebration in honor of an existing regime becoming what appears to a modern observer to be an expression of acute social unrest. Central institutions of the social hierarchy—the university and the legal system—were attacked by the crowds, and the forces of order were unable to cope with the situation. N. Z. Davis has suggested some explanations for the social function of comparable forms of group behavior in sixteenth-century France. See "The Reasons of Misrule" and "The Rites of Violence," both recently reprinted in her *Society and Culture in Early Modern France* (Stanford, 1975), pp. 47-123, 152-88. In this instance, Niccolò di Leonello may have been encouraged to attempt his attack on Ercole by what might have appeared to him an indication of popular disaffection for the regime. This was a serious miscalculation, although there was clearly a number of dissidents ready to rally to his cause.

23. See my *Ferrara*, pp. 180-83. The standard account of Niccolò's career is still A. Cappelli, "Niccolò di Leonello d'Este," *Atti e Memorie della Deputazione Modenese di Storia Patria*, 5 (1870): 413-58, with documents; and further bibliography in L. Chiappini, *Gli Estensi* (Verona, 1967), pp. 525-26.

24. Caleffini, fol. 85v.

25. Under Ercole, the Milanese alliance became a cornerstone of Ferrarese diplomacy, designed as it was to offset the danger posed both by Venetian expansionist aims and the growing effectiveness of papal territorial administration. Ercole's general goal was to keep these powers at

bay through diplomatic and marital alliances with Naples and Milan, reciprocal agreements with the smaller states of Urbino and Mantua, and military collaboration with Florence whenever possible. Gardner, *Dukes and Poets*, gives the best English account.

26. R. Bacchelli, *La Congiura di don Giulio d'Este* (Milan, 1958; first published, 1931), provides a stirring and comprehensive account of the tragic events of 1505-6. For Ippolito I, see also T. Gerevich, "Ippolito d'Este arcivescovo di Strigonio," *Corvina* (Budapest, 1921); C. Marcora, "Il cardinale Ippolito d'Este arcivescovo di Milano (1494-1519)," *Memorie storiche Diocesanale di Milano*, 5 (1958); H. Hauvette, *L'Arioste et la Poésie Chevaleresque à Ferrare au Début du XVIe Siècle* (Paris, 1927), pp. 88-125; M. Catalano, *Vita di Ludovico Ariosto* (Geneva, 1931).

27. Zambotti, p. 62: "Eleonora parturi uno fiolo maschio in Castello Vechio, per il che de alegreza fu sonate tutte le campane e facto fogo denanti a la porta del dicto Castello, tragando schiopiti e bombardelle insino à di."

28. See his essay, "Womanhood and the Inner Space," in *Identity, Youth and Crisis* (New York, 1968), pp. 261-94; repr. in J. Strouse, *Women and Analysis* (New York, 1974), pp. 291-319, where it is accompanied by a follow-up essay, "Once More the Inner Space: Letter to a Former Student," pp. 320-40, in which the argument is further developed. The passage quoted appears on p. 311, where Erikson argues that particular historical conditions have led to a form of biological determinism, which social change may serve to undermine and perhaps even destroy.

29. Caleffini, fol. 55v.

30. These have been published by L. Chiappini, *Eleonora d'Aragona*, pp. 67-74.

31. Until the last months of their marriage, Eleonora was clearly a person of greater physical vitality than Ercole, who suffered chronically from pain resulting from a serious injury to his right foot at the battle of La Molinella. From the 1480s on, he often walked with a cane, and his correspondence with Eleonora indicates that many of his travels took him to spas, where he could try new treatments for this debilitating condition. See, e.g., Chiappini, *Eleonora d'Aragona*, p. 58, where in a letter dated May 30, 1485, Ercole writes: "Continuemo ogni zorno quisti bagni, et ben che in questi quatro di che siamo stati qua, se possi mal judicare che fructo habino anchora facto al nostro piede, pur a nuy pare et cusi anche al Medico che habino giovato et operato qualche cosa, et speremo de bene in meglio." Eleonora took the cure on at least one occasion, which produced several interesting letters from Montegrotto, where she seems to have been treated for apoplexy. See the texts in Chiappini, pp. 59-60.

32. This was especially true during the most critical days of the war of Venice and Ferrara. See Zambotti, pp. 119-20, for the best account; for a brief summary, see my *Ferrara*, pp. 215-17.

33. L. A. Muratori, *Antichità Estensi ed Italiani*, 2 (1740): 259. Given the source, the remark may be apocryphal.

34. Caleffini, fol. 280: "Et dà audentia al populo et spaza supplicatione et è accepta al populo ferrarese. *Et il Duca se attende a dare piacere et zugare et fare il barcho"* (italics mine).

35. Caleffini, fol. 280.

36. On religious life in Ferrara during this period, see my *Ferrara*, pp. 193-200; see also W. L. Gundersheimer, ed., *Art and Life at the Court of Ercole I d'Este: The 'De triumphis religionis' of Giovanni Sabadino degli Arienti* (Geneva, 1972), pp. 32-37, 107-10. Lockwood, p. 114, describes Ercole's "deep personal religiosity, amounting almost to fanaticism." In a forthcoming article, I shall discuss the impact of ducal piety on public welfare and popular culture in Ferrara. See also two brief studies by L. Chiappini, "Ercole I d'Este e Girolamo Savonarola," and "Un brucia-mento delle vanità a Ferrara nel 1474," both in *Atti e Memorie della Deputazione Ferrarese di Storia Patria*, 7, pt. 3 (1952).

37. For excerpts, and a note on other memorial writings, see Zambotti, pp. 229-30, esp. n. 9; also Chiappini, *Eleonora d'Aragona*, pp. 96-98.

38. Chiappini, *Eleonora d'Aragona*, p. 96: After praising her virtues and describing her suffering and her Christian death, Ercole admonished his fourteen-year-old son not to give in to grief, for that would not be politic: "Il vi bisogna questa volta portarvi per modo che siasi reputato savio et prudente Cardinale et homo et non giovene et di grande animo et non pusillo et apto a tollerare le adversita sicome a temperare le prosperità et questo è veramente un caso da dar inditio dela virtù del anomo vostro et dela constantia che debe havere un vostro pare prelato et constituo in tale dignità quale è il cardinalto. . . . Sichè fati come confidimo in voi." Given Eleonora's strenuous efforts to gain this new rank for her second-born son, she would doubtless have approved Ercole's strong admonition.

39. G. Pardi, ed., *Diario di Ugo Caleffini*, 2: 424-51.

40. *La biblioteca estense e la cultura ferrarese ai tempi del duca Ercole I, 1471-1505* (Turin, 1903), pp. 229-33.

41. For Goggio and his important treatise *De laudibus mulierum*, see Conor Fahy, "Three Early Renaissance Treatises on Women," *Italian Studies* 12 (1965): 30-55, and my forthcoming article, "Bartolommeo Goggio: A Feminist in Renaissance Ferrara," *Renaissance Quarterly* (1980).

42. Of special interest in this context is the correspondence between

Ercole and Eleonora concerning Hippolito's advancement in the church. See Chiappini, *Eleonora d'Aragona*, pp. 91-92.

43. *De regis et boni principis officio*, first printed in Naples in 1668. The Biblioteca Estense in Modena has a manuscript, MS Est. lat. 679 (Alpha T9, 16) including the oration and a letter from Eleonora to Caraffa informing him of the Latin version.

44. See n. 41, above. For Goggio's arguments on female superiority, see British Library, MS Additional 17415, esp. bks. II and V.

45. *De claris mulieribus* (Ferrara, 1493).

CHAPTER 4

Book-Lined Cells:
Women and Humanism In The Early Italian
Renaissance

Margaret L. King[*]

"Shall I marry, or devote my life to study?" Alessandra Scala asked Cassandra Fedele. "Do that for which your nature has suited you," responded Fedele, not very helpfully.[1] Both women understood that marriage and scholarship might be incompatible. Both understood that the pursuit of learning required deliberate choice, the repudiation of ordinary goals, and an extraordinary commitment of energies. Both married.

I shall endeavor to describe here the condition of the learned woman in the early Renaissance, so that we may begin to understand not only why Scala and Fedele chose as they did, but why they felt they had to choose at all. First, I shall outline some common patterns in the careers of learned women. Then I shall explore the perceptions learned women had of themselves and the perceptions of them held by learned men. I shall conclude by assessing the

[*] I am indebted to Professor Paul Oskar Kristeller, who has assisted me in all my work on the learned women of the Renaissance, and to Professor Albert Rabil, Jr., who generously shared with me his work on Laura Cereta, and in collaboration with whom I intend to publish a selection of works by women humanists.

66

significance of the phenomenon of the learned woman of the early Italian Renaissance for the later development of woman's role in the society of the learned. Her achievements and her failures are still with us.

Thwarted Ambitions

By participating in the humanist movement as it emerged in fourteenth- and fifteenth-century Italy, women took part in a community of learning essential to the development of Renaissance civilization and consequential for the evolving intellectual life of modern Europe. Women constituted a small minority among humanists; yet their participation was significant. There were perhaps a dozen who could easily be named; perhaps another twenty, less visible, could be identified; others perhaps existed whose identities will elude us; perhaps three, in these centuries, were famous. But their significance is not in numbers.[2]

The women humanists typically came either from the court cities of northern Italy, ruled by despots, or from the Veneto. They came from prominent families. Some (such as Battista Montefeltro, Cecilia Gonzaga, Costanza Varano) were the daughters of ruling families. Some (such as Isotta Nogarola, Cassandra Fedele, Laura Cereta) belonged to the urban aristocratic and professional elite. Often they were born in families that specialized in learning. Some even came from families that specialized in learned *women*. Battista Montefeltro, Costanza Varano, Cecilia Gonzaga, and the sixteenth-century poet Vittoria Colonna were all related, as were the three Nogarolas (Angela, Isotta, and Ginevra) and the later poet Veronica Gambara.[3] Learned women, therefore, came from a limited set of environments specifically favorable to their education and advancement.

They were educated, typically, by men. Some were educated by their fathers. Alessandra Scala was trained by her father Bartolommeo, one of Florence's great humanist chancellors in the fifteenth century.[4] Laura Cereta studied with her father Silvestro, a member of Brescia's solid governing elite.[5] Caterina Caldiera studied assiduously with her father Giovanni, a physician, whose enthusiasm for his daughter's genius is revealed in the prefaces to two works he wrote for her.[6] His words may suggest the pride in their learned daughters felt by other fathers whose words have not survived: "[Our] little daughter," Giovanni wrote his brother, "exceeds all others in excellence of mind, in depth of character, and in knowledge of the liberal arts, not according to my judgment alone but to that of the wisest men who flourish in this [barbarous] age." [7]

Other women were educated by tutors. The Nogarola sisters were taught by Martino Rizzoni, himself a student of Guarino Veronese.[8] Cassandra Fedele was taught by Gasparino Borro, for whom she expresses deep respect in a letter written after her training had ended.[9] Olimpia Morata studied with two brothers, one expert in Greek, one in medicine and natural philosophy.[10] Cecilia Gonzaga's education is best known. She joined her brothers as pupils of Vittorino da Feltre in the Casa Giocosa (joyous house), a pioneering humanist school founded and protected by the marquis of Mantua, her father.[11]

Trained by wise fathers and excellent teachers in the languages, literature, history, poetry, and moral philosophy of the ancients, the learned women of this epoch often showed early and brilliant promise.[12] Costanza Varano was sixteen when she recited a Latin oration, universally acclaimed for its fineness, to Bianca Maria Visconti.[13] Cecilia Gonzaga had mastered Greek by age eight.[14] Isotta Nogarola and Cassandra Fedele were still young when their glory was at its peak.[15] Laura Cereta's literary career was well under way before her marriage at age fifteen, and it may have culminated at age eighteen, twelve years before her death.[16] Olimpia Morata's career flowered soon after her entry to the d'Este court at age fourteen.[17] The precocity of these women was remarkable even in an age that valued precocity. But their early achievements form an intriguing contrast with the difficulties several of these women experienced when advancing age necessitated hard decisions about adult roles.

A young woman was free to be studious. There were no other demands made of her, and the period of adolescence for those with literary interests was a period of freedom. But that freedom could not last into adulthood. A young woman eventually confronted a choice between two futures: marriage and full participation in social life on the one hand; or abstention from marriage and withdrawal from the world.[18] For learned women, the choice was agonizing. To marry implied the abandonment of beloved studies. Not to marry implied the abandonment of the world. It was this dilemma that faced Alessandra Scala, with whose question of Cassandra Fedele this essay began. Both understood the implications of a decision for marriage. Some learned women did in fact marry, and their studies virtually ended with their marriage: among these, in addition to Scala and Fedele, were Costanza Varano and Ginevra Nogarola. Others withdrew from the world, either to a convent, like Cecilia Gonzaga, or to a self-imposed solitude at home, like Isotta Nogarola. Others, having married, survived their husbands to devote years of solitary widowhood to renewed pursuits of knowledge: among these, Laura Cereta.[19] The community of marriage, it seems, inhibited the learned woman from pursuing studious interests, and certainly prevented her from realizing ambitions she might have cherished for greatness. The freedom of solitude permitted, in some cases, the learned woman to develop intellectual capacities—but that freedom, perhaps more apparent than real, was purchased at the cost of solitude. I shall return to consider what feelings experienced by learned women might have persuaded them to seek freedom in the book-lined cells of the solitary life. First, some preliminary judgment should be made about the achievements of the learned women of the early Italian Renaissance.

Learned women achieved competence in the difficult material of humanist studies and composed works in most of the usual genres: letters, orations, dialogues, treatises, and poems. Much of their writing is mediocre; but then much that was written by male humanists is mediocre as well. The greatest number, perhaps, of their works constitute mere declarations of competence. Chief among these is Cassandra Fedele's oration on the liberal arts, recited at the University of Padua in 1487.[20] The oration is unoriginal—though it won Cassandra great fame. It is remarkable not in itself but because a woman had acquired the skills necessary to compose it without error and to deliver it with poise to an audience of some of Europe's most learned men. Other works by learned women were written to achieve political or social ends sought by male relatives: Costanza Varano's oration to Bianca Maria Visconti and letter to

King Alfonso of Aragon were written to obtain for her brothers the lordship of Camerino, and Battista Montefeltro's oration to Emperor Sigismund was designed to enlist that monarch's aid in restoring her husband and her son-in-law to ancestral lands.[21] Perhaps the finest works produced by learned women are those that directly or indirectly describe their authors' struggles to gain recognition and pursue their studies. These include Isotta Nogarola's dialogue on Adam and Eve and Laura Cereta's letters on her own life.[22] The achievement of learned women in this age was substantial: they participated more than adequately in the secular society of the learned.

Yet their achievement is flawed. Its deficiency is seen not in what learned women did in fact achieve, but in what they failed to achieve. Their accomplishments, on the whole, did not match their early promise. Their ambitions, too often, were not realized. Their success was disturbed by too many defeats.

Only a few learned women continued to write—and presumably to labor at their studies—after the brilliant years of youth. Among the learned women whose mature years yielded little or no intellectual activity are Maddalena Scrovegni, known for her learning in the Paduan years of her early widowhood; Cecilia Gonzaga, whose youthful retirement to a convent was encouraged by the Venetian cleric Gregorio Correr; Ginevra Nogarola, who had enjoyed in her adolescence the same acclaim as her sister; Cassandra Fedele, whose productive years ended with her marriage at age thirty-three but who lived in near silence for sixty thereafter, pursued perhaps by the memory of past glory. And Isotta Nogarola and Laura Cereta, two among those who continued their studies, perhaps until death, did not find the tranquillity they sought in dedicating themselves to the pursuit of knowledge. The ambitions of the learned women of the Renaissance were thwarted: some never achieved goals they were capable and apparently desirous of achieving; others achieved partial goals at inordinate cost.

This pattern of failure in the careers of learned women was due, certainly, in part, to the absence of opportunities for them to enter learned professions—but I shall leave this issue to another place. I shall be concerned, instead, here with the attitudes held by women and men that also help to explain this pattern of failure. They were not less important than social obstacles to the realization of ambitions among learned women, and they are more elusive.

Book-lined Cells

Remarkable people sometimes know they are remarkable. Laura Cereta did. She enjoyed her studies; she understood her talents; she delighted in describing to those who asked and to some who didn't how she had progressed to her present stage of knowledge. Gradually her talents emerged, she reported; as her mind acquired small particles of knowledge, she learned to supply words to adorn them; her mind yearned for studies even more challenging; as her understanding expanded, so did her diligence; she loved philosophy above all; she burned with desire for mathematics; she delved deeply into theology, and she found there knowledge not "shadowy and vaporous" but "perpetually secure and perfect." [23] At birth she had been given the name of Laura, whom Petrarch had immortalized in his sonnets; now she labored in imitation of Petrarch to lend that name still grander eternity.[24] Cereta was proud of her mind. She was unique.

Learned women more typically betray their fragile self-confidence. "Even the wisest and most famous men would fear to attempt to praise you adequately," Costanza Varano wrote in her oration to Bianca Maria Visconti; "What then can I, an ignorant, unlettered, and inexperienced girl hope to do?"[25] Cassandra Fedele began her oration to the learned doctors of Padua with a more elaborate but similar demurral: "I must put an end to my timidity, and many of you no doubt will see it as audacious, that I, a maiden, who even if I were older could possess no learning, disregarding the boundaries of my sex and mental powers, have come forth to speak in this radiance of learned men, and moreover in this city, in which in our age (as once in Athens) the studies of the liberal arts flourish." [26] Isotta Nogarola apologizes not only for being a woman with pretenses of learning but for being a woman at all, in a work which is, I believe, the most important written by a woman in the early Italian Renaissance: the *De pari aut impari Evae atque Adae peccato,* a dialogue on the relative responsibility of Adam and Eve for the fall of mankind from grace.[27] Nogarola condemned Adam in this dialogue, but based her defense of Eve, paradoxically, on the weakness of female nature. Eve, who had been created imperfect, could not be held responsible for universal sin: "for where there is less sense and less constancy," Nogarola wrote, "there there is less sin; and this is the case with Eve, wherefore she sinned less." [28] Eve's ignorance was natural and deliberately planted by God; but Adam had been created perfect and could be expected to behave perfectly: "When God created man, from the beginning he created him perfect, and the potencies of his soul he made perfect, and gave him a greater understanding and knowledge of truth, and also a greater profundity of wisdom." [29] Nogarola's uncertainties about her role as a woman—put into question by her confrontation with the world of male learning—culminate here in the clear conviction that woman was in fact created inferior to man and that all women had to bear the burden of this first act of creation.

Nogarola gives voice in this dialogue and in her other works to a concern shared certainly to some degree by several and perhaps by all. Her success in the society of the learned was inhibited by her membership in the female sex. The acuity of her mind could be undermined by the frailty of her nature. Not surprisingly, learned women on occasion regretted having been born female and attempted to distance themselves from other women. Not surprisingly, other women despised them.

Both Nogarola and Cereta were attacked by other women and fought to distinguish themselves from the unlettered members of their sex. Nogarola had addressed a letter to her compatriot, Guarino Veronese.[30] When Guarino did not reply after several months, the women of Verona ridiculed Nogarola, condemning her arrogance in approaching so great a man and rejoicing in her humiliation by his silence. Desperately, she wrote Guarino a second time, reproaching him for having exposed her to the mockery of her sex:

There are already so many women in the world! Why then . . . was I born a woman, to be scorned by men in words and deeds? I ask myself this question in solitude. I do not dare to ask it of you, who have made me the butt of everyone's jokes. . . . For they jeer at me throughout the city, the women mock me. [I, a woman, in turning to you, a man, am like a donkey yoked to an ox; when I fall in the mud, as I must, when dragged by so strong a beast, neither my own kind, nor yours, will have anything to do with me.] I cannot find a quiet stable to hide in, and the donkeys tear me with their teeth, the oxen stab me with their horns.[31]

Nogarola's literary ambitions had exposed her to the envy and hostility of her sex. Laura Cereta, too, was the object of fierce criticism by women. She responded with spirit, understanding both the envy that may have motivated the attacks and the self-destructiveness implicit in any attack on women by women: these women search out others who have risen above them by their genius and destroy them with poisonous envy, she wrote. "I cannot bear these babbling and chattering women who, aflame with wine and drunkenness, do injury by their impudent words not only to the [female] sex but above all to themselves." "Burning with the fires of hatred, the more they gnaw others, spewing forth words, the more are they wordless, gnawed within." Virtue and learning, she concludes, are not acquired through destiny but through effort; these women who are unable to ascend to knowledge fall into sloth and sink into the filth of pleasures.[32]

Less pained than Nogarola by the attacks of other women, Cereta more easily defends herself and more aggressively turns on her enemies.[33] She ruthlessly condemns empty women, who strive for no good but exist to adorn themselves and do not understand that their condition is one of servitude: these women of majestic pride, fantastic coiffures, outlandish ornament, and necks bound with gold or pearls bear the glittering symbols of their captivity to men who are proud enough to be free.[34] For Nogarola, women's inferiority derived from the order of things, from a divine decree asserted at the hour of creation; for Cereta it is derived from women themselves, who lacked the will to be good, to be learned, to be free: "For knowledge is not given as a gift, but through study. . . . The free mind, not afraid of labor, presses on to attain the good." [35]

Nogarola and Cereta clearly reveal their attitudes toward themselves as women and as learned women; others speak less fully, but sufficiently to persuade us that the consciousness of womanhood in the quest for intellectual integrity was probably general.[36] Being women, they were burdened. To succeed wholly, they would have had to cast off that burden—but it is a burden that cannot be cast off. Or they would have had to elevate the whole of their sex—but this they were powerless to do. The ambitions of the learned women of the Renaissance were thwarted *in part* because, being women, they were vanquished from within: by their own self-doubt, punctuated by moments of pride; and by their low evaluation of their sex, which undermined their confidence further and which was confirmed by the behavior of other women for whom the intellectual strivings of a few threatened their condition of comfortable servitude.

The learned women, conquered from within, capitulated and withdrew from battle. They withdrew from study altogether, into marriage, or into grief. They withdrew to convents and to good works and to silence. They withdrew from secular studies, where men excelled, and took up sacred studies, appropriate for women, and formed cloisters of their minds. They withdrew from friendships, from the life of their cities, from public view, to small corners of the world where they worked in solitude: to self-constructed prisons, lined with books—to book-lined cells, my symbol for the condition of the learned women of this age.

There, they fascinated men. Matteo Bosso recalled years later his after-school visits to Isotta Nogarola in her "libraria cella"—literally, her book-lined cell.[37] Ludovico Foscarini was struck by the same image of that learned woman—by then committed to sacred study and religious exercises—in her solitude: "In my mind I see again your little cell [*cellulam tuam*] redolent of sanctity." [38] Years earlier, Antonio Loschi had been inspired by a similar image of Maddalena Scrovegni: "Your virtues, your manner of life . . . so moved me, and a vision of your little cell [*sacellum*], that one place in your father's house which you had chosen and set aside for silence, for study, and for prayer, was so fixed in my soul that it first gave birth to this meditation within me." [39] Women enclosed themselves in studious solitude, and men applauded. And women sought their approbation. When learned women withdrew from the public discourse of the learned, they may have been moved in part by the powerful spur of male opinion. They were defeated, I have suggested, from within—but the attitudes toward them held by male contemporaries were sharp probes that could penetrate deep within the hearts where that battle raged that ended in surrender.

Armed Maidens

Male humanists praised learned women extravagantly.[40] Angelo Poliziano went to Venice, he said, specifically to meet Cassandra Fedele. His famous letter to her, which followed upon their meeting, praises her highly indeed; for he compared her favorably with Giovanni Pico della Mirandola, his friend and one of that century's monumental geniuses.[41] Costanza Varano's first public oration won Guiniforte Barzizza's warm commendation of Varano and of her grandmother, the learned Battista Montefeltro, who had had the wisdom to cultivate in her young relative a simulacrum of her own excellence.[42] In an age when learning was prized, learning in women was prized as well—all the more because it was rare.

But such praise is treacherous. For the women who competed with learned men and who had the boldness to equal or exceed them were not in recognition of their excellence admitted to the company of men—yet they were excluded from the company of women.[43] Like divine miracles, they were both wondrous and terrible; as prodigies, they had exceeded—and violated—nature. Male by intellect, female in body and in soul, their sexual identity was rendered ambiguous: they were, to borrow Nogarola's imagery, rejected by donkeys and oxen alike, expelled from either stable, abandoned, restless, and sleepless. Not quite male, not quite female, learned women belonged to a third and amorphous sex.

The ambiguous sexual identity of learned women was assumed from the early age of humanism. In dedicating his book *De claris mulieribus (Concerning Famous Women)* to Andrea Accaiuoli, Boccaccio declared that learned woman to have so far exceeded the rest of womankind that her sexual being had in fact been transformed by a miraculous divine act: "and when I saw that what Nature has taken from the weaker sex God in His liberality has granted to you, instilling marvelous virtues within your breast, and that He willed you to be known by the name you bear (since in Greek *andres* means "men"), I [judged] that you should be set

equal to the worthiest men, even among the ancients." [44] Her very
greatness, Boccaccio reasons, in which she equals male greatness,
suggests that Andrea was not so much a talented female as a
woman transformed by the Creator himself and made—not a man—
but a being of compound and indefinite sexuality.

Other men in the next century would, like Boccaccio, in the
rhetoric of praise question and transform the sexual identity of
intelligent women. Lauro Querini found that Isotta Nogarola had
attained greatness by overcoming her biological nature: "The
greatest praise is justly bestowed upon you, illustrious Isotta, since
you have . . . overcome your own nature. For that true virtue,
which is essentially male, you have sought with singular zeal . . .
such as befits the whole and perfect virtue that men attain." [45]
Pietro Dabuson said of Cassandra Fedele that she was the "miracle" of the age; for a male soul had been born in one of female
sex.[46] Angelo Poliziano understood that Fedele had, by attaining
deep learning, detached herself from her sex, abandoning symbolic
objects associated with women in favor of those associated with
men: instead of wool, books; instead of a needle, a pen; instead of
white dyes to blanch the skin, black ink to stain the page in the
process of poetic creation.[47] Not the muses, not the sibyls, not the
Delphic priestesses, nor any of the learned women of antiquity,
Greek or Roman, however eloquent, could compare with her: "For
this we know indeed, this we know," he wrote, "that she was not
damned along with her sex to dullness and stupidity." [48] She, too,
had overcome her sex, had created a man within her womanliness,
and had become a creature of ambiguous identity, belonging to a
third and unknown sex beyond the order of nature. The learned
women of the Renaissance, in the eyes of their male contemporaries and friends, ceased, in becoming learned, to be women.

Whatever they were—and shortly I shall sketch the image I believe was applied to them—they aroused fear and anger in male
contemporaries, who then joined to constrain these brilliant creatures perceived as threats to the natural and social order. Perhaps
the most brutal attack was an anonymous one upon Isotta Nogarola: she was accused of incest. Having aroused her enemy's anger
by repudiating through her intellectual activity a role proper for

women, he responded, not surprisingly, with an assault on her sexual integrity. He wrote:

[She], who has won such praise for her eloquence, does things which little befit her erudition and reputation—although this saying of many wise men I hold to be true: that an eloquent woman is never chaste; and the behavior of many learned women also confirms its truth. . . . But lest you approve even slightly this excessively foul and obscene crime, let me explain that before she made her body generally available for promiscuous intercourse, she had first permitted, and indeed even earnestly desired that the seal of her virginity be broken by none other than her brother, so that by this tie she might be more tightly bound to him. Alas for God in whom men trust, "who does not mingle heaven with earth nor the sea with heaven," when she, who sets herself no limit to this filthy lust, dares to engage so deeply in the finest literary studies.[49]

Other women were the victims, not of overt hostility, but of kind persuasion: male friends urged them to retreat from full participation in intellectual life, offering advice perhaps as inimical to their progress as heated opposition. Leonardo Bruni, in outlining for the daughter of Battista Montefeltro a program of humane studies, cautioned against the study of rhetoric—the one discipline the knowledge of which would enable a woman to participate publicly in intellectual discourse: "To her [i.e., the woman student] neither the intricacies of debate nor the oratorical artifices of action and delivery are of the least practical use, if indeed they are not positively unbecoming. Rhetoric in all its forms . . . lies absolutely outside the province of woman."[50]

Learned women, then, were sometimes attacked, and sometimes urged to achieve less than could be expected of their talents and their hopes. They were also urged to be chaste. Cassandra Fedele and Isotta Nogarola were praised for their chastity; the latter, clearly influenced by men who preferred that she, as a learned woman, maintain her chastity, voluntarily committed herself outside the boundaries of organized religious life to celibacy.[51] Now, the social function of chastity in the Italian Renaissance is a complex problem that calls for serious exploration. I hesitate to generalize, but given that the theme of chastity in relation to the learned women is so prominent, I feel a tentative hypothesis is required. I would suggest that when learned women (or men, for that matter) themselves chose a celibate life, they did so at least in part because they sought psychic freedom;[52] when, on the other hand, men urged chastity upon learned women, they did so at least in part to constrain them. These fearful creatures of a third sex threatened male dominance in both the intellectual and the social realm. Chaste, they were perhaps less awesome. And chastity suited the stony asexuality that they possessed, or that they were seen as possessing. Learning and chastity were indissolubly linked—for in undertaking the life of learning women repudiated a normal life of reproduction. *She* rejected a sexually active role for the sake of the intellectual life; *he* insisted on her asexuality because by means of intellect she had penetrated a male preserve. Chastity was at once expressive, I propose, of the learned woman's defiance of the established natural order and of the learned man's attempt to constrain her energies by making her mind the prison for her body. In the first case, chastity is a source of pride and independence; in the second, it is an instrument of repression.

The tension between these two facets of chastity in relation to the learned woman is evident in Antonio Loschi's poetic tribute to Maddalena Scrovegni.[53] Scrovegni, widowed while still young, had returned to her father's house in Padua and undertaken a life of study there in a small *sacellum,* as I mentioned earlier. There Loschi, a young humanist, had conversed with her, and impressed by her learning and virtue, was inspired to write a poem, accompanied by a dedicatory letter and exposition, in her honor. Struck by the image of this learned woman in her book-lined cell, Loschi built for her, as he put it, "on poetic foundations," a grander edifice, in which she might sit and reign. He called this larger and worthier edifice the Temple of Chastity, and Scrovegni herself the personification of chastity. The temple was perched on a mountain; the mountain itself rose from a broad plain; the broad plain, an island, was bounded by sea; temple, mountain, plain, and sea were set in the frozen land of Scythia, the home of the Amazons. The temple was huge, white, immaculate, symbolic of virtue. Within the temple's deepest recess was a room—reminiscent of Scrovegni's cell—on the walls of which were carved images in relief of ancient and mythological figures noted for their chastity. Like the mind itself, one of whose principal functions is memory, this cave contained images of the past—for it was in fact the analogue, not only of Scrovegni's studious cell, but of her mind as well, by both of which she was enclosed. There in the center she sat imperious on a crystal throne, surrounded by her handmaidens Modesty, Virginity, Frugality, and others. A powerful, monumental figure, she dominates the space around her—and yet she is dominated by it. She is queen within her own domain, but she is constrained: rigid on her throne, engulfed by the massive weight of temple walls, denied access to the realm of sensation and pleasure by the very guard who, defending her, repels the assaults of Venus and her son, isolated on an uncharted island in a remote and frigid land. Loschi's tribute to Scrovegni is ambivalent indeed: as it honors her for that virtue concomitant with knowledge, it confines her to a timeless and frozen desert.

The ambivalence discernible in Loschi's encomium of Scrovegni is characteristic, I believe, of male attitudes toward learned women. At the very moment that they praised learned women, learned men undermined them. They perceived such women as desexualized, or of distorted sexuality, as neither male nor female, but as members of a third sex; and these creatures of a third sex aroused in them fear and anger that provoked, sometimes hostile retaliation, and sometimes sweet persuasion to passive roles and to the ultimate passivity of chastity. For the phenomenon of the learned woman, whose learning destroyed the integrity of her sexual identity, they fashioned a fitting image: that of the armed maiden, a fusion of the icons of Athena, the chaste goddess of wisdom, and of the Amazons, fierce warriors ruthless to men. Male admirers repeatedly likened learned women to the Amazon queens and to other female warriors of myth and history. Angelo Poliziano's encomium of Cassandra Fedele opens with the words that Virgil wrote for Camilla, the warrior maiden of the Aeneid: "*O decus italiae virgo.*"[54] Boccaccio's catalogue of famous women includes a great number of armed women, of warrior maidens, of female aggressors, several of whom combined with their martial energy a love of learning, and who suffer, interestingly, gross humiliation.[55] And behind these visions of female warriors lay the vision of Athena, martially armed, unnaturally born, coldly virginal, and though female, defined not by sex but by intellect. The chill refinement of the symbol of wisdom coalesced with the ferocity of the Amazons. These images from antiquity were invested with fresh meaning when they were jointly applied to the learned woman: they expressed the relation men perceived between wisdom in women and preternatural aggression. Learned women fascinated learned men, and men applauded, *of course,* their retreat to quiet studies apart from male society. There, in solitude, they were both magnificent and chained: fierce goddesses in book-lined cells. Thus confined, it is no wonder that they won no battles.

The Phenomenon of the Learned Woman in the
Early Italian Renaissance: An Assessment

Let us not leave her there, but reflect for a last few brief moments on the achievement of the learned woman of the Renaissance. She received no degrees. She wrote no truly great works. She exerted no great influence on emerging trends in the history of ideas. She was probably unhappy. But she was perhaps the earliest figure of the type of the learned woman who is still with us. She was educated and excelled in the highest tradition of learning available to male contemporaries—not in needlework, not in graceful conversation, not in tinkling accomplishments, but in the languages and literature that were the vehicles of the most profound thoughts the age produced. And she exercised her knowledge publicly, at least at some point in her career—not in the cloister, not in hermitage, nor merely within the well-insulated walls of domesticity— but in the marketplace, for the learned to hear and to judge.

The achievement of the learned women of the Renaissance, I suggest in closing, was enormous, and has not wholly been surpassed. Certainly, many more women are educated now than were educated then; many more seek careers in the public realm; and many are successful in attaining positions of authority—success that no Renaissance woman I know of enjoyed. But the inward experience of today's learned women is perhaps no more tranquil than that of the women I have discussed. Many learned women still doubt themselves—more than men do. Many men still view learned women with hostility—and their hostility is still often blended with fascination. Many women still choose between marriage and learning; and many, many must adjust their expectations of love, of marriage, of motherhood in order to pursue an active intellectual life, or, in order to permit themselves the warmth of these relationships, must adjust their intellectual goals. Few women, in my experience, have *not* had to face these choices; few men, in my experience, have had to. This is perhaps the last barrier to the achievement of female equality in the society of the learned—and it is obstinate. What the learned women of the Italian Renaissance attained, we have attained, in greater quantity; but what they suffered we have not escaped. We have confined their demons in a Pandoran box, from which they erupt to haunt us: book-lined cells; armed maidens; the thwarting of ambitions.

Notes

1. Fedele's response to Scala, on the basis of which Scala's query can be assumed, is in G. F. Tomasini, *Clarissimae feminae Cassandrae Fidelis venetae epistolae et orationes posthumae* . . . (Padua, 1636), p. 167: "Mea itaque, Alexandra, utrum Musis an Viro te dedas ancipitem esse; id tibi de hac re eligendum censeo, ad quod te magis proclivem natura constituit."

2. I am concerned with the period 1350-1530. Laura Cereta, Cassandra Fedele, and Isotta Nogarola (all fifteenth century) achieved considerable fame. Nine others, to my knowledge, achieved some visibility: Cecilia Gonzaga, Battista Montefeltro (or Malatesta, her name by marriage), Olimpia Morata, Angela Nogarola, Ginevra Nogarola, Alessandra Scala, Maddalena Scrovegni, Ippolita Sforza, and Costanza Varano. For the learned women of the Renaissance, see especially P. O. Kristeller, "Learned Women of Early Modern Italy: Humanists and University Scholars," in this collection, pp. 91-116, and my "Thwarted Ambitions: Six Learned Women of the Early Italian Renaissance," *Soundings* 76 (1976): 280-300, with bibliography, pp. 301-04. In addition to the works already cited in that bibliography, the following may be useful for a reconstruction of the experience of the learned women of the Renaissance: for Laura Cereta, A. Rabil, Jr., "Laura Cereta, Quattrocento Humanist," paper

delivered to the University Seminar on the Renaissance, Columbia University (December 1978), the typescript of which cites additional bibliography; and an edition of her work by G. F. Tomasini, *Laurae Ceretae brixiensis feminae clarissimae epistolae jam primum e manuscriptis in lucem productae* (Padua, 1640); on Isotta Nogarola, my "The Religious Retreat of Isotta Nogarola (1418-1466)," *Signs* 3 (1978): 807-22; on Battista Montefeltro (Malatesta), A. Fattori and B. Feliciangeli, "Lettere inedite di Battista da Montefeltro," R. Accademia dei Lincei, Classe di Scienze Morali, Storiche e Filologiche, *Rendiconti*, ser. 5, 26 (1917): 196-215; G. Franceschini, "Battista Montefeltre Malatesta, signora di Pesaro," *Studia oliveriana* 6 (1958): 7-43, with a bibliography of editions of her poems on p. 9, n. 2; A. degli Abati Olivieri Giordani, *Notizie di Battista Montefeltro moglie di Galeazzo Malatesta signore di Pesaro* (Pesaro, 1782); and W. H. Woodward, *Vittorino da Feltre and other Humanist Educators: Essays and Versions* (Cambridge, 1897; rept., ed. E. Rice, New York, 1963), introduction to his translation of Leonardo Bruni's *De studiis et litteris*, pp. 119-22; on Olimpia Morata, G. Agnelli, *Olimpia Morata* (Ferrara, 1892); R. Bainton, *Women of the Reformation*, vol. 1, Germany and Italy (Minneapolis, 1971), pp. 253-66; J. Bonnet, *Vie d'Olympia Morata: épisode de la Renaissance et de la réforme en Italie*, 3d ed. (Paris, 1856); C. A. B. Southey, *Olympia Morata, Her Times, Life, and Writings* (London, 1834); R. Turnbull, *Olympia Morata, Her Life and Times* (Boston, 1846); D. Vorländer, "Olympia Fulvia Morata—eine evangelische Humanistin in Schweinfurt," *Zeitschrift für Bayerische Kirchengeschichte* 39 (1970): 95-113; and editions of her works by C. S. Curione, *Olympiae Fulviae Moratae foeminae doctissimae ac plane divinae orationes, dialogi, epistolae, carmina, tam Latina quam Graeca*, 3d ed. (Basel, 1570); and L. Caretti, *Opere*, Deputazione Provinciale Ferrarese di Storia Patria, *Atti e memorie*, n.s. 11 (1954), Parti I *(Epistolae)* and II *(Orationes, dialogi et carmina)*; on Maddalena Scrovegni, A. Medin, "Maddalena degli Scrovegni e le discordie tra i Carraresi e gli Scrovegni," *Atti e memorie della regia accademia di scienze, lettere ed arti in Padova* 12 (1896): 243-72; V. Zaccaria, "Una epistola metrica inedita di Antonio Loschi a Maddalena Scrovegni," *Bollettino del Museo Civico di Padova* 46 (1957-58); 153-68; and my "Goddess and Captive: Antonio Loschi's Poetic Tribute to Maddalena Scrovegni (1389), Study and Text," forthcoming in *Medievalia et Humanistica* (1980); on Ippolita Sforza, the editions of two orations; one before Pope Pius II published by G. G. Meersseman in his "La raccolta dell'umanista fiammingo Giovanni de Veris 'De arte epistolandi,' " *Italia medioevale e umanistica* 15 (1972): 250-51; and one in honor of her mother Bianca Maria, published most recently by C. Corvisieri in his edition of the *Notabilia temporum di*

Angelo de Tummulillis de Sant'Elia, Fonti per la storia d'Italia, 7 (Livorno, 1890): 231-32; on Costanza Varano, P. M. Chiappetti, *Vita di Costanza Varano* (Jesi, 1871); B. Feliciangeli, "Notizie sulla vita e sugli scritti di Costanza Varano-Sforza (1426-1447)," *Giornale storico della letteratura italiana* 23 (1894): 1-75; D. Michiel, *Elogio di Costanza da Varano,* Nozze Varano-Dolfin (Venice, 1807); and editions of her works by T. Bettinelli, C. *Varaneae Sfortiae Pisauri Principis orationes et epistolae,* in *Miscellanea di varie operette* 7 (Venice, 1743): 295-330, by G. Lami, in *Catalogus codicum manuscriptorum qui in Bibliotheca Riccardiana Florentiae adservantur . . .* (Livorno, 1756), pp. 145-50, and by Feliciangeli, "Notizie sulla vita . . . di Costanza Varano-Sforza," pp. 50-75. For manuscript versions of works by these and other learned women, see also the indices of P. O. Kristeller, *Iter Italicum, a Finding List of Uncatalogued or Incompletely Catalogued Humanistic Manuscripts of the Renaissance in Italian and Other Libraries,* 2 vols. (Leiden, 1963, 1967). I have focused here on women learned in the humanists' sense of the term and have excluded women patrons, religious writers, and poets. For a full understanding of the situation of the learned women, attention must be given to these as well, and to the wider problems of the role of women—learned or un-learned—in Renaissance culture and society.

3. Costanza Varano, Cecilia Gonzaga, and Vittoria Colonna were grand-daughters and great-granddaughter of Battista Montefeltro; Angela Noga-rola was the aunt of Isotta and Ginevra, and Veronica Gambara was Ginevra's granddaughter.

4. Fedele's letter to Bartolommeo Scala, ed. Tomasini, *Cassandrae Fidelis . . . epistolae et orationes,* no. 109, congratulates him for having undertaken his daughter's education. It has been speculated that Ales-sandra may have studied at the university in Florence; but she could not, as a woman, be admitted, and pursued instead higher studies with the aid of several professors engaged to give her private instruction. This informa-tion has reached me recently by the kind communication of P. H. La-balme, citing C. B. Schmitt's review of A. F. Verde, *Lo studio fiorentino, 1473-1503, Ricerche e documenti,* vol. 3 (Pistoia, 1978), in the *Times Liter-ary Supplement,* October 13, 1978, p. 1177; I have not yet seen Verde's work.

5. Rabil, "Laura Cereta," p. 1.

6. His *Catonis expositio pro filia erudienda* and his *De concordantia poetarum, philosophorum et theologorum;* for manuscripts and editions, see my "Personal, Domestic, and Republican Values in the Moral Philosophy of Giovanni Caldiera," *Renaissance Quarterly* 28 (1975), nn. 7 and 9, respectively.

7. "Tam praeclaro ingenio, tanta optimorum morum experientia et liberalium disciplinarum eruditione filiola nostra excellére cunctos non meo juditio, sed etiam sapientissimorum omnium hominum qui nostra hac sevissima temporum tempestate floruerunt vissa est." *Catonis expositio*, Modena, Biblioteca Estense, cod. Campori, app. 293, fol. 1.

8. E. Abel, *Praefatio* to his edition of the works, *Isottae Nogarolae Veronensis opera quae supersunt omnia, accedunt Angelae et Zeneverae Nogarolae epistolae et carmina*, 2 vols. (Budapest, 1886), 1: xvi-xvii.

9. Tomasini, ed., *Cassandrae Fidelis . . . epistolae et orationes*, preface, pp. 21-25 and no. 14.

10. Caretti, ed., *Opere* of Olimpia Morata, "La vita," 1: 37-38; see among several letters particularly no. 3, to Chilianus Sinapius, pp. 59-60.

11. Woodward, *Vittorino da Feltre*, pp. 29-92, for the Mantuan school.

12. For indications óf the kinds of studies women pursued, see the letters of Leonardo Bruni to Battista Montefeltro (trans. Woodward, in *Vittorino da Feltre*, pp. 123-33), and of Lauro Quirini to Isotta Nogarola (*Isottae Nogarolae . . . opera*, ed. Abel, 2, no. 53).

13. The oration *Pro adventu Dominae Blancae in Picenum* (ed. Feliciangeli, "Notizie sulla vita . . . di Costanza Varano-Sforza," pp. 50-54; also in the editions of Bettinelli and Lami) was delivered in 1442, when Varano was sixteen. For her age at this time, see the same work, p. 24, n. 1.

14. Ambrogio Traversari reported her accomplishment in a letter to Niccolò Niccoli, in L. Mehus, ed., *Ambrosii Traversarii Generalis Camaldulensium aliorumque ad ipsum et ad alios de eodem Ambrosio latinae epistolae*, 2 vols. (Florence, 1759), 2, no. 50, and in E. Martène and U. Durand, eds., *Veterum scriptorum et monumentorum historicorum, dogmaticorum, moralium, amplissima collectio* 3 (Paris, 1724), no. 20.

15. Nogarola was already famous at age eighteen and participated most actively in the world of humanism in the five ensuing years (see my "Religious Retreat," pp. 807-11); Cassandra Fedele's most remarkable achievement is dated 1487, when at age twenty-two she spoke to an assembly at the University of Padua (her *Oratio pro Bertuccio Lamberto suo consanguineo Canonico Concordiensi liberalium artium insignia suscipiente*, in her *Epistolae et orationes*, ed. Tomasini, pp. 193-200, and other editions).

16. Rabil dates her letters, our main evidence of her literary activity, between January 1485 and March 1488; at the latter date, she was eighteen years old. Cereta died at age thirty in 1499. "Laura Cereta," pp. 11, 1.

17. Caretti, introduction to Morata's *Opere*, pp. 37 ff.

18. Giovanni Caldiera provides supporting evidence for this statement. He defined the following different conditions of women: virgins destined for marriage; married women; widows; nuns; servants (slaves); prostitutes. Since maidens and widows would pass through the condition of matrimony at some time or would already have done so, respectable women, neither servants nor prostitutes, were seen to have only two choices: marriage and the convent. See my "Personal, Domestic, and Republican Values," pp. 555-56.

19. For the choices made by Fedele, Gonzaga, and the Nogarolas, see my "Thwarted Ambitions." For Scala's marriage, see G. Pesenti, "Alessandra Scala, una figurina della Rinascenza fiorentina," *Giornale storico della letteratura italiana* 85 (1925): 259 ff.; for Varano's, who died less than three years after her marriage, Feliciangeli, "Notizie sulla vita . . . di Costanza Varano-Sforza," pp. 42-45; for Cereta's marriage and widowhood, Rabil, "Laura Cereta," pp. 21-26.

20. See n. 15, above.

21. For Varano's oration to Bianca Maria, see n. 13, above; her letter to the King of Aragon in her *Orationes et epistolae,* ed. Bettinelli, pp. 310-14, and Lami, *Catalogus,* pp. 149-50. Battista Montefeltro's oration is published by G. B. Mittarelli, *Bibliotheca codicum manuscriptorum monasterii S. Michaelis Venetiarum prope Murianum* (Venice, 1779), cols. 701-2.

22. Nogarola's dialogue in her *Opera,* ed. Abel, 2: 185-216. Many of Cereta's letters were published by Tomasini in the edition cited above, n. 1; among these, those most revelatory of her own life and feelings I judge to be the prefatory letter and numbers 31, 37, 45, 46, 50, 54, 56, 58, 59, 64, 65, 66, and 71.

23. Cereta, *Epistolae,* ed. Tomasini, p. 3: "His igitur sat eram contenta litteris quae possint non umbram mihi, vel fumum, sed perpetuo securum aliquid, perfectumque largiri."

24. Ibid., p. 20: "Ego potius omnem hanc insumpsi operam mihi, ut Laurae nomen, miro Petrarcae preconio cantatum, novior altera in me custodiat aeternitas. . . ."

25. I have condensed this passage from Feliciangeli's edition, "Notizie sulla vita . . . di Costanza Varano-Sforza," pp. 50-52: "Quam gravissimum onus ac viribus impar meis, illustrissima ac excellentissima Domina, meis invalidis humeris imponatur, id certe exploratissimum habeo. Quo enim stilo orationis, qua dicendi facundia nobilitatem, sapientiam, pietatem, indulgentissimam humanitatem, ceterasque virtutes tuas meis tumultuariis ac tantae rei minime condignis efferam verbis? Qua in re non modo incultus et inexpolitus ac puellaris sermo non sufficeret, sed sapientis-

simorum virorum ac praeclarissimorum oratorum ingenia palpitarent et quod plus est, eloquentissima Ciceronis, invicta floridaque oratio conticeret atque deficeret. Quid igitur indocta, rudis, inexpertaque puella faciam?"

26. Fedele, *Epistolae et orationes*, ed. Tomasini, p. 193: "Timiditas itaque finem accipiat, etsi non dubitem plerisque vestrum facinus audax videri posse, quod ego et virgo et cui per aetatem altior nulla eruditio contingere potuit, neque mei sexus, neque ingenii memor, in tantam eruditorum hominum lucem, et praesertim in ea urbe, in qua his temporibus (ut olim Athenis) liberalium Artium studia florent oratura processerim."

27. See n. 22, above. I have also discussed this work in my "Religious Retreat," pp. 818-20, and "Thwarted Ambitions," p. 288.

28. Nogarola, *Opera*, ed. Abel, 2: 188: ". . . nam ubi minor sensus minorque constantia, ibi minus peccatum; et hoc in Eva, ergo minus peccavit."

29. Ibid., 2: 199: "Deus quum hominem creavit, ab initio creavit illum perfectum et animae eius potentias perfectas, et dedit ei maiorem veritatis rationem et cognitionem, maiorem quoque sapientiae profunditatem. . . ." Also quoted in my "Thwarted Ambitions," p. 288.

30. This exchange is also discussed, with fuller documentation, in my "Religious Retreat," pp. 809-10, and "Thwarted Ambitions," pp. 284-85.

31. "Sepissime mihi cogitanti mulieres quanti sint, venit in mentem queri fortunam meam, quoniam femina nata sum, que a viris re atque verbis derise sunt. Hanc enim coniecturam domi de me facio, ne queram foris, qui me sic ludibrio habueris. Nam tanta erumna afficior ut nihil supra. . . . Gaudebam cum hanc ad te dedi; arbitrabar equidem id valde ad laudem meam pertinere, quoniam testimonio sententie tue nihil erat quod me assecutam esse non putarem. 'Nunc pol merores antevortunt gaudiis,' cum aliter evenire intelligam. 'Usa sum te nequiore meque magis haud respectus es quam si nunquam gnata essem. Per urbem enim irrideor, meus me ordo deridet, neutrobi habeo stabile stabulum, asini me mordicus scindunt, boves me incursant cornibus.' " My free translation is based on the text in R. Sabbadini, ed., *Epistolario di Guarino Veronese*, R. Deputazione Veneta di Storia Patria, ser. 4: Miscellanea di Storia Veneta, ser. 3, vols. 8, 11, 14 (Venice, 1915-19), 11: 305-306; also published by Abel in Nogarola's *Opera*, I: 79-82. I have included the words in brackets, exercising due caution; they are implied by Nogarola's elaborate allusion to Plautus' *Aulularia*, 226-35. Her reference is to a scene in which a poor man refuses to marry his daughter to a rich man, comparing himself with a donkey, the prospective bridegroom with an ox. When a donkey presumes

to consort with an ox, the poor man complains, and stumbles in the mud, he can expect sympathy from neither the poor (the donkeys) nor the rich (the oxen). In adapting these words which comment on the abyss between social classes, Isotta apparently had in mind not the divisions between the poor and the rich (she was vastly richer than Guarino), but a social division more pertinent to her own case, that between males and females. Here, then, she sees herself as the female "donkey," dragged down by the male "ox" and consequently ostracized by both her kind and his. Nogarola has borrowed heavily from Plautus but omitted a section that would make her thought complete. The omitted sentence, which her reader—the learned Guarino—would have understood from context, I have supplied. Furthermore, I have translated "ordo" as "sex." It is those of Isotta's sex, the women of Verona, who mock her, as we know from Guarino's reply (Sabbadini, *Epistolario,* XI: 306-309). Interestingly, a man's "ordo" was the social group to which he belonged—the noble "order," the secretarial "order," the "ordo litteratorum;" a woman, though, belonged to the "order" of women.

32. I have paraphrased Cereta, *Epistolae,* ed. Tomasini, no. 54; passages quoted are from pp. 122-25: "Sed garrientes blaterantesque foeminas ferre non possum, quae temulentia vinoque flagrantes non sexui modo, sed sibi plerumque dictis petulantibus injuriantur"; "Conticescant igitur insolentes illae mulierculae ab omni honestatis jure disjunctae, quae odii incendiis ardentes, ni loquacius rodant alios, ipsae intro mutae roduntur"; "sola a nobis ipsis virtus acquiritur, nec possunt ad rerum arduarum cognitionem ascendere, quae luto voluptatum sorditates, in torpore segnius hebescunt."

33. Yet she is sympathetic to the plight of women in general—she comforts them in grief, and praises their capacity for loyalty; see, e.g., ibid., letters nos. 47 and 64.

34. Ibid., p. 68: "Intueantur eas, quae maiestate superba medium per plateas populum secant. Harum hanc, atque illam ex alienis capillis in summum verticem turritus nodus adstringit. Huic crines in frontem undatim crispi dependent. Illa fulvos, ut colla denudet, auro molli subnectit. Haec humero, illa brachio, ista collo in pectus habet monile demissum: aliae gulam sufferunt margaritarum nexu substrictam, tanquam ex liberis glorientur haberi captivae: Radiantes item pleraeque digitos gemmis ostendunt."

35. Ibid., p. 192: "Neque enim datur dono scientia, sed studio. Nam liber animus labori non cedens acrior semper surgit ad bonum."

36. Costanza Varano, for example, saw the rejection of marriage and the choice of a life of studious solitude as particularly "fruitful" for a woman;

see my "Religious Retreat," p. 815. Olimpia Morata well understood that she was in some way denying her sex in undertaking a studious life when she wrote:

I, a woman, have dropped the symbols of my sex,
Yarn, shuttle, basket, thread,
I love but the flowered Parnassus with the choirs of joy
Other women seek after what they choose
These only are my pride and my delight.

(trans. from the Greek by R. Bainton, in *Women of the Reformation in Germany and Italy*, p. 25). Both these women and others understood an unstated conflict between woman's conventional role and the life of the mind, and the uniqueness of their quest *as women* to participate in that life.

37. Nogarola, *Opera*, ed. Abel, 2: 128.

38. Ibid., 2: 123: "Memoria repeto cellulam illam tuam, quae undique sanctitatem redolet." Also quoted in my "Thwarted Ambitions," p. 286, and "Religious Retreat," p. 812.

39. In his *Domus pudicicie*, prose exposition, Leiden, Bibliotheca Universitatis Leidensis, cod. Vulcanianus 90, fol. 4v: "Sic michi mores tui, sic vita, sic etas atque habitus persuasere, et sacellum tuum quem unum locum in paternis penatibus aptum silencio, studiis, et orationibus elegisti, ita sese animo meo affixit, ut ab eo michi primum talis meditacio nata sit." A critical edition of Loschi's work, which was brought to my attention by Professor P. O. Kristeller, will appear in my "Goddess and Captive."

40. None known to me, however, matched the enthusiasm of Bartolommeo Goggio, whose *De laudibus mulierum* argued not merely the equality, but the superiority of women to men in all regards; see W. Gundersheimer, "Bartolommeo Goggio: A Feminist in Renaissance Ferrara," forthcoming in *Renaissance Quarterly* (1980).

41. Poliziano's letter to Fedele in her *Epistolae et orationes*, ed. Tomasini, no. 101, and in *Angeli Politianii operum*, Tomus primus, *Epistolarum libros xii, ac miscellaneorum centuriam* (Leiden, 1539), 3: 84-86; in the former edition, p. 157: "Mirari equidem antehac Ioannem Picum Mirandulam solebam, quo nec pulchrior alter mortalium, nec in omnibus (arbitror) doctrinis excellentior. Ecce nunc etiam te Cassandra a post illum protinus cepi, fortasse iam cum illo quoque, venerari." Also quoted in my "Thwarted Ambitions," p. 296.

42. Guiniforte Barzizza wrote to congratulate Varano on June 2, 1442, commenting on her worthy imitation of her maternal grandmother, Bat-

tista Montefeltro; *Gasparinii Barzizzii Bergomatis et Guiniforti filii opera,* ed. G. A. Furietti (Rome, 1723), pp. 135-36: "Gratulor inclytae illi Baptistae ex Monteferetrio maternae aviae tuae: quae cum humanitatis arctium peritissima judicetur, eloquentiae suae monumenta permulta confinxerit: nullum pulchrius, nullum certius, nullum majori sibi gloriae futurum optare potest, quam ut te neptem virtutis suae quasi simulachrum quoddam relinquat."

43. Contemporaries found it difficult to believe that women could write worthy works. Laura Cereta was accused of having presented her father's works as her own—and was proud of the accusation, since the quality of her own work was established, she felt, if it could be mistaken for that of a learned man. See her *Epistolae,* ed. Tomasini, no. 50. Ambrogio Miches wrote Cassandra Fedele that her learning would arouse wonder had it been attained by a man—let alone by a woman!; see her *Epistolae et orationes,* ed. Tomasini, p. 138: "[your learning] non solum in foemineo sexu, verum etiam in virile stupore forent." Greeted by such responses, women may have felt that the attainment of recognition for learning entailed the abandonment of sexual identity.

44. *Concerning Famous Women,* trans. G. A. Guarino (New Brunswick, N.J., 1963), pp. xxxiii-xxxiv; also *De mulieribus claris,* in *Tutte le opere di Giovanni Boccaccio,* ed. V. Branca, 10, 2d ed. (Verona, 1970): 18-21, text in Latin and Italian.

45. Nogarola, *Opera,* ed. Abel, 2: 12: "Iure igitur es tu quoque, Isota praeclara, summis laudibus prosequenda, quippe quae naturam, ut sic dixerim, tuam superasti. Virtutem enim veram, quae virorum propria est, singulari industria es consecuta, nec eam quidem mediocrem, ut plerique virorum, sed ut integerrimae perfectaeque sapientiae virum decet."

46. Fedele, *Epistolae et orationes,* ed. Tomasini, p. 142: "Ambigendum inscrutabili sapientia inauditum dedit seculo nostro miraculum. Virilem quippe animum muliebri sexui innasci et foeminas sexu quidem paulisper immutato virorum claros mores nancisci praestitit."

47. Ibid., p. 156: "At vero aetate nostra, qua pauci quoque virorum caput altius in literis extulerunt, unicam te tamen existes puellam, quae pro lana librum, pro fuco calamum, stylum pro acu tractes, et quae non cutem cerussa, sed atramento papyrum linas."

48. Ibid., pp. 155-56: "Scimus hoc profecto scimus, nec cum sexum fuisse a natura tarditatis, aut hebetudinis damnatam."

49. From the text published by A. Segarizzi in his "Niccolò Barbo, patrizio veneziano del secolo XV e le accuse contro Isotta Nogarola," *Giornale storico della letteratura italiana* 43 (1904): 53: "que sibi tantam ex dicendi facultate laudem acquisierit, ea agat, que minime cum tanta erudi-

tione et tanta sui existimatione conveniant, quamvis hoc a multis longe
sapientissimis viris acceperim: nullam eloquentem esse castam, idque
etiam multarum doctissimarum mulierum exemplo comprobari posse. . . .
Nisi vero hoc nimium sane tetrum atque obscenum scelus sit aliquantulum
a te comprobatum quod ante quam corpus suum assiduis connubiis di-
vulgaret primo fuerit passa atque etiam omnino voluerit virginitatis sue
specimen non ab alio nisi a fratre eripi hocque modo vinclo propiore
ligari. Proh deum atque hominum fidem, 'quis celum terris non misceat et
mare celo' [Juvenal, *Sat.*, II, 25] cum illa, que in tam spurcissima libidine
modum sibi non inveniat, audeat se tantum in optimis litterarum studiis
iactare." Also quoted in my "Thwarted Ambitions," p. 284, and "Religious
Retreat," p. 809. Nogarola learned, perhaps from this or other attacks, that
the world of male learning was slow to recognize learning in women; for
men considered learning in women, she wrote her uncle, "virus ac pestem
publicam" (*Opera*, ed. Abel, 1: 42). Cereta was also attacked by hostile
critics—and she defended herself so valiantly and so frequently that her
championship of learning in women emerges as a major theme of her
opera; see Rabil, "Laura Cereta," pp. 26-34, and her *Epistolae*, ed.
Tomasini, esp. no. 65.

50. *De studiis et litteris*, trans. Woodward, *Vittorino da Feltre*, p. 126.
Also cited in my "Thwarted Ambitions," p. 281. Gregorio Correr, with
great kindliness, urged Cecilia Gonzaga, in a similar vein, to give up her
secular studies for sacred ones, so that she could translate into the vernacular sacred works for the instruction of "unlettered virgins"—an intellectual
task of great merit but certainly not of the same seriousness as the composition of original Latin works; see his *Epistola ad Caeciliam virginem de
fugiendo saeculo*, in G. B. Contarini, *Anecdota veneta nunc primum col-
lecta et notis illustrata* (Venice, 1757), p. 42.

51. See particularly the letters to Nogarola by Paolo Maffei and
Ludovico Foscarini, in her *Opera*, ed. Abel, 2: nos. 54 and 67, respectively.

52. For two instances where men associate celibacy and freedom, see G.
Correr, *Soliloquium ad deum de vita sua*, in Contarini, *Anecdota veneta*,
pp. 12-24, and E. Barbaro, *De coelibatu*, ed. V. Branca, Nuova collezione
di testi umanistici inediti o rari, 14 (Florence, 1969).

53. See n. 39, above.

54. Fedele, *Epistolae et orationes*, ed. Tomasini, p. 155.

55. Boccaccio, *De mulieribus claris;* note especially the cases of Zenobia
and Pope Joan.

CHAPTER 5

Learned Women of Early Modern Italy: Humanists and University Scholars

Paul Oskar Kristeller*

The contribution of women to history, and especially to cultural and intellectual history, is a worthwhile subject that has not yet been adequately studied and that may eventually benefit from the current enthusiasm for women's studies, provided that there is a serious effort to study rather than to argue or to eulogize. The subject, and even the limited part of it that I propose to discuss, is large and complicated, and I cannot do more in a brief chapter than to survey some of the general facets of the problem. I shall focus my attention on Italy because I am better informed about the history of that country than about that of others. I shall not limit myself entirely to the Renaissance period, however defined, but venture some excursions into the Middle Ages and into the seventeenth and eighteenth centuries.[1]

The considerable role played in Italian history by women rulers, and by the wives or mistresses of male rulers, does not belong to our

* I am indebted for some references in this paper to Robert Connolly, Margaret L. King, Julius Kirshner, Dorothy Latz, Edward P. Mahoney, Herbert S. Matsen, Leo Mladen, and Sesto Prete.

topic, nor do the important functions assigned at all times to the wives and mothers of patricians and businessmen,[2] as we find them described in the family treatises of Francesco Barbaro or Leon Battista Alberti,[3] to mention but the two most famous examples of a larger literary genre. We are also not concerned with the beloved ladies, idealized but no doubt real, who inspired the great Italian poets, Dante's Beatrice, Petrarch's Laura, or Boccaccio's Fiammetta, or the women characters, fictitious but modeled after living persons, who appear in the poems of Ariosto, Tasso, or others.

More closely related to our subject are the women artists who appeared between the sixteenth and the eighteenth century, such as Sofonisba Anguissola, Artemisia Gentileschi, and Rosalba Carriera.[4] We might add Angelika Kauffmann, who was not an Italian but lived and worked in Italy and thus belongs to Italy as did Claude, Poussin, and even Rubens.[5] These artists belong to intellectual history, not merely because they painted, but because they lived in a period in which an artist did not have to prove his creativity by ignoring the previous history of his art and the general culture of his time, but was usually educated and even learned, and was constantly commissioned to present and interpret religious and classical subjects that required a good deal of literary knowledge from the artist, or at least from his patrons or advisors.

Apparently there were more women poets and writers than there were women painters, and they began to appear at an earlier date. The list begins with Christine de Pisan, a celebrated French poet of the late fourteenth and early fifteenth centuries who was born in Venice as the daughter of a physician and astrologer from Bologna, Tommaso Pizzani.[6] In the Florence of the late fifteenth century, we find at least two ladies who excelled as Tuscan poets. Lucrezia Tornabuoni,[7] the wife of Piero di Cosimo de' Medici, was one of the leading writers of religious hymns (*Laudi*), and her son Lorenzo de' Medici undoubtedly inherited from her his poetic gifts, if not his scholarship or his political skill. Antonia Pulci, who was married to the poet Bernardo Pulci and thus related to his brothers Luca and Luigi, was a poet in her own right and wrote several of the religious plays (*sacre rappresentazioni*) that were performed by the lay religious guilds of the city.[8] The sixteenth century saw a larger number of women poets, some of them quite famous: Veronica

Gambara, Gaspara Stampa, and above all, Vittoria Colonna. We may add Laura Battiferri, Veronica Franco, and Isabella Morra.[9] Tullia d'Aragona composed not only lyrical poems but also a prose treatise on the infinity of love,[10] a major specimen of a literary genre that was much cultivated during the sixteenth century and that includes among its authors Ficino, Pico, Bembo, Castiglione, Diacceto, Leone Ebreo, Tasso, and Francesco Patrizi. Later in the century we encounter Tarquinia Molza, a noted friend and patron of poets and scholars who also wrote poetry, some of it in her native Modenese dialect.[11] All these ladies displayed considerable talent and also a good deal of literary training and scholarship.

Among the ruling women we find many that are not so much known for their political activities, but rather for their role as patrons of the arts and of learning. When writers and scholars dedicated their works to these princesses, they gave high praises to them in exchange for the material rewards they expected or received from them, but they must also have assumed that these ladies read and appreciated the books dedicated to them. Although some of these writings dealt with illustrious ladies or with the praise of women and thus appealed directly to the dedicatees,[12] others were of a more general content and thus show that the women to whom these treatises were addressed shared the intellectual and literary interests of their male contemporaries. It is no coincidence that most of the works dedicated to princesses and other ladies are in the vernacular rather than in Latin. Among the ladies who appear most frequently in this role of patrons and dedicatees, we find Eleonora of Aragon, duchess of Ferrara; [13] her sister Beatrice, queen of Hungary; [14] and Isabella d'Este Gonzaga, marchioness of Mantua.[15] We may add Caterina Cornaro, queen of Cyprus, who was celebrated by Pietro Bembo in his dialogue on love, *Gli Asolani*.[16]

Other ladies who received the dedication of Latin works by contemporary humanists or were celebrated by them in Latin verse or prose must have enjoyed a strictly humanist education. Maddalena degli Scrovegni of Padua, to whom Antonio Loschi addressed a Latin poem and letter, was also the author of several Latin letters.[17] Battista da Montefeltro Malatesta, to whom Leonardo Bruni dedicated his *De studiis et litteris*, addressed a Latin speech to the

emperor Sigismund; [18] and Cecilia Gonzaga, to whom Gregorio
Correr dedicated a Latin treatise in praise of the monastic life, had
been educated with her brothers by Vittorino da Feltre.[19] Battista
Sforza da Montefeltro, wife of Federico of Urbino, was praised
after her death in many Latin orations, letters, and poems.[20]
Jolanthe of France, duchess of Savoy, received from the French
humanist Guillaume Fichet a dedication copy of his treatise on
rhetoric.[21] We know less about Albiera degli Albizzi of Florence,
whose early death was the theme of poems and letters by Poliziano,
Ficino, and many others,[22] or of Ginevra de' Benci, famous through
her portrait by Leonardo da Vinci, who was praised by several
humanists in verses addressed to her admirer, Bernardo Bembo.[23]

Another area in which women played an important part is that
of religious life and of the literature connected with it. In medieval
and Renaissance Italy, girls as well as boys received a religious
education. There were numerous female convents affiliated with
several religious orders, and it was a common practice for unmarried daughters of prominent and of more modest families to enter a
convent and to live in it for the rest of their lives. Many nuns
excelled in ecclesiastic administration and politics, and in pious
exercises and activities, and some of them also wrote on religious
subjects. Many women mystical writers of note appeared in medieval Germany and England, and later in France and in Spain. In
Italy we find St. Catherine of Siena whose letters played an important role in bringing the popes back from Avignon to Rome, and
who also wrote an influential dialogue on Providence.[24] In the fifteenth and sixteenth century there were many authors of religious
letters and treatises, including Battista da Varano, St. Catherine of
Genoa, and S. Maria Maddalena de' Pazzi.[25] S. Angela Merici of
Brescia founded the order of the Ursulines, which is still active in
our day.[26]

Most nuns who were not active as writers were assiduous readers
of religious literature, especially in the vernacular, and there is a
large body of religious writings explicitly written for nuns and dedicated to them, which includes lives of saints, many of them translated from Greek or Latin, vernacular versions of patristic writings,
and above all a whole literature of spiritual letters containing
moral and religious exhortations and meditations.[27] We must keep

in mind this religious and monastic tradition if we want to understand the religious overtones in the life and work of such women scholars as Isotta Nogarola or Elena Cornaro. Several women were also active and prominent in both the Catholic and Protestant Reformation, such as Vittoria Colonna, Giulia Gonzaga, and Renée de France, duchess of Ferrara.[28]

We come closer to the heart of our problem when we enquire about the role of women in Renaissance humanism, not merely as patrons, but also as active students and writers. This role can be studied and evaluated only on the basis of extant writings, and the rule "publish or perish" applies not only to modern academic life but also to intellectual history and bibliography.

Renaissance humanism is a broad and complex movement which has often been misunderstood by modern historians. A twentieth-century humanist is mainly an advocate and preacher of human values, however vaguely understood, but usually he is not committed to literature or learning, let alone to classical learning. The Renaissance humanists may have been concerned with human values, but their major interest was the world of letters and of scholarship, and especially that of classical scholarship. The fields that attracted their professional interest included moral philosophy, but also grammar and rhetoric, history and poetry, and all aspects of Greek and Latin learning. The terms "humanism" and "humanist" are not derived from humane or humanitarian but from the humanities, or *studia humanitatis.* The literary and scholarly works of the humanists are for the most part written in Latin, not in the vernacular, and their interests do not immediately include such fields of academic instruction as theology, logic, natural philosophy, metaphysics, medicine, mathematics, or astronomy, although in due time humanism was to have an impact on all these fields. It is a mistake to identify humanism with the sum total of Renaissance learning or literature. It merely constitutes one limited sector of it, though an important and influential one. Thus, humanism had a limited influence in the area of university instruction, but it soon came to dominate the secondary schools. The study of the classical languages and of Greek and Latin literature came to occupy the central place in the curriculum of the humanist school, and it retained this place until the early decades of our century. The hu-

manistic school disappeared only during the last few decades, and I
seem to be one of its last products.

The role of women in humanist education and learning was not
prominent, but it was significant. It was primarily the daughters of
princely, noble, or patrician families who received, when intelligent, a humanist education from private tutors, along with their
brothers. We are here essentially concerned with those ladies who
were active as humanist writers and whose works have come down
to us. We find many women among the authors of individual Latin
letters, poems, or orations. They include many persons of whom we
otherwise know very little, but also some that are well known or
even famous. We had occasion to mention Maddalena degli
Scrovegni for her letters and Battista Malatesta for her oration, and
we might add Angela Nogarola, who composed several Latin
poems and letters.[29] A Bolognese lady, Niccolosa Castellani Sanuti,
achieved a certain celebrity when she addressed a Latin speech to
Cardinal Bessarion, then the papal legate in Bologna, asking him to
repeal a decree in which he had prohibited the wearing of sump-
tuous dresses by the ladies of Bologna.[30] More famous still is Ippolita Sforza, daughter of Francesco Sforza, the duke of Milan, and
later the wife of Alfonso II of Aragon, duke of Calabria and king of
Naples. On a solemn occasion, during the Congress of Mantua in
1459, Ippolita addressed a short Latin speech to the humanist Pope
Pius II, who made an improvised reply; this speech must have
greatly impressed her contemporaries, for it survives in numerous
manuscript copies.[31] Another short speech of Ippolita's, in praise of
her mother, was less popular, and it has been recently discovered
and published.[32]

Much more important and famous as a scholar was Isotta Nogarola of Verona,[33] a member of a noble family that also produced
several male scholars of note. Isotta is the author of numerous Latin
letters and also wrote a disputation on the question whether Adam
or Eve was the greater sinner. Her correspondence included letters
of Guarino of Verona, the elder Ermolao Barbaro, bishop of Verona, Ludovico Foscarini, and many other distinguished scholars. It
survives in many manuscript copies and was published in a critical
edition in 1886. Isotta's sister, Ginevra Nogarola, also started out as
a promising author of Latin letters and poems but ceased to be

active as a humanist after getting married.[34] I found a beautiful manuscript of the Roman historian Justinus in the Yale Library that was copied by Ginevra in her youth.[35] Another author of humanist letters and speeches was Costanza da Varano Sforza.[36]

Less well known than the Nogarola sisters, but equally interesting, is Laura Cereta of Brescia, whose letters and orations appear in two manuscripts and were for the most part published by Bishop Giacomo Filippo Tommasini in Padua in 1640.[37] She was in correspondence with Cardinal Ascanio Sforza, with Bonifacius Bembus, Michael Carrariensis, and Ludovicus Cendrata; and she also wrote a few orations, an invective, a dialogue, and a theological question. Better known is Cassandra Fidelis of Venice, wife of the physician Johannes Maria Mapellus. Her letters and orations were published by Tommasini in 1636. She was very famous in her day, corresponded among others with Angelo Poliziano, and delivered a speech at the University of Padua.[38]

In Florence we find Alessandra Scala, daughter of the chancellor Bartolomeo Scala, and wife of the poet Michael Marullus.[39] She was a student of Demetrius Chalcondylas, of Johannes Lascaris and of Poliziano, perhaps at the University of Florence, and she won great praise from Poliziano and others for her knowledge of Greek. She wrote a Greek epigram that has been preserved, indicating that she reached a command of classical Greek that was attained by only a few Western scholars of her century, such as Francesco Filelfo, Lianoro Lianori of Bologna, and Angelo Poliziano.

In the sixteenth century, we encounter Olimpia Morata of Ferrara, daughter of the humanist Fulvio Pellegrino Morato.[40] She married a German Protestant and spent the latter part of her life in Germany. Her writings were repeatedly printed in Basel. They include orations, letters, and poems, some of them in Greek; two Latin versions of Novelle from Boccaccio's *Decameron;* and a paraphrase of the Psalms in Greek.

I should be inclined to think that Elena Lucrezia Cornaro Piscopia belongs to the same line of women humanists whom we have been describing. Her works, most of which were printed in Parma in 1688, consist mainly of orations, letters, and poems in Italian and Latin, and of a few poems in Greek and other languages.[41] She lived in the seventeenth century, to be sure, but we begin to see more and more that the literary and scholarly tradition of Renaissance humanism remained alive in the seventeenth and even in the eighteenth century, alongside with the new philosophical and scientific currents that began to rise and expand during the same period.

I do not claim to have given a complete list of women humanists. Some of them are relatively obscure and appear only as authors of single letters or poems, and these I have at least duly recorded in my *Iter Italicum*. Many more occur only as recipients of letters or poems written by male humanists, and these I have often failed to record when their names were unknown to me. In doing so, I may have been guilty of unconscious "male chauvinism," but I must add in excuse that I have done the same with many male recipients of letters or poems whose names were unfamiliar to me. I mention this fact in order to indicate that more research on the women scholars of the Renaissance is needed, especially in the numerous miscellaneous collections of letters and poems that have come down to us in manuscripts and in printed editions.

As to Elena Cornaro, I am afraid that the many eulogies which she has received so far have not always been based on a careful reading and study of her writings. The study of Elena Cornaro and her works requires the ability to decipher old editions and manuscripts, and to read her works in Latin, Greek, and Italian, as they were written. For better or worse, this lady did not write in English, although we are told that she did learn some English from an Englishman residing in Venice; this was quite unusual for her time, since the number of continental scholars who knew English was regrettably small before the eighteenth century. Thus, I should like to encourage women students and scholars who want to become proficient in women's studies and to do justice to Elena Cornaro and other ladies of her kind, to study Latin, Greek, and Italian, something that is useful for scholars anyway, and necessary for students of the Renaissance, and especially for those who want to produce a scholarly monograph on the life and works of Elena Cornaro. We also learn from Elena's biographers that her learning included mathematics and music; Hebrew, which she learned from a local rabbi; as well as Arabic and Chaldaic. Elena's religious inclinations link her, as Isotta Nogarola before her, with the traditions of female monasticism and lay piety and confirm the view, which I have tried to defend elsewhere, that humanism and monasticism were not incompatible during the Renaissance period.[42]

Elena Cornaro was not only a humanist scholar but also a student of theology and of Aristotelian philosophy, and she obtained a doctorate in philosophy at the University of Padua in 1678. She thus set a precedent of great significance in the history of women scholars, and it is her university degree that has aroused so much interest in her life and career, especially with the tercentenary of her graduation. It is therefore appropriate for us to discuss the place of women at the Italian universities, as students, as graduates, and as faculty members.

The university, unlike other schools or cultural institutions, is a creation of the high Middle Ages, and especially of the twelfth century.[43] The earliest universities, some of them of short duration, sprang up in different parts of Europe, mainly in France, England, and Italy. They differed among each other in their curriculum as well as in their institutional structure. They began as free associations of students and of teachers, patterned after the guilds and the new city communities, and soon obtained legal recognition from the authorities of the church and of the state. A university was not a *universitas litterarum,* as commencement speakers of the nineteenth and twentieth century have often claimed, but a *universitas scholarium et magistrorum,* an association of students and teachers, as modern historical research has conclusively shown. The subjects of instruction differed for each of the early universities, but a standard program gradually emerged that included the liberal arts and philosophy, theology, civil and canon law, and medicine. This was not a unified curriculum, for the arts and philosophy were usually studied as a preparation for one of the other fields, and the study of theology, of law, and of medicine consisted of entirely separate programs that led to different degrees and different careers. If specialization is such a regrettable thing, as many educators have been trying to make us believe, the fault began at least with the twelfth century when the accumulation of knowledge for the first time reached a point where it could no longer be mastered within the liberal arts program of the earlier medieval schools. The universities were self-governing bodies which soon established their admission standards, their course requirements, and also their examinations and degrees. They were not schools of general education but graduate and professional schools which prepared their students for specific careers; their graduates became teachers and scholars, church or state officials, lawyers or physicians. There was no attempt to cover all fields of learning, and there were many professions, activities, and even branches of learning that required no university training.

The Italian universities, unlike their Northern sisters, had only two, not four faculties: law and, as a later addition, arts and medicine. There was no separate faculty of theology at the Italian universities, as there was in the North. There were sporadic courses on theology given in the faculty of arts and philosophy. The courses were given each year by appointed teachers on assigned subjects. For the University of Bologna, we have for each academic year, beginning with the late fourteenth century, a published list (rotulus), comparable to a modern college or university catalogue, in which the teachers are enumerated, along with their titles, courses, and even textbooks.[44]

The examinations were not given at the end of a course or of an academic year but after the completion of all course work and prior to the degree, usually in the form of oral disputations on assigned topics (called puncta). They were administered, not by the university corporation or by the professors as such, but by a special corporate body called collegium. There was a college of philosophers and physicians, and a college of jurists, permanent and self-perpetuating bodies to which new members were elected by a vote of the older members, and which had their official statutes and privileges. One of their main functions was to appoint examining committees and to confer degrees on the candidates who had successfully passed their examinations.[45] These colleges have often been confused by historians with the teaching faculties of the respective universities, but they are in fact different institutions with different functions and also with different membership, although the latter usually overlaps with that of the teaching faculty. For a senior member of the teaching faculty is normally also a member of the college corresponding to his faculty. But not every member of the teaching faculty is also a member of the college, for many junior teachers have not yet been elected to the college, and even senior teachers were sometimes excluded from the college if they were not citizens of the town in which the university was located. Vice versa, the college included respected professionals, lawyers or physicians, who were not members of the teaching faculty of the university.

In the fourteenth century many old and new Italian universities received from the popes the right, which they had previously lacked, to confer degrees in theology.[46] This led to the establishment of a college of theology, but not of a separate teaching faculty of theology, and this distinction has also been overlooked or blurred by many historians. The membership of a college of theology included, to be sure, those persons who happened at the time to teach courses on theology at the university. But they were at all times quite few in number, and the majority of the college of theologians always consisted of scholars who held a degree in theology, usually from a Northern university; who belonged to the local monastic communities; and who often had taught, and continued to teach, theology, not at the university, but in the schools of their own respective orders. They were members of the college of theologians because they were rightly assumed to have the necessary qualifications for supervising the conferral of theological degrees and of upholding their standards. As other Italian universities, Padua had a theological college since the fourteenth century, and it was the responsibility of this college to arrange for examinations and to confer a degree in theology.[47] Elena Cornaro, or rather her father for her, applied for a degree in theology, and this request was rejected.[48] This fact is not surprising, for the degree usually prepared for ecclesiastical offices or for teaching positions from which women were excluded, and I know no instance of a theological degree conferred upon a woman until very recent times.

In the other disciplines or faculties, the picture is a bit brighter, but the number of documented cases is still fairly small. I shall discuss the cases known to me and do not exclude that further research may turn up additional ones.

In the case of jurisprudence, I know of no woman until recent times who appears to have taught or studied civil or canon law. However, there is one famous episode that should be mentioned.

According to Christine de Pisan, Giovanni d'Andrea, a famous professor of canon law at Bologna in the early fourteenth century, had
several well-educated daughters; one of them, called Novella, recited her father's lectures before his classes, when he was ill or
absent, and lectured behind a veil or curtain in order not to distract
the students by her beauty. The anecdote sounds very much like an
invented story, but it is reported by a trustworthy source, and
hence has been accepted by most authorities.[49]

Much more can be said about women in medicine. In older books
on the history of medicine, we find frequent mention of a lady
named Trotula who is often treated as a teaching member of the
medical school of Salerno, which was in a sense the earliest Italian
and Western university.[50] Trotula is even called the wife and
mother of well-known Salerno physicians. Yet we have really no
documentary evidence of her professional status or of her family
relations, or even of her historical existence. We have a treatise on
gynecology which goes under the name of Trotula, which was composed at Salerno in the eleventh or the twelfth century and which
had a considerable manuscript diffusion for several centuries. The
name "Trotula" may be a title rather than an author or person, and
most historians of medicine have questioned the historical existence
of a woman named Trotula who would be the author of the treatise
and prefer to take Trotula as a conventional title of the book. Since
the title is the only evidence we have for Trotula, I am afraid
women doctors will have to give up this precedent, at least for such
an early period. When we go further down in time and study the
history of medicine in Salerno, Naples, and the rest of southern
Italy, we do find a number of women, beginning in 1307, who
received royal licenses to treat specified diseases.[51] These women
were examined by royal physicians, and they must have received
private instruction from their relatives or from other physicians,
but there is no indication that they had attended university courses;
and in the case of some of them it is explicitly stated that they
knew no Latin, which was the language of all university instruction
at that time. A notable exception is Costanza Calenda, the daughter of a medical professor in Naples, who appears in 1422 as a
doctor of medicine.[52] I am afraid that she seems to beat the precedent of Elena Cornaro and of Padua by several centuries, if we

accept the testimonies about her as valid. However, Costanza's degree was in medicine and not in philosophy, and we cannot argue in her case that her degree in medicine would have to be preceded by a degree in philosophy, as was the case at Bologna, Padua, and the other universities of northern Italy after the thirteenth century. Moreover, the school of Salerno, although the oldest Italian and Western center of advanced medical instruction, was never fully organized along institutional lines comparable to the younger universities of northern Italy. Thus, there is no compelling reason to take the glorious precedent of a woman doctor of philosophy away from Padua, the oldest university whose date of origin is precisely known, and to which I am linked by special personal ties. Apart from Costanza Calenda, I have not come across any other women physicians before the nineteenth century.

We are in a somewhat better position for the arts and philosophy. Alessandra Scala, whom we mentioned before may have attended courses at the University of Florence, but there is no evidence that she ever obtained a doctoral degree. In the case of Elena Cornaro, we may make the opposite statement: we have no evidence that she ever attended regular courses at the University of Padua, and if some Padua professors appear as her teachers, they must have instructed her as private tutors. On the other hand, we have ample documentary evidence that Elena obtained her doctorate in philosophy at Padua on June 25, 1678.[53] We also learn that in the good tradition of Paduan and Italian Aristotelianism, she had two topics or passages *(puncta)* assigned for her examination and disputation, one from Aristotle's *Posterior Analytics* and one from his *Physics*.[54] For centuries, at Padua as elsewhere, the main philosophical subjects taught in the faculty of arts were logic and natural philosophy, and the textbooks used for these subjects were the logical and physical writings of Aristotle in Latin translations. Hence it was quite normal to select for a doctoral examination in philosophy a passage from the logical and another from the physical works of Aristotle. We may assume that Elena had thoroughly studied Aristotelian philosophy before she successfully passed her examination. As a matter of fact, her doctorate in philosophy is our main evidence that she combined the study of Aristotelian philosophy with that of the humanities, as many scholars had done before her. The teaching of Aristotelian logic and physics, at Padua and other universities, continued without interruption, though not without some changes, from the Middle Ages through the seventeenth and far into the eighteenth century. Elena's examiners, according to the documents not yet published, were Carolus Renaldinus, Angelus Montagnana, and Ermenegildus Pera, but the examination was actually attended and approved by the full membership of the *collegium*, which included Carolus Patinus, the son of the French physician Guy Patin, who was a correspondent and perhaps also a tutor of Elena. In any case, her graduation complied with all the customary formalities prescribed by the statutes. It was sponsored by the bishop of Padua, Gregorio Barbarigo, as chancellor of the university, and by the *collegium philosophorum* which assigned the examination topics, appointed the examiners *(promotores)*, and presumably issued the diploma, which does not seem to have survived. This is in marked contrast with the procedures followed for Protestant students who received degrees at Padua or elsewhere in Italy, as we can see from the extant diploma of William Harvey.[55] Since the *collegium* required of the candidate a sworn affirmation of his Catholic faith, the university used for Protestant candidates the device of substituting for the *collegium* a resident Count Palatine who was entitled by imperial privilege to confer doctoral degrees. He, and not the *collegium*, selected the examining committee, which consisted of the same university professors who would have served also under the auspices of the *collegium*, and he also signed the doctoral diploma in the place of the bishop. Since the requirements for the degree were fully complied with, the doctoral diplomas issued by the Counts Palatine were recognized everywhere as legally valid.

After Elena Cornaro, we encounter at least two illustrious ladies who distinguished themselves as scholars connected with the University of Bologna during the eighteenth century. The first is Laura Maria Caterina Bassi, who obtained her degree in philosophy at Bologna in 1732, again with an examination based on Aristotle's *Posterior Analytics* and *Physics*. She taught philosophy in the arts faculty at Bologna from 1732 to 1778.[56] The other is Gaetana Agnesi, who held a chair of mathematics at Bologna for many years and was the author of a widely used textbook in her field.[57] These are the examples of women graduates and university teachers in Italy which I have been able to collect for the period prior to the nineteenth century. They are few in number, and they are illustrious exceptions, which confirm the rule that women were excluded from university studies and degrees and from the careers of university teaching and of the academic professions.

It is only during the nineteenth and twentieth centuries that we find an ever increasing number of women students, graduates, professors, and professionals.[58] I know from the reports of older friends that there were still restrictions at the turn of our century. A distinguished woman philologist who had completed a regular course of study at the University of Leipzig was refused admission to the degree in that university and had to obtain it at the University of Heidelberg, which at that time was more open-minded.[59] As a student, I still heard stories of older professors who refused to admit women in their lectures or seminars, or who insulted them with offensive remarks after they had been admitted. At the time when I studied at various German universities in the 1920s, this situation had completely changed. There was a large number of women students at all universities and in all fields, although their number and percentage may have varied for the different faculties and disciplines. They were less numerous in mathematics or philosophy than in history, literature, classics, or art history, but their studies and careers were not significantly different from those of their male colleagues, and in recent decades women scholars have distinguished themselves through their published contributions to many fields of science and of scholarship. Women graduates have asserted themselves more slowly as professionals and as academic teachers, but there has been, in my memory, a continuous progress. I heartily approve of this development and strongly oppose any remnants of past discrimination, but I also oppose quotas and other forms of reverse discrimination, under whatever name they are disguised, and favor a system strictly based on individual merit and individual industry. The training of scholars and professionals, women or men, on which the future of our civilization depends, is accomplished only by a steady and strenuous effort to learn and to read, to think and to understand, to criticize and to formulate. I hope that our colleges and universities will continue to help their students to develop their talents and to become educated persons, accomplished professionals, and responsible citizens.

Notes

1. William Boulting, *Woman in Italy* (London, 1910); E. Rodocanachi, *La femme italienne à l'époque de la Renaissance* (Paris, 1907), and *La femme italienne avant, pendant et après la Renaissance* (Paris, 1922); Ruth Kelso, *Doctrine for the Lady of the Renaissance* (Urbana, 1956); Joan Kelly-Gadol, "Did Women Have a Renaissance?" in *Becoming Visible: Women in European History*, ed. Renate Bridenthal and Claudia Koonz (Boston, 1977), pp. 137-64; S. Chojnacki, "Patrician Women in Early Renaissance Venice," *Studies in the Renaissance* 21 (1974): 176-203. For more detailed information on individual women, see L. Frati, *La donna italiana secondo i più recenti studi* (Turin, 1899; a second edition of 1928 was not accessible to me); Isidoro Del Lungo, "La donna fiorentina nel Rinascimento e negli ultimi tempi della libertà," in *La vita italiana nel Rinascimento* (Milan, 1910), pp. 99-146; A. Mazzeo, *Donne famose di Romagna*, 2d ed. (Bologna, 1973; not seen); *Poetesse e Scrittrici: Enciclopedia biografica e bibliografica Italiana*, ser. 6, 2 vols. (Milan, 1942); Jolanda De Blasi, *Le scrittrici italiane dalle origini al 1800* (Florence, 1930), and *Antologia delle scrittrici italiane dalle origini al 1800* (Florence, 1930).

2. P. D. Pasolini, *Caterina Sforza*, 3 vols. (Rome, 1893); E. Breisach, *Caterina Sforza: A Renaissance Virago* (Chicago, 1967). For other Renaissance princesses, see below. Alessandra Macinghi negli Strozzi, *Lettere di una gentildonna fiorentina del sec. XV ai figliuoli esuli*, ed. C. Guasti (Florence, 1877). For Alessandra Macinghi, see also Lauro Martines, "A Way of Looking at Women in Renaissance Florence," *Journal of Medieval and Renaissance History* 4 (1974): 15-28. Vespasiano da Bisticci, "Vita dell'Alexandra de' Bardi," in his *Vite*, ed. A. Greco, 2 (Florence, 1976): 467-99.

3. Francesco Barbaro, *De re uxoria*, ed. A. Gnesotto, *Accademia Patavina di scienze, lettere ed arti, Atti e Memorie*, n.s. 322 (1915-16): 6-105; Leon Battista Alberti, *I libri della famiglia (Opere volgari*, ed. C. Grayson, 1 [Bari, 1960]): 1-341.

4. *Women Artists: 1550-1950*, by Ann Sutherland Harris and Linda Nochlin (New York, 1976), pp. 106-8, 118-24, 161-64, et passim.

5. Ibid., pp. 174-78.

6. M. G. Pinet, *Christine de Pisan* (Paris, 1927).

7. *Le laudi di Lucrezia de' Medici*, ed. G. Volpe (Pistoia, 1900; not seen);

A. Parducci, "La ystoria della devota Susanna di Lucrezia Tornabuoni," *Annali delle Università Toscane*, n.s. 10 (44, 1925-26): 177-201. G. Levantini-Pieroni, "Lucrezia Tornabuoni," in his *Studi storici e letterari* (Florence, 1893), pp. 1-83; B. Felice, "Donne medicee avanti il Principato: II. Lucrezia Tornabuoni moglie di Piero di Cosimo," *Rassegna Nazionale* 146 (1905): 645-60.

8. Her four plays are listed by Colomb de Batines, *Bibliografia delle antiche rappresentazioni italiane sacre e profane stampate nei secoli XV e XVI* (Florence, 1852), pp. 15-18. One of them, the *Rappresentazione di Santa Guglielma*, was reprinted in *Sacre Rappresentazioni dei secoli XIV, XV e XVI*, ed. A. d'Ancona, 3 (Florence, 1872): 199-234. A. D'Ancona, *Origini del teatro italiano*, 1 (Turin, 1891; repr. Rome, 1966): 268-69; M. Apollonio, *Storia del teatro italiano*. 2d ed., 1 (Florence, 1943): 242.

9. Others were Lucia Bertani, Chiara Matraini, and Barbara Torelli. There are numerous old and modern editions of the poems and letters of these ladies, and many monographs dealing with them, some of them in English, but few of their poems have been translated into English. There is an old anthology of women poets: *Rime diverse d'alcune nobilissime e virtuosissime donne*, ed. Lod. Domenichi (Lucca, 1559; not seen). See also *Gaspara Stampa e altre poetesse del '500*, ed. F. Flora (Milan, 1962). On Gaspara Stampa, there is an unpublished Columbia thesis by Joseph H. Satin (1952). On Isabella Morra, see B. Croce, *La Critica*, 27, ser. 3, 3 (1929): 12-35, 126-40, 186-94; the introductory essay alone, without the texts, was reprinted in his *Vite di avventure, di fede e di passione (Scritti di storia letteraria e politica* 30 [Bari, 1936]: 283-319.

10. Tullia d'Aragona, *Dialogo della infinità di amore* (Venice, 1547); repr. in *Trattati d'amore del Cinquecento*, ed. G. Zonta (Bari, 1912), pp. 185-248. Cf. John Charles Nelson, *Renaissance Theory of Love* (New York, 1958), pp. 129-32.

11. Some of her writings, including Italian versions of Plato's *Charmides* and of part of the *Crito*, are printed in Francesco Maria Molza, *Delle poesie volgari e latine*, ed. Pierantonio Serassi, 3 vols. (Bergamo, 1747-54), 2 (1750): Appendix (Opuscoli inediti di Tarquinia Molza Modenese) and 3 (1754): 22-27. Cf. G. Tiraboschi, *Biblioteca Modenese*, 3 (Modena, 1783): 244-53. Verses by Pincetta and others addressed to Tarquinia Molza are found in Modena, MS Est. ital. 224 (Alpha T 7.1). See also British Library, MS Add. 22336.

12. Conor Fahy, "Three Early Renaissance Treatises on Women," *Italian Studies* 11 (1956): 30-55; he also gives a "list of treatises on the equality or superiority of women written or published in Italy during the fifteenth and sixteenth centuries" (pp. 47-55). He deals especially with

Bartolomeus Gogius (Goggio), *De laudibus mulierum,* a treatise in Italian dedicated to Eleonora of Aragon in British Library MS Add. 17415, on which Werner Gundersheimer is preparing a more detailed study, and with treatises by Mario Equicola and Agostino Strozzi, an Augustinian Canon, both dedicated to Margherita Cantelma. He also mentions Boccaccio, *De claris mulieribus,* dedicated to a lady, Andrea Acciaiuoli (ed. Berne, 1539); Ant. Cornazzano, *De mulieribus admirandis,* in terza rima, to Bianca Maria Sforza (MS Est. ital. 177, Alpha J 6, 21); Vespasiano da Bisticci, *Delle lodi delle donne* (MS Ricc. 2293); and Jacobus Philippus Bergomas (Foresti) OESA, *De claris mulieribus,* to Beatrice of Aragon (in *De memorabilibus et claris mulieribus aliquot,* ed. J. Ravisius Textor [Paris, 1521], fols. 14v-176; first printed in 1496). We may add Giovanni Sabadino degli Arienti, *Gynevera de le clare donne,* dedicated to Ginevra Sforza Bentivoglio, ed. C. Ricci and A. Bacchi della Lega *(Scelta di curiosità letterarie 223* [Bologna, 1888]).

13. L. Chiappini, *Eleonora d'Aragona, Prima Duchessa di Ferrara* (Deputazione Provinciale Ferrarese di Storia Patria, n.s. 16 [1956]). Cf. Werner L. Gundersheimer, *Ferrara: The Style of a Renaissance Despotism* (Princeton, 1973), pp. 215-17. For works dedicated to her, see P. O. Kristeller, *Iter Italicum, a Finding List of Uncatalogued or Incompletely Catalogued Humanistic Manuscripts of the Renaissance in Italian and Other Libraries,* 2 vols. (Leiden, 1963-67), 1:254 and 381 (Diomede Caraffa, on the duties of a prince, translated into Latin at Eleonora's request by Baptista Guarinus), p. 429 (another Latin translation by Colantonius Lentulus, cf. Leningrad, Ermitazh, Otdelenie rissunkov, no. 78159), pp. 384, 438. See also n. 12, above. For a list of Eleonora's books, see G. Bertoni, *La Biblioteca Estense e la coltura ferrarese ai tempi del Duca Ercole I* (Turin, 1903), pp. 229-33.

14. A. Berzeviczy, *Beatrice d'Aragon, reine de Hongrie,* 2 vols. (Paris, 1911-12). For works dedicated to her, see *Bibliotheca Corviniana,* by C. Csapodi and K. Csapodi-Gardonyi (New York, 1969), pp. 45-46, no. 29 (Agathias, Latin by Christophorus Persona); p. 47, no. 34 (Ant. de Bonfinis, *Symposion de virginitate et pudicitia coniugali*). Kristeller, *Iter,* 1:438 (Diomede Caraffa); 2:49, cf. 1:433 (Diomede Caraffa, Latin by Colantonius Lentulus). See also n. 12, above.

15. A Luzio and R. Renier, "La coltura e le relazioni letterarie di Isabella d'Este Gonzaga," *Giornale storico della letteratura italiana* 33-42 (1899-1903), and *Mantova e Urbino* (Turin, 1893). Julia Cartwright (Mrs. Ady), *Isabella d'Este Marchioness of Mantua,* 2 vols. (London, 1903). Edith Patterson Meyer, *First Lady of the Renaissance: A Biography of Isabella d'Este* (Boston, 1970). *Mostra dei codici Gonzagheschi,* by U. Meroni (Man-

tua, 1966). C. Malcolm Brown, "Lo insaciabile desiderio nostro de cose antiche: New Documents on Isabella d'Este's Collection of Antiquities," in *Cultural Aspects of the Italian Renaissance*, ed. Cecil H. Clough (Manchester, 1976), pp. 324-53. Even Clarice Orsini, Lorenzo de' Medici's wife, who was not noted for her cultural interests, received from Marsilio Ficino the dedication of his Tuscan version of an abridged psalter (P. O. Kristeller, *Supplementum Ficinianum* 2 [Florence, 1937]: 185-87). Vespasiano da Bisticci sent her a manuscript containing vernacular versions of Jerome *(Vita S. Paulae)* and Augustine *(De vita Christiana)*, adding a complimentary prologue: Rome, Accademia Nazionale dei Lincei, MS Corsin. 1858 (44 B 27), fols. 1-1v. The letter will be published by Miss Albinia de la Mare (Oxford).

16. Pietro Bembo, *Gli Asolani*, ed. C. Dionisotti-Casalone (Turin, 1932; first published, 1505). Marcel Brion, *Catherine Cornaro, reine de Chypre* (Paris, 1945).

17. A. Medin, "Maddalena degli Scrovegni e le discordie tra i Carraresi e gli Scrovegni," *Atti e Memorie dell'Accademia di Padova*, n.s. 12 (1895-96): 243-72. He publishes a Latin letter (pp. 260-62). There are three other letters in MS Ambr. C 141 inf. (Kristeller, *Iter*, 1: 319-20.) The verse epistle addressed to Maddalena by Antonio Loschi is mentioned by L. Frati, "Le epistole metriche di Antonio Loschi," *Giornale storico della letteratura italiana* 50 (1907): 88-104, and published by V. Zaccaria, "Una epistola metrica inedita di Antonio Loschi a Maddalena Scrovegni," *Bollettino del Museo Civico di Padova* 46-47 (1957-58): 153-68. A prose letter of Loschi to Maddalena will be published by Margaret L. King.

18. Leonardo Bruni, *De studiis et litteris*, in his *Humanistisch-Philosophische Schriften*, ed. H. Baron (Leipzig and Berlin, 1928), pp. 5-19. Her Latin oration is printed in J. B. Mittarellius, *Bibliotheca codicum manuscriptorum monasterii S. Michaelis Venetiarum prope Murianum* (Venice, 1779), cols. 701-14. A Latin letter and two sonnets are given by James Dennistoun, *Memoirs of the Dukes of Urbino*, 1 (London, 1851): 411-13.

19. Gregorius Corrarius, *Epistola ad Ceciliam virginem de fugiendo saeculo*, ed. J. B. M. Contarenus, *Anecdota Veneta* 1 (1757): 33-44.

20. They are found in cod. Vat. Urb. lat. 1193 (C. Stornaiolo, *Codices Urbinates Latini* 3 [1921]: 198-203) and partly published by A. Cinquini, *Classici e Neolatini* 1-7 (1905-11).

21. P. O. Kristeller, "An Unknown Humanist Sermon on St. Stephen by Guillaume Fichet," *Mélanges Eugène Tisserant* 6 (Studi e Testi 236) (Vatican City, 1964): 459-97, at p. 472.

22. F. Patetta, "Una raccolta manoscritta di versi e prose in morte d'Albiera degli Albizzi," *Atti della R. Accademia delle Scienze di Torino* 53 (1917-18): 290-94, 310-28.

23. John Walker, "Ginevra de'Benci by Leonardo da Vinci, *National Gallery of Art, Report and Studies in the History of Art 1967* (Washington), pp. 1-38. To the poems published and translated in this article, a Latin poem by Naldo Naldi *(Epigrammaton Liber,* ed. A. Perosa [Budapest, 1943], p. 39, no. 121) should be added, according to a communication of Dr. George Szabó.

24. There are several editions of her letters and of the dialogue, and many biographies. Cf. R. Fawtier, *Sainte Catherine de Sienne,* 2 vols. (Paris, 1921-30).

25. St. Catherine of Genoa (Caterina Fiesca Adorna), *Treatise on Purgatory and the Dialogue,* trans. Ch. Balfour and Helen D. Irvine (London, 1946). V. Puccini, *The Life of Suor Maria Maddalena de' Patsi* (1619, English translation; repr. 1970).

26. T. Ledochowska, *Angela Merici and the Company of St. Ursula,* trans. M. T. Neylan, 2 vols. (Rome, 1969).

27. Girolamo Benivieni dedicated his Tuscan version of Cassian's *Collationes* to the nuns of Sangaggio in Florence (Biblioteca Laurenziana, MS Acquisti e Doni 55). His brother Domenico Benivieni addressed five spiritual letters to various nuns (Kristeller, *Iter* 1:219). Ermolao Barbaro the Elder dedicated his Latin life of St. Athanasius to the nuns of S. Croce in Giudecca in Venice *(Iter,* 2: 444-45). The subject evidently is in need of further investigation.

28. Roland H. Bainton, *Women of the Reformation in Germany and Italy* (Minneapolis, 1971). A. von Reumont, *Vittoria Colonna* (Freiburg, 1881). Eva-Maria Jung, "Vittoria Colonna: Between Reformation and Counter-Reformation," *Review of Religion* 15 (1950-51): 144-59. Maud F. Jerrold, *Vittoria Colonna* (Freeport, N.Y., 1969). K. Benrath, *Julia Gonzaga* (Halle, 1900). Christopher Hare (Marian Andrews), *A Princess of the Italian Reformation: Giulia Gonzaga* (London, 1912). Siro Attilio Nulli, *Giulia Gonzaga* (Milan, 1938). Bart. Fontana, *Renata di Francia,* 3 vols. (Rome, 1889-99).

29. Angela Nogarola's poems and her letter to Maddalena degli Scrovegni are published with the writings of her niece Isotta Nogarola *(Opera,* ed. E. Abel [Vienna, 1886], 2:291-326). For Maddalena Scrovegni and Battista Malatesta, see nn. 17 and 18, above.

30. For the text of the decree (1453), see G. B. Comelli, "Di Nicolò Sanuti primo conte della Porretta," *Atti e Memorie della Deputazione di storia patria per la Romagna III* 17 (1898-99): 101-61, at pp. 148-52. Nic-

colosa's Latin speech was published by Lod. Frati, *La Vita privata in Bologna dal secolo XIII al XVII*, 2d ed. (Bologna, 1928), pp. 251-62 (from a manuscript in Vicenza). In MS Vat. Ottob. lat. 1196, the oration is attributed to Franciscus Philelphus, and this attribution is accepted by G. Benadduci, "Contributo alla bibliografia di Francesco Filelfo," *Atti e Memorie della R. Deputazione di storia patria per le province delle Marche* 5 (1901): 459-535, at p. 490, no. 26. In a letter that is perhaps fictitious, Niccolosa suggests that she had asked a prominent scholar to express her thoughts in Latin prose ("intitularmi del mio proprio nome su l'opera solamente da me tracta e pensata, avenga che a uno uomo di grande eccellentia e virtu la facesse per piu dignita descrivere et autenticamente porre in latino idioma"; see Lod. Frati, "Lettere amorose di Galeazzo Marescotii e di Sante Bentivoglio," *Giornale storico della letteratura italiana* 26 (1895): 305-49, at pp. 320 and 333-39. In his reply, Matthaeus Bossus indicates that he does not consider Niccolosa as the author of the oration which he criticizes, but he fails to identify the author, and may use this device out of courtesy toward Niccolosa *(Opera varia* [Bologna, 1627], pp. 156-65). Also Guarino of Verona wrote a letter against the decree of Bessarion *(Epistolario,* ed. R. Sabbadini 3 [Venice, 1919]: 526-34, no. 982) and corresponded with Matthaeus Bossus about the matter (ibid., pp. 650-52, nos. 906-7).

31. G. Voigt, *Enea Silvio Piccolomini,* 3 (Berlin, 1863; repr. Frankfurt, 1967): 44-45. L. Pastor, *Geschichte der Paepste* 2 (Freiburg, 1889): 42-43. Cecilia M. Ady, *Pius II* (London, 1913), p. 165. The text was printed in *Pius II, Orationes,* ed. D. M. Mansi (Lucca, 1757) 2: 192-93, not seen, and in Angelus de Tummulillis, *Notabilia temporum,* ed. C. Corvisieri, *Fonti per la Storia d'Italia* 7 (Livorno, 1890): 231-33. Cf. G. Meerssemann, "La raccolta dell'umanista fiammingo Giovanni de Veris 'De arte epistolandi,'" *Italia Medioevale e Umanistica* 15 (1972): 215-81, at 229.

32. Meerssemann, 250-51.

33. Isotta Nogarola, *Opera quae supersunt omnia,* ed. E. Abel, 2 vols. (Vienna, 1886). Cf. R. Sabbadini, "Notizie sulla vita e gli scritti di alcuni dotti umanisti del secolo XV raccolte da codici italiani, V: Isotta Nogarola," *Giornale storico della letteratura italiana* 6 (1885): 163-65. Dorothy M. Robathan, "A Fifteenth-Century Bluestocking," *Medievalia et Humanistica* 2 (1944): 106-14. Margaret L. King, "Thwarted Ambitions: Six Learned Women of the Italian Renaissance," *Soundings* 59 (1976): 279-304 (which also deals with Costanza Barbaro, Cecilia Gonzaga, Ginevra Nogarola, Cataruzza Caldiera, and Cassandra Fedele), and "The Religious Retreat of Isotta Nogarola," *Signs* 3 (1978): 807-22. See also Dr. King's article in this volume.

34. Several letters of Ginevra (Zenevera) Nogarola are found in Isotta Nogarola, *Opera*, 2: 327-42. Cf. M. L. King, "Thwarted Ambitions."

35. Yale University Library, MS Marston 279, fol. 2 (in gold letters): "Cenevra anogarolis scripsi manu mea immaculata." Rome, Biblioteca Nazionale, MS Vittorio Emanuele 1335, containing Giovanni Dominici, *Libro d'amore di carità*, was copied by Giovanna de Piero di Martinozzi. Cf. Viviana Jemolo, *Catalogo dei manuscritti in scrittura latina datati o databili*, 1, Biblioteca Nazionale Centrale di Roma (Turin, 1971), pp. 136-37, no. 126.

36. Constantia Varanea Sfortia, *Orationes et Epistolae*, ed. D. A. Sancassania, in *Miscellanea di Varie Operette* 7 (Venice, 1743): 295-330. B. Feliciangeli, "Notizie sulla vita e sugli scritti di Costanza Varano-Sforza (1426-1447)," *Giornale storico della letteratura italiana* 23 (1894): 1-75 (with many texts). Costanza's correspondents include Isotta Nogarola, Cecilia Gonzaga, Guarino, and Guiniforte Barzizza.

37. Laura Cereta, *Epistolae*, ed. Jac. Phil. Tomasinus (Padua, 1640). Cf. Pia Sartori Treves, *Una umanista bresciana del secolo XV* (Brescia, 1904; not seen). I am indebted for much information to Dr. Albert Rabil, Jr., who is preparing a monograph on Laura Cereta.

38. Cassandra Fidelis, *Epistolae et orationes posthumae*, ed. J. Ph. Tomasinus (Padua, 1636). Her *Oratio pro Bertucio Lamberto*, delivered in Padua 1487 on the occasion of his doctorate in the liberal arts, was printed several times in and after 1488, with letters and poems to and on Cassandra (Hain 4553-56 and Copinger 1474). H. Simonsfeld, "Zur Geschichte der Cassandra Fedele," in *Studien zur Litteraturgeschichte, Michael Bernays gewidmet* (Hamburg and Leipzig, 1893), pp. 97-108; C. Cavazzana, "Cassandra Fedele erudita Veneziana del Rinascimento," *Ateneo Veneto* 29 (1906), 2: 73-91, 249-75. A. Cappelli, "Cassandra Fedele in relazione con Lodovico il Moro," *Archivio Storico Lombardo* III vol.4 (1895): 387-94. Poliziano's letter to Cassandra, *Opera* (Lyons, 1539) 1: 84-86, begins with the words *O decus Italiae virgo* (Virg., Aen., XI 508). Another letter of Poliziano to Cassandra was published by G. Pesenti, "Lettere inedite del Poliziano," *Athenaeum* 3 (1915): 284-304, at pp. 299-301. For a letter of Poliziano to Lorenzo de' Medici in which he speaks of his visit to Cassandra, see A. Poliziano, *Prose volgari inedite e prose latine e greche edite e inedite*, ed. I. Del Lungo (Florence, 1867), pp. 78-82; repr. in A. Poliziano, *Opera omnia*, ed I. Maïer, 2 (Turin, 1970). Cassandra's husband, the physician Johannes Maria Mapellus of Vicenza, edited a collection of logical texts by William Heytesbury and others (Venice, 1494; Hain 8437) and dedicated it to Manfredus de Medicis, a professor of philosophy at Pavia.

39. G. Pesenti, "Alessandra Scala," *Giornale storico della letteratura italiana* 85 (1925): 241-67. Her Greek epigram is printed along with those of Politian, several of which are addressed to her (Poliziano, *Epigrammi Greci*, ed. A. Ardizzoni [Florence, 1951], pp. 37-38, App. 1). She corresponded with Cassandra Fedele (Cassandra Fidelis, ed. Tomasinus, pp. 163-64 and 167). In a letter to Cassandra, Politian praises Alessandra for playing the role of Electra in a performance of Sophocles' Greek play in the house of her father, Bartolomeo Scala (Pesenti, *Athenaeum* 3 [1915]: 299-301).

40. Olympia Fulvia Morata, *Opera omnia* (Basel, 1580). There are several other editions including the following: *Opere*, ed. L. Caretti (Deputazione Provinciale Ferrarese di Storia Patria, *Atti e Memorie*, n.s. 11 [1954], two parts; reference supplied by Dr. Albert Rabil, Jr.). J. Bonnet, *Vie d'Olympia Morata*, 3d ed. (Paris, 1856).

41. Helena Lucretia Cornelia Piscopia, *Opera*, ed. B. Bacchini (Parma, 1688). No copy is listed in the National Union Catalogue, but the Columbia University Library has acquired a microfilm copy so that American scholars may now read and interpret her writings. Cf. Mons. Nicola Fusco, *Elena Lucrezia Cornaro Piscopia* (Pittsburgh, 1975), with a bibliography by Maria Tonzig and John Halmaghi. See now F. L. Maschietto, *Elena Lucrezia Cornaro Piscopia* (Padua, 1978), who lists Elena's extant writings, some of them included in the *Opera* of 1688, and others scattered in rare editions and manuscripts (pp. 152-64).

42. P. O. Kristeller, "The Contribution of Religious Orders to Renaissance Thought and Learning," in my *Medieval Aspects of Renaissance Learning*, ed. E. P. Mahoney (Durham, 1974), pp. 95-158. Elena translated a Latin work of devotion by Johannes Lanspergius from Spanish into Italian (*Opera*, pp. 179-310) and was an oblate of the Benedictine order (Maschietto, pp. 176-82).

43. C. H. Haskins, *The Rise of Universities (New York, 1923); H. Rashdall, The Universities of Europe during the Middle Ages*, new ed. by F. M. Powicke and A. B. Emden, 3 vols. (Oxford, 1936).

44. U. Dallari, *I Rotuli dei Lettori Legisti e Artisti dello Studio Bolognese dal 1384 al 1799*, 4 vols. (Bologna, 1888-1924).

45. A. Gherardi, *Statuti della Università e Studio Fiorentino* (Florence, 1881), pp. 81-82 and 172. *Il "Liber Secretus Juris Caesarei" dell'Università di Bologna*, 1, ed. A. Sorbelli (Bologna, 1938). *Storia della Università di Bologna*, 1, by A. Sorbelli (Bologna, 1944), pp. 178-82.

46. Gherardi, pp. 116-18, no. 6 (bull of Clement VI for Florence, May 31, 1349). *I più antichi statuti della Facoltà teologica dell'Università di Bologna*, ed. F. Ehrle (Bologna, 1932), pp. 1-6 (bull of Innocent VI for

Bologna, June 30, 1362). G. Brotto and G. Zonta, *La facoltà teologica dell'Università di Padova* (Padua, 1922), pp. 253-54 (bull of Urban V for Padua, April 15, 1363).

47. Brotto and Zonta, p. 30 et passim. Cf. Ehrle for the analogous situation at Bologna.

48. Maschietto, pp. 112-19.

49. G. Tiraboschi, *Storia della letteratura italiana* 5, 1 (Venice, 1823): 478-80. F. C. von Savigny, *Geschichte des Roemischen Rechts im Mittelalter* 6 (Heidelberg, 1831): 97. The source is Christine de Pisan, *La Cité des Dames*, bk. 2, chap. 36, and the French text which is still unpublished is cited by Tiraboschi. It was kindly copied for me by Professor Charity Cannon Willard of Ladycliff College from Bibliothèque Nationale, Fonds Français, MS 1179, fol. 82v: "Pareillement a parler de plus nouviaulx temps sans querre les anciens histoires, Jehan Andri, le sollempnel legiste a Boulogne la Grace n'a mie soixante ans, n'estoit pas d'oppinion que mal fust que femmes fussent lettrees quant a sa belle et bonne fille que il tant ama, qui ot nom Nouvelle, fist apprendre lettres, et sy avant es loys que quant il estoit occupez d'aucun essoine par quoy ne povoit vacquer a lire les lecons a ses escolliers, il envoyoit Nouvelle sa fille en son lieu lire aux escolles en chayere, et affin que la biaute d'elle n'empeschast la pensee des oyans, elle avoit une petite courtine audevant d'elle, et par celle maniere suppleoit et allegoit aucunesfoiz les occupacions de son pere, lequel l'ama tant que pour mettre le nom d'elle en memoire fist une nottable lecture d'un livre de loys que il nomma du nom de sa fille la Nouvelle." According to Mrs. Willard, the word "courtine" should be understood as curtain rather than veil. In the early English version *(The boke of the Cyte of Ladyes* [London, 1521], fol. H 4) it reads as follows: "John Andry a solempne legyster of Boloyne la Grace was not of the same opynyon that it was evyll that women were lettered. As to his fayre doughter and good that he loved so moche whiche was named Nouvelle made her to lern letters and she had the lawes ye when he was occupyed in ony busynesse by ye which he myght not extende to rede ye lessons of his scolers he sent Nouvelle his doughter in his place to rede to ye scolers in ye chayre and to ye entente ye her beaute sholde not hurte ye thought of them ye she taughte she had a lytell curtyne before her and by suche manere she fullylled [sic] ye occupacyons of her fader."

50. P. O. Kristeller, *Studies in Renaissance Thought and Letters* (Rome, 1956), p. 505. Edward F. Tuttle, "The *Trotula* and Old Dame Trot: A Note on the Lady of Salerno," *Bulletin of the History of Medicine* 50 (1976): 61-72. The treatise entitled *Trotula de mulierum passionibus* appears in many

medieval manuscripts and was repeatedly printed in the sixteenth century, for the first time in the *Experimentarius medicinae* (Strasbourg, 1544).

51. C. H. Talbot, "Dame Trot and her Progeny," in *English Association, Essays and Studies*, n.s. 25 (1972), *Essays and Studies in honour of Beatrice White*, ed. T. S. Dorsch (London, 1972), pp. 1-14. For the documents, see S. De Renzi, *Storia documentata della Scuola Medica di Salerno* (Naples, 1857; repr. Milan, 1967), p. cxiii, no. 262; p. cxxiii, no. 308. R. Calvanico, *Fonti per la Storia della medicina e della chirurgia per il Regno di Napoli nel Periodo Angioino* (Naples, 1962), gives or lists many more documents (p. 119, no. 916, dated 1307; pp. 124-25, no. 966, dated 1307; p. 141, nos. 1165 and 1168; p. 145, no. 1234; p. 156, no. 1413, not in the index under Lauretta; p. 159, no. 1451; pp. 194-95, no. 1872, identical with De Renzi, no. 262; p. 195, nos. 1874 and 1875; p. 204, no. 1981; p. 214, no. 3006; p. 222, no. 3119; p. 224, no. 3127; p. 229, no. 3195; p. 232, nos. 3226 and 3227; p. 239, no. 3327; p. 243, no. 3371; p. 256, no. 3534; p. 261, no. 3571; p. 268, no. 3598; pp. 269-70, no. 3610; pp. 277-78, no. 3643). Some of the same persons occur in more than one document. One document in De Renzi (no. 308, cf. p. 560) does not occur in Calvanico. For women medical practitioners in Florence, see R. Ciasca, *L'Arte dei Medici e Speziali nella storia e nel commercio fiorentino dal secolo XII al XV* (Florence, 1927), pp. 287-88, who refers to archival documents but gives no details.

52. De Renzi, p. cxxx, no. 338, cf. p. 569. The two documents cited but not transcribed by De Renzi (Archivio Angioino, Reg. 1422, fol. 20, and 1423, fol. 20) were destroyed during the last war, according to a communication from Dottoressa Iolanda Donsì, director of the Archivio di Stato in Naples, but there is a modern copy of Reg. 1423, fol. 20, that gives "Nobilis Mulier Costannella Calenda de Salerno filia Salvatoris uxor Baldassaris de Sancto Mango viri nobilis de Salerno filii nobilis mulieris Manselle Iscilliate" (MS Soc. Stor. Nap. XX A 16, p. 94). The copy does not confirm that Costanza held the title of a doctor of medicine, according to a communication from Dottoressa M. Antonietta Arpago.

53. Maria Tonzig, "Elena Lucrezia Cornaro Piscopia (1646-1684) prima donna laureata," *Quaderni per la storia dell'Università di Padova* 6 (1973): 183-92, at p. 184 and the document facing p. 185. A fuller reproduction of the document (Archivio Antico dell'Università di Padova, MS 365, fols. 24v-26v) was kindly supplied to me by Dott. Lucia Rossetti. See now a partial reproduction on Tav. XVIII, 1-2, following p. 110 in Maschietto.

54. Fol. 25: Ex Primo Posteriorum Textus 9 (?), si igitur scire ut poscimus etc. The text is *Analytica Posteriora*, 1, 2, 71 b 19-20, and we should read *posuimus* rather than *poscimus*. Ex Primo Physicorum Textus

42, quod igitur contraria quodammodum (i.e., quodammodo). The text is *Physica*, 1, 5, 189 a 9-10.

55. A *Facsimile Reproduction of the Diploma of Doctor of Medicine granted by the University of Padua to William Harvey 1602*, With a translation by J. F. Payne (London, 1908).

56. Laura Maria Caterina Bassi Verati was also a member of the Collegium philosophorum, but although she appears on the Rotuli for many years (Dallari, 3, 1 [1891]: 336, and 3, 2 [1919]: 111), she taught only at her home. See *Dizionario Biografico degli Italiani* 7 (1965): 145-47.

57. Maria Gaetana Agnesi appears on the *Rotuli* of Bologna from 1750 to 1799 (Dallari, 3, 2 [1919]: 71 and 322), but she lived in Milan and apparently never actually taught at Bologna. She was a member of the Accademia delle Scienze dell'Istituto in Bologna and wrote a textbook on calculus *(Instituzioni analitiche ad uso della gioventù italiana*, 2 vols. [Milan, 1748]) that appeared also in French (Paris, 1775) and in English (London, 1801). See *Dizionario Biografico degli Italiani* 1 (1960): 441-43 (by M. Gliozzi and G. F. Orlandelli). Maria Amoretti obtained a degree at Pavia in 1777 (Tonzig, p. 184; Maschietto, p. 139).

58. For a preliminary list of women doctorates, see Maria Tonzig's article cited in n. 53, above.

59. This story was told to me by my late friend, Dr. Erla Hittle Rodakiewicz. She obtained her doctoral degree at Heidelberg in 1900, and her thesis was published the next year (Erla Hittle, *Zur Geschichte der altenglischen Praepositionen 'mid' und 'wid'*, Anglistische Forschungen 2 [Heidelberg, 1901]). I am indebted to Mr. J. Arthur Funston, archivist of Earlham College, for his help in verifying this information.

CHAPTER 6

Learned Women in the Europe of the Sixteenth Century

Roland H. Bainton

I was honored by the invitation to contribute to this collection of essays. My remarks are largely culled from the three volumes of my *Women of the Reformation* and my *Erasmus of Christendom* and may be summarized under these headings: the mastery of languages, ancient and modern; the range of writing accomplished by learned women; a review of certain exceptional women; and the important question of how their learning affected the attitudes of these women. Two final voices are heard: that of a highly learned man speaking on women's education and that of a highly learned woman describing her own experience.[1]

Women in the upper echelons of society were versed in the humanist disciplines involving acquaintance with the ancient classical and Christian literature and ability to handle Latin and Greek. Latin was, of course, still a spoken tongue in which the cultivated could communicate from Sweden to Spain. A smaller number were proficient in Greek. A few ventured into Hebrew. As for the literature of antiquity, the learned were so well versed that there was no need to footnote an allusion. A woman of the Neapolitan circle wrote a tract *Della Vera Tranquillita dell'Animo*, in which she said

117

that everyone desires to reach a ripe age but no one wishes to be congratulated on having made it. It was not necessary for her to remind her readers that Cicero had said this first in *De Senectute*.[2]

Mastery of modern tongues was not infrequent. In England these were French and Italian, but not German. Catherine Parr betrays dependence on the *Del Beneficio de Giesu Christo Crucifisso*, esteemed by the liberal Italian Catholics.[3] As for Queen Elizabeth, there is a book of her *Devotions* consisting of prayers of her own composition in English, Latin, Greek, Italian, and French, and all quite idiomatic.[4] The widest linguistic range I have anywhere encountered was that of Katerina Jagellonica, the queeen of Sweden. A volume of her correspondence is in seven languages. She had Polish from her father; Italian from her mother; Latin, of course, from her education; Swedish from her subjects; German from her craftsmen; and French and Italian from the diplomatic relations.[5]

The range of writing open to women authors was limited. Translation was always appropriate. Queen Elizabeth at the age of ten translated Marguerite de Navarre's *Mirror of the Sinful Soul*.[6] Anne Locke, a friend of John Knox, in the preface to her translation of Taffin's *Markes of the Children of God* (original in French), made references to the limitations imposed upon her by reason of her sex. She wrote, "But because great things by reason of my sexe, I may not doe, and that which I may, I ought to doe, I have according to my duety, brought my poore basket of stones to the strengthening of the wals of that Jerusalem, wherof (by Grace) we are all both Citizens and members." [7]

One may well wish that she had not felt impeded in essaying "great things," for she had a lively fancy. In the preface to her translation from the French of Calvin's commentary on King Hezekiah's song of thanksgiving, she observed that physicians are quite as needful for the soul as for the body. Wherefore God, the great physician, wrote a prescription. His apothecary, John Calvin, compounded it, and she now was sending it to her friend in an English pillbox.[8]

No restriction appears to have been placed on devotional literature for women. One would judge that they were not deemed competent to write on theology after the manner of Aquinas and

Calvin. St. Teresa certainly thought this was not her province. When it came to the analyzing of mystical states she was so acute that she is still referred to in works on psychology, but as for the Trinity, "Oh, that's for the doctors!" she would say.[9] But whether by conviction or convention, women did compose devotional tracts. Witness the *Rime Religiose* of Vittoria Colonna, the *Chansons Spirituelles* of Marguerite de Navarre, the meditations of Katherine Zell, and the *Lamentation of a Sinner* of Catharine Parr. Polish women composed *Modliwity* (prayers).

And now for a glance by country. In Germany we have the case of Margaret Peutinger, whose husband discovered the road map of the Roman Empire. Despite a large family, she kept up her studies. Her husband wrote as follows to Erasmus:

My wife and I were working at separate desks. She had before her your Latin translation of the New Testament and along with it an Old German version. She said to me, "I'm reading Matthew 20. I see that Erasmus has added something which is not in the German." "And what?" I asked. She answered, "The words: 'Can you be baptized with the baptism with which I am baptized?'" Then we looked it up in the Vulgate of St. Jerome and found that it is not there. We looked then at your *Annotations*, where you mention Origen and Chrysostom. My wife said, "Let's read them." We did and found there what you have added. We trust you won't be offended, etc.

Then Margaret in her own hand added a page in a mixture of German and Latin.[10]

In Italy, Vittoria Colonna was highly esteemed in literary circles. Bembo, the *arbiter elegantarum* in Latin and Italian, lauded her skill, and Castiglione submitted to her judgment a manuscript of his *Cortegiano*. Michelangelo carried on with her a love affair consisting of an exchange of sonnets. Here is an example of her work, her sonnet on the "Star of the Wise Men":

What joy, oh star and blessed sign
Twinkling on the cattle stall,

From the fabled east you call
Wise men to the birth divine!
Behold the King amid the kine
Swaddled in no lordly hall.
Above, what love surpassing all
Lifts our hearts and makes them thine!
The place, the beasts, the cold, the hay,
The lowly coverlet and bed
Of thy love what more could say?
Then, for the star which hither led
And gave such proof of thy design
To joyful praise our hearts incline.[11]

Olympia Morata was the daughter of a professor of classics at the court of Renée of Ferrara. Olympia married a German physician at the court, and he was a Protestant. With him she left for Germany. In her twenties she was renowned for her classical erudition. She was able even to translate the Psalms from Hebrew into Greek. And she wrote a lively dialogue on matters of religion. But most of her writings perished in the siege of Schweinfurt. All that survived was published by her fellow countryman and admirer, Curio, a refugee in Basel. She died at the age of twenty-nine.[12]

Renée of Ferrara composed no writings, to my knowledge. But she harbored Calvin and the poet Clement Marot and corresponded with Marguerite de Navarre,[13] herself an author in varied genres. If Marguerite did not write on theology, she understood it. When Pope Paul III heard her in conversation with Cardinals Sadoleto and Contarini, he marveled at her saintliness and erudition. She has been considered an anomaly because she wrote both mystical meditations and a collection of love stories. How could she treat of earthly love and be enraptured of the love of God? But that was her point: How can one love God whom one has not seen if one love not the brother whom one has seen? The earthly love rises in the scale of being until it becomes heavenly. A neoplatonic strain suffuses her poetry. The longest and greatest poem was entitled *Prisons*, for such said she, are all the delights of earth if they be tarnished by greed, lust, ambition, and the love of self. Even the church is not without alloy.[14] Some verses in my own condensed

translation and a brief prose summation strive to catch the essence
of her thought:

Churches entrance me with their ancient towers
Triumphant portals and chimes that mark the hours
Altars within, with silver marked and gold,
Given lavishly by those of old.
They hoarded not their goods and lands but gave
As if by prayers perpetual mankind to save;
The candles flicker and the torches flare,
While bells harmonious reverberate in air.
"Paradise is this," I say to me,
"Chants melodious, organs with holy glee
Reverent priests with sermons that console
To bring the seeker to his cherished goal.
I am in rapture; Lord, my altar Thou.
My pilgrimage in Thee is ended now."
Then in my fancy comes hypocrisy
With sweet seduction she entices me.
For honor says I should a church endow.
Or give a fee to break my wedding vow.
Let me devote some of my sordid gain
To house a relic brought by Charlemagne.[15]

"Vanity of vanities!" So is it with life's every charm, the spacious
firmament, the starry sky, gardens, woods and flowering nooks,
games and the diversions at the courts of kings, all give but a mo-
mentary flush of mirth, then wither or are tarnished by the sons of
Cain. Only in the realm above this mortal flesh, above the strivings
vain and lust of power, only beyond the last frontier shall we find
peace, merely approximated now as we the naught are drawn into
the whole, in the rapturous union of the bridegroom and the bride,
in loss of self within the Saviour's wounded side. Marguerite has
been rapt into a realm where learning itself may be relegated also
to the realm of vanity.

Our information about women in the lower social brackets comes
largely from the martyrologies. They did not have the humanist
training but knew their Bibles in the vernaculars from "In the be-

ginning" to the last trump of Revelation and could overwhelm inquisitors with massive citations from the Word of God. Isabel de la Cruz was such a woman; through the spirit she could confound the doctors.[16]

After one has amassed data on the content of education one is prompted to ask what difference it made in the attitudes and behavior of these women. My concern has been primarily with their religious positions, and at this point the education appeared to have made no difference. In England, Lady Jane Grey, Mary Tudor, and Elizabeth all had the same humanist education. Yet Lady Jane was an ardent Protestant; Mary sent the Protestant leaders to the fires of Smithfield; and Elizabeth tried to comprehend all England in a latitudinarian frame, excluding only recusant Catholics and radical Puritans. One must at the same time remember that the classical sources offered a wide spectrum. One could go from Socrates to the Sophists and the Cynics.

Yet there was one woman in the sixteenth century who imbibed the classical concept of *humanitas* and *concordia*. She was Maria of Hungary and Bohemia, sister of Ferdinand of Austria and Charles, the emperor.[17] The brothers were ardent for the house of Hapsburg and the Catholic faith. Ferdinand kept lecturing his sister for leniency toward heretics. She replied that persuasion is more effective than the stake. Then their aunt died, the regent of the Netherlands, and Charles begged his sister to succeed her. She loathed the burden but yielded for the honor of the house of Hapsburg. The emperor then constrained her to sign edicts of increasing severity against heretics. She signed, then mitigated sentences or tipped off the victims to escape. Did she get her irenicism from the *philanthropia* of Panaitios or the *humanitas* of Cicero? I suspect that rather she imbibed the spirit of her mentor, John Henkel, a Catholic priest, a reformer who declined a bishopric and tried to heal the breach with Luther. After ascertaining the content of instruction, we need to inquire as to the character of the instructor.

Perhaps the best witnesses to what was possible in educational theory and practice are Erasmus, the greatest educator of the sixteenth century, and Lady Jane Grey, one of the century's most learned ladies. Erasmus, in a tract on marriage, assigned to the mother the early education of the girls and then proceeded to discuss in general the education of women.[18] Girls, he said, are harder to train than boys. Both are slippery, but girls are more crafty. Their disposition is weaker and they make a bigger fuss over a failure. Like boys, they are to be treated with gentleness. A mother who beats her daughters deserves to be beaten. The first step in physical education is physical care. Girls are not to be victimized by parental pride into wearing heavy and cumbersome attire, pompous headpieces, superfluous underwear, dresses trailing to the ground and impeding movement.[19] How long should the education of women continue? It should never stop. The mind of the adolescent girl is to be filled with study. She should be shielded only from obscenity in art and music. After marriage, though encumbered with children, her interests should be cultivated. Her husband will rejoice in partnership on an intellectual level.[20] This point is made by a married woman in a discussion with an abbot who insists in one of the colloquies that women should confine themselves to the distaff, or if they have books, certainly let them not be in Latin. The lady reminds him that in pictures of the Annunciation the Virgin Mary is commonly shown reading a book. "Yes," rejoins the abbot, "she was reading the canonical hours of the Benedictine order." The lady informs him of the learned women in Spain, Italy, England, and Germany.[21]

Erasmus was personally acquainted with a number of them and enjoyed their companionship. In several instances we can fill in the details. His commentary on the nativity hymn of Prudentius was dedicated to Margaret More,[22] who in turn translated into English his meditation on the Lord's Prayer. Erasmus rejoiced that the Princess Mary was able to write Latin letters and, save for ill health, would have done the translation of John for the English version of the *Paraphrases*. To Maria of Hungary, an irenicist like Erasmus and a woman who delighted in Latin codices, he dedicated his work on *The Christian Widow*.[23] The tract *On Matrimony* was dedicated to Catherine of Aragon. The sisters of Pirckheimer, Caritas and Clara, both nuns, elicited his praise for their learning.[24]

As to the way a lady of the aristocracy enjoyed her education, we

have a charming picture from the pen of Roger Ascham who tells
us of how, about to go abroad, he came to take

> leave of that noble Lady Jane Grey, to whom I was exceeding
> much beholden. Her parents, the duke and the duchess, with
> all the household, gentlemen and gentlewomen, were hunting
> in the park. I found her in her chamber, reading *Phaedon
> Platonis* [the *Phaedo* of Plato] in Greek, and that with as much
> delight as some gentlemen would read a merry tale in *Boccace*.
> After salutation and duty done, with some other talk, I asked
> her, why she would leese such pastime in the park. Smiling she
> answered me, "I wisse, al their sport in the park is but a
> shadow to that plesure that I find in Plato. Alas! good folk,
> they never felt what true plesure meant."
>
> "And how came you, madam," quoth I, "to this deep knowl-
> edge of pleasure, and what did chiefly allure you unto it,
> seeing not many women, but very few men, have attained
> thereunto?"
>
> "I will tell you," quoth she, "and tell you a troth, which
> perchance ye will marvel at. One of the greatest benefits that
> ever God gave me is, that he sent me so sharp and severe
> parents and so gentle a schoolmaster: for when I am in pres-
> ence either of father or mother, whether I speak, keep silence,
> sit, stand or go, eat, drink, be merry or sad, be sewing, playing,
> dancing, or doing anything else, I must do it as it were in such
> weight, measure and number, even so perfectly as God made
> the world; or else I am so sharply taunted, so cruelly threat-
> ened, yea presently sometimes with pinches, nipps, and bobbs,
> and other ways, (which I will not name for the honour I bear
> them) so without mesure misordered, that I think myself in
> hell, till time come that I must go to Mr. Aylmer, who teach-
> eth me so gently, so pleasantly, with such fair allurements to
> learning, that I think all the time nothing whiles I am with
> him. And when I am called from him, I fall on weeping, be-
> cause whatsoever I do else but learning, is full of grief, trouble,
> fear, and wholly misliking to me. And thus my book hath been
> so much my plesure and more, that in respect of it, al other
> plesures in very deed be but trifles and troubles unto me." [25]

The conclusion to be drawn from these random samplings is that the women of the aristocracy were quite able to vie with the men in the humanistic disciplines. Indeed, women in high station in the age of the Reformation often found intense relief in the pursuit of learning from the banalities of recreation and the trivialities of etiquette in court circles. Although women were not trained for the professions through the study of theology, jurisprudence, and medicine, they might be self-taught. We have noted how Marguerite of Navarre astounded the theologians by her erudition. In the lower social brackets we find extensive biblical knowledge, whether by reading or memorization from listening. As for the curricula for boys and girls at the elementary level, we suffer from paucity of information. There is a great deal yet to be learned.[26]

Notes

1. All references for the essay, unless otherwise indicated, are to my *Women of the Reformation,* vol. 1, Germany and Italy (Minneapolis, 1971); vol. 2, France and England (Minneapolis, 1973); vol. 3, Spain to Scandinavia (Minneapolis, 1977).

2. Bainton, 3: 136-37, 153-54, n. 9.

3. Bainton, 2: 167-68, and 180, n. 5.

4. Bainton, 2: 251, n. 45. Elizabeth's *Devotions* have been recently republished (*A Book of Devotions,* trans. Adam Fox [Gerrards Cross, 1970]).

5. Bainton, 3: 183. The only library in the United States in which I could find a copy was that of Brigham Young University at Provo, Utah. The Mormon missionaries pick up and send home such items.

6. Bainton, 2: 233, 250, n. 5.

7. Bainton, 3: 93.

8. Bainton, 3: 91-92.

9. Bainton, 3: 60, 64, n. 97. *Ob* stands for *Obras Completas,* see p. 61.

10. Desiderius Erasmus, *Opus Epistolarum Des. Erasmi Roterodami,* ed. P. S. Allen (Oxford, 1906-58), vol. 4, letter 1247, pp. 608-9: "Communis interpretacio Germanica hoc solum habet, 'Mögend ir trincken den kelch den ich wird trincken?' Sy sprachen, 'Wir mögen.' Vnd der Herr sprach: 'Ja, mein kelch werden ir trinken' ecz. Hic de baptismate nihil. Margarita Peutingerin Augustana."

11. Vittoria Colonna, *Le Rime di Vittoria Colonna*, ed. Pietro Ercole
Visconti (Rome, 1840), Sonnet CIX, p. 269:

Quanta gioia, tu segno e stella ardente,
   Allor che i vivi bei raggi fermaste
   Sul tugurio felice, al cor mandaste
   Dei saggi re del bel ricco oriente!
E voi quanto più basso il re possente
   Fasciato, picciolin, pover trovaste,
   Più grande alto il vedeste e più l'amaste,
   Ch'al ciel tanta umiltà v'alzò la mente!
Il loco, gli animali, e'l freddo, e'l fieno
   Davano, e i panni vili, e'l duro letto
   Dell'alta sua bontà securo segno.
E per la stella, e per lo chiaro aspetto
   Della possanza, avendo in mano il pegno,
   L'adoraste col cor di gioia pieno.

The translation of the sonnet is my own.
   12. Bainton, 1: 253-67.
   13. Bainton, 1: 235-51.
   14. Bainton, 2: 13-41.
   15. Marguerite de Navarre, *Les Dernières Poésies*, ed. Abel Lenfranc
(Paris, 1896), pp. 152-54:

Eglises viz belles, riches, anticques,
Clochers, portaulx triumphans, autanticques.
Entrant dedans, j'y viz divers ouvraiges,
Tables d'autelz fort couvertes d'ymaiges
D'or et d'argent, monstrant n'estre pas chiches
Ceulx qui les ont donnez si beaulx et riches,
Et qui plus est grandes fondations,
Sans espargner terres, possessions.
Tant qu'il sembloit que ces fundateurs
Tous les prians fussent les redempteurs,
En rachaptant leurs pechez par prieres
Dont j'en oÿs en diverses manieres.
               ⁕   ⁕   ⁕
Je prins plaisir d'ouyr ces chantz nouveaulx,
De veoir ardans cierges et flambeaux,

D'ouyr le son des cloches hault sonnantes
Et par leur bruyt oreilles estonnantes:
"C'est paradis icy, me dis je alors,
Se le dedans est pareil au dehors;
Je n'oÿs riens que chantz melodieulx,
Orgues sonnant pour resjouir les dieulx;
Je n'y entendz sinon parolles sainctes,
Prestres devotz, predications mainctes,
Pour consoler tous les devotz espritz
Et ramener à bon port les perilz."

   o   o   o

Parquoy bientost dedans ma fantasie
Se vint loger madame Hypocrisie,
Me remonstrant que j'aquerroys honneur
Si à l'église estoys devot donneur;

   o   o   o

Car, pour six blancz faisant dire une messe,
Quicte j'estois de rompre ma promesse,
Voire et absoubz de ce qu'en mariage
Povoys faillir, en donnant quelque ouvrage,
Ou de l'argent, ou quelque reliquaire
Que Charlemaigne apporta du grant Quaire.

16. Bainton, 3: 18-27.
17. Bainton, 3: 205-15.
18. See my *Erasmus of Christendom* (New York, 1969), pp. 231-33.
19. *Desiderii Erasmi Roterdami Opera Omnia*, 10 vols. (Leiden, 1703-6), 5: 716 D, 712 C, 711 C-D.
20. *Erasmi Epistolae*, ed. P. S. Allen, vol. 4, letter 1233.
21. Desiderius Erasmus, *Colloquies*, ed. Craig Thompson (Chicago, 1965), pp. 217-23.
22. *Erasmi Epistolae*, vol. 5, letter 1404.
23. *Erasmi Epistolae*, vol. 8, letter 2215.
24. *Erasmi Epistolae*, vol. 2, letter 409.
25. Roger Ascham, *Schoolmaster*, fol. IIb, reproduced in John Strype, *Life of Bishop Aylmer, Works* (Oxford, 1812-24), 5: 3-4.
26. Gerald Straus has just published a detailed account of education in the Lutheran provinces of Germany in the sixteenth century, under the title *Luther's House of Learning: Indoctrination of the Young in the Ger-*

man Reformation (Baltimore, 1978). At the elementary level he notes no distinction between the training of boys and girls; and, as for professional training, this the girls in the lower echelons did not receive. A useful survey is also provided by Lowell C. Green's essay, "The Education of Women in the Reformation," *History of Education Quarterly* (Spring, 1979), pp. 93-116.

CHAPTER 7

Women's Roles in Early Modern Venice: An Exceptional Case

Patricia H. Labalme

On June 25, 1678, in the old university town of Padua, a Venetian woman thirty-two years of age prepared to receive her doctorate. A crowd had gathered, so large that the ceremony had to be moved out of the university halls into the great cathedral chapel dedicated to the Virgin Mary. There, in the presence of her professors and the principal figures of the university and the city, Elena Lucrezia Cornaro Piscopia defended the Aristotelian theses assigned to her the day before and earned the symbols of the *laurea:* the book, the doctor's ring, the ermine cape, the poet's laurel crown.[1] Her academic performance was flawless, her acclaim resounding. Yet we are told by her early biographers that before she began, she faltered, nearly fainting. It was evidently a characteristic loss of confidence, and on another occasion of public appearance, she revealed its source: "This I cannot do," she said, "because in the end I am a maiden." [2] She was, then, not a married lady, not a nun, but a maiden, thirty-two years old, one whose life was conditioned by roles she had not assumed and by expectations she had not realized. It is only against the background of those roles and

129

expectations that her achievement and her limitations can be clearly assessed.

It is an appropriate moment for a reassessment of women's roles in early modern Venice. Thanks to the work of Stanley Chojnacki, James Davis, and Margaret King, we are in a better position to understand women in medieval and Renaissance Venice than was Pompeo Molmenti, the great nineteenth-century chronicler of Venetian society. For Molmenti, the earlier history of Venetian women was obscure, and he found a moral rationale for that obscurity. He refers to the silent and discreet shadow that hides the life of women in the earlier and more vigorous centuries of the republic, a shadow which, for him, increased their attractions. He wrote:

> For women appear to us more beautiful and dear when they do not try to compete with men, when they do not involve themselves with civic affairs but pass their days in sheltered peace, sweet symbols of domestic virtue. So, in the ancient period of Venice, when it was strong and glorious, women had absolutely no importance in public life but remained ignored amidst the ardor of struggle, the glories of victory, the fervent pursuit of business. But when the succeeding ages came in which splendor and pomp concealed the germs of decadence, the Venetian woman appeared in all the luxuriant brilliance of her beauty, amid the ceremony of public festivities or in salons lit by the lamps of Murano, with walls covered by tapestries or adorned with the paintings of Titian, of Veronese, of Tintoretto.[3]

Molmenti's sigh is almost audible as he regrets the passage of that masculine age of triumphant endeavor and invokes the feminine presence only when Venice begins her long decline, amid artistic magnificence and the glow of Murano glass. It is an ambivalent and incomplete presentation. For as the shadows that hide the lives of women in the Venetian past are dispersed, a far more interesting, complex, even powerful feminine presence is perceived than the older historian could possibly have imagined.[4]

To be sure, Molmenti's sense of shadow reflects a historical fact.

There did seem to be a scarcity of information about women. *Maritar o monacar:* to marry or take the veil. That was their choice. Those who went to the cloister apparently faded into a separating silence. Those who married were absorbed into the families of their husbands where their traces are made elusive by the Venetian concern for continuity of line through the male patrician. "Everyone knows," opined a Venetian lawyer in the sixteenth century, "it is men who continue families." [5] Such a view explains the genealogies of Venetian society that list only the male lines, with women appearing, when they are included, as wives and daughters and with no additional information beyond their names.[6] Yet women, when they passed into other families, brought dowries with them, and information about these dowries and the regulations concerning them have begun to provide us with a new sense of a woman's position in her society.

The dowry of a Venetian bride might represent a fortune. Since the fifteenth century, the amounts of dowries had steadily escalated, in spite of governmental prohibitions that attempted to restrict their increases.[7] The Senate considered this trend gravely detrimental to the economy. "Our youth," it stated in 1535, "no longer devotes itself to business affairs in the city, nor to navigation, nor to other praiseworthy industry, placing all its hopes in these excessive dowries." [8] Marriage had become a business in itself. James Davis has found for one Venetian family a log in which dowry income was balanced against dowry expense over a period of two centuries. In that case, the books showed a handsome profit.[9] It was, in a sense, a shopper's market, since a larger number of well-dowered ladies were available than there were worthy candidates for their hands. This was because in most noble families, eager to preserve the patrimony from subdivision among too many heirs, only one male married and carried on the line, while the others concentrated on politics and business, sharing the same *palazzo* and contributing their funds and efforts to the power and position of the clan. Competition for a highly eligible male pushed up the price, because a suitable marriage was essential to social status. The burden grew for families with daughters, and the reward grew for the men who married them.

It was, however, a qualified reward, for the dowry never became the husband's; it remained the property of the woman. It was her share in the patrimony, to the extent that if she was unwed and undowried she would have to receive a proper share of the inheritance. If married, her dowry was her own: either the dowry itself or something of equal value had to remain intact in order to support the wife after the death of the husband.[10] Since it was assumed, moreover, that the husband would use or invest part of the dowry, dowry restitution took priority over all other creditors of a husband's estate, even over the claims of his children, so that both his ascendants and descendants were financially liable if the husband's estate was not sufficient to repay the entire dowry of his widow. Whereas the wife could not invest her dowry without the husband's consent, the husband could invest it only when he paid his wife interest. If the marriage proved childless, the dowry reverted to the wife's original family. If there were children, the wife left her dowry to them, sometimes in equal shares, sometimes to the daughters only, in order that they too might enjoy substantial dowries.[11]

These dowries, then, and the many laws that regulated their use, tell us something of the private respect a wealthy married woman could command. Subordinate to her husband in every way, she still retained a certain economic power within the home, although that power was used at her husband's discretion. Ultimately, her wealth remained hers, as much hers as her family connections: both were vitally important to the clan into which she married. It should be remembered that the Venetian nobility exclusively controlled every aspect of this vast, long-lived, much admired republic. Politics, as practiced by this ruling patrician class, depended on a network of family alliances, just as commerce and industry presupposed the combination of economic wealth from several families. When women passed into other families, they brought with them a nexus of aristocratic connections, essential to the political and economic success of their husbands. It was not an insignificant role. As one seventeenth-century Venetian nobleman put it, "a woman is a kind of merchandise which must be carefully protected because it is easily damaged." [12] She could be a very valuable merchandise.

As dowry regulations tell us something of the role of women within the family, so do the sumptuary laws reveal public attitudes toward, and public activities of, Venetian patrician women. A woman's costume and style of life was meant to reflect that sobriety and thrift which patrician moralists held forth as ideal and traditional virtues, exemplified, so they claimed, in the simplest lives of the earliest aristocracy.[13] But Venice from the Middle Ages on was an opulent city, where goods and luxuries of every sort were readily available. Pomp and wealth, whether public or private, whether exhibited in the many religio-civic ceremonies of the city, or displayed in private homes and personal costume, were demonstrations of power. That is why the Venetian sumptuary laws that closely regulated a woman's dress, cuisine, and household furnishings were so continuously defied, and defied with impunity.

The purpose of the sumptuary laws, like that of the dowry laws, was to conserve patrician wealth and to preserve patrician equality, *ugualianza*. Such laws exist from the thirteenth century on and deal with a wide range of luxuries: trimmings of fur, buttons of amber or gold, linings of taffeta, silver belts, embroidery of pearls, dresses with trains, false hair, tapestries and hangings, stuccoed ceilings, silken sheets, the size of betrothal and wedding feasts, silver damascened plates, marzipan and sugared fruits—there were proscriptions and prescriptions for every aspect of a lady's life.[14] Yet the continued repetition and reinforcement of these laws show how much difficulty there was in their application. The government said: only a single strand of pearls was permissible; women promptly hung their single strands to their waists. The government prohibited the use of certain expensive fabrics: women faced their sleeves and skirts with these fabrics and then slashed them so their luxury might show. So many men as well as women chose to violate the restrictions and pay the fines that *pagar le pompe*—to pay for the sumptuary violations—became a proverbial expression for accepting the consequences of illegality.[15] Those who were meant to supervise these laws found their task well-nigh impossible, and their office was considered, according to a sixteenth-century observer, "officio odioso," an odious office.[16] The women would have their way, and that way was paved with the complicity of the male patricians for whom luxury represented the power of the purse.

Parte veneziana dura una septimana: Venetian law lasts but a week. How could personal sumptuary restrictions be maintained in a city which prided itself on lavish festivals, the splendid *andate* of

the year, when civic ceremonies brought forth the signoria, the
senators, the guilds, in great costumed processions winding across
the fairy-tale Piazza of San Marco? A city that advertised its own
beauty and wealth could not but take pride in its beautiful women.
Marino Sanudo, the conservative chronicler of the early sixteenth
century, in his *Laus Venetiae*, a panegyric of his city, describes the
palaces, the gondolas, and the nobility, and he boasts of the Venetian women as most beautiful, magnificently dressed, wearing rings
of rubies, sapphires, and emeralds. Even poor ladies, he said, dis-
play expensive rings and pearl necklaces.[17] Much of this jewelry
was hired, and for prices so high that the rental fees had to be
controlled by law.[18] On certain occasions the government waived
its own regulations so that Venetian women could appear in impressive elegance. The most famous of these occasions was the visit
of Henry III of France in 1574, when two hundred young women,
dressed in white, covered with pearls and diamonds, danced before
the French king in the great hall of the ducal palace.[19]

There is no doubt that such types of civic exhibition and such
tolerance of women's extravagance ultimately fortified Venetian
patriarchal pride and political panache. Yet already in the fifteenth
century, some women claimed their costume as their right. When
the patriarch of Venice had prohibited a variety of necklaces, bra-
celets, rings, and embroidered garments, a Venetian lady wrote a
letter to the pope, claiming that her noble birth and her acknowledged wealth entitled her to wear her jewels *ad honor dei parenti e
per propria bellezza,* for the honor of her family and for her own
beauty. At the same time, a committee of like-minded ladies also
wrote to the pope claiming that in Venice, a city noted among the
others of Italy for its riches and reputation, women had always
covered themselves *a capite usque ad pedes,* from head to feet with
jewels and finery of every sort. To all these enterprising women
who had so cleverly identified their personal beauty and reputation
with that of the city and its nobility, the pope granted a three-year
release from the patriarchal decree.[20]

Costume and jewelry, then, define the Venetian woman's role in
several ways. Partly feminine magnificence served patriarchal
pride; partly it served a feminine mystique. From the sixteenth
century on, there may well have been an emphatic insistence on

the part of women that they be more visible, more socially prominent. Stanley Chojnacki has put forward this hypothesis, suggesting
even that there was a female campaign to be noticed, an attempt to
compensate in the social sphere for what was denied them in politics and business. For traces of this, he looks not only to their
sumptuary assertiveness but to the sensuality of contemporary art,
to the emotive realities of literature dealing with human relationships, to the expression of family sentiments.[21] By the seventeenth
century, the defense of women's costume is associated with a claim
for her superior qualities and forms part of the "querelle des
femmes." Lucrezia Marinella, whose book on *The Nobility and Excellence of Women together with the Defects and Deficiences of
Men*, published in Venice in 1600, points out that women have
always proved their superiority by the use of ornaments, allowed to
only those men who were rulers and princes. She wrote:

> It is an amazing thing to see in our city the wife of a shoe-
> maker, or a butcher, or a porter dressed in silk with chains of
> gold at the throat, with pearls and a ring of good value on her
> finger, accompanied by a pair of women sustaining her on both
> sides . . . and then in contrast to see her husband cutting the
> meat, all smeared with cow's blood, poorly dressed, or bur-
> dened, like an ass, clothed with the stuff from which sacks are
> made. . . . It might seem an incongruity [una deformità], to see
> the wife dressed as a gentlewoman and the husband as the
> basest of men, more like her slave or household servant; but
> whoever considers this carefully will find it reasonable, be-
> cause it is necessary that the lady, even if low-born and hum-
> ble, be draped with such clothes for her natural excellence and
> dignity, and that the man be less adorned as if a slave, or a
> little ass, born to her service.[22]

And in 1644 Arcangela Tarabotti, a literary nun, wrote a defence
of female luxury insisting that beautification was the *proprietà*, the
right of a woman. A woman is sacred and godly; she should embel-
lish her feminine beauty with the most luminous, lovely, and precious accessories, so that her divine splendor might shine forth. As
for those men who lamented that the purchase of grain or cattle

was sacrificed to the cost of a bejeweled ribbon, she gave a shrewd answer: jewelry does not lose its value. It is a far better investment than the dissolution and debauchery for which men make such continual expense.[23]

It appears that women controlled their costumes, whether men approved or disapproved. Take, for example, the use of the *zoccoli,* those very high-platformed shoes that were originally devised to keep the feet free of mud but that grew to such remarkable heights that a woman wearing them would have to be supported on each side to make safe progress. Often criticized as extravagant and out-landish—one wit said that Venetian women were *mezzo carne, mezzo legno,* half flesh and half wood and he would have none of them[24]—these shoes also served to impede the mobility of the female sex. It was an impediment which some Venetian men apparently found desirable. According to St. Didier, a chatty French visitor to the city in the 1670s, when the doge's wife and daughters introduced the style of more practical shoes and another foreign observer commented how much more convenient these would prove, a Venetian nobleman gravely replied, *purtroppo commodo, purtroppo commodo,* all too convenient, all too convenient.[25]

For Venetian patrician women were not encouraged to convenience of movement. Brought up in the strictest privacy to protect that valuable merchandise, even after marriage a woman's life was relatively restricted. St. Didier considered their existence almost savage. Some husbands were so jealous, he wrote, that without scruple they confined their wives for entire years to their homes.[26] That is probably a sophisticated Frenchman's exaggeration. We know that ladies sampled the many pleasures of Venice. The literary nun mentioned above compares, in one passage, her bleak fate with that of the young bride, enjoying her cosmetics and jewels; her lessons with a dancing master that would render her body attractive in society; her perfumes, gardens, gondolas, liveries, the masks and *comedies* of her new life.[27] A group of Florentine noblewomen, Strozzi ladies living in exile in Venice, were much aggrieved when, because their husbands had dabbled in Venetian political secrets, they were required to leave their adopted city, so pleasing to them for its quiet, its delights, its security.[28] But these were foreign ladies whose lives were undoubtedly freer than those of their Venetian counterparts.[29] The world of proper Venetian women was closely circumscribed, their main function being the maintenance of their homes, at least for those who achieved marriage and homes of their own.

Just as many Venetian men did not marry, in order that the substance of a family might not be overly divided, so many Venetian women were placed in convents for the same reason. Few families could afford to marry more than one or two daughters. Convents had provided a protected education for girls when they were young, and many returned to these convents as novices later on, some willingly, with a genuine vocation. Many, however, had no real choice. The decision might well depend on a family's finances or father's determination. A monastic dowry was a fraction of a marital dowry, and with it, the young woman signed a waiver for any other claim to the paternal estate.[30]For this reason, the numbers of patrician women who entered Venetian convents was large, so large that Venetian women's alternative role of the cloistered nun must now be considered.

It should be said that our evidence here is not extensive. We have the reports of a few patriarchs; the records of reforms discussed in the Senate; some letters of papal nuncios; some private diaries; the remarks of a number of foreign visitors; and the tirades of Arcangela Tarabotti, the literary nun referred to earlier who was an unwilling and ill-humored witness. But what is clear is that in some monasteries life was hardly cloistered at all.[31] St. Didier remarked that Venetian nuns preferred their convents to the paternal home because they could enjoy more liberty and see whomever they pleased.[32] Occasionally, that liberty became scandalous. Priuli, the Venetian diarist, remarked in 1509 that some nuns were no better than "public prostitutes" for whom no other remedy would serve "but to burn down the aforesaid convents together with the nuns for the salvation of the Venetian State."[33] Such dereliction was probably infrequent. More common were uncanonical comings and goings, frequent visitors, parties held in the convent parlor, illicit books in the cells, bleached curls instead of shaven heads, and an immodest *décolletage*.[34] St. Didier almost purred as he reported:

"The most attractive are never without flowers which they attach to their garments or place in their bosom. . . . No sight could be more agreeable." [35]

Such monastic freedom was often criticized but rarely reformed. One sympathetic patriarch in 1629 even softened the monastic regulations, explaining that these women were noble, brought up and nourished with delicacy and respect. "If they had been of the other sex," he wrote, "they would have commanded and governed the world." Instead, he commented, they made a gift of their liberty, a gift to God and to their country and to the families who could never have otherwise supported them.[36] Less indulgent was Pope Gregory XIII, who proposed an apostolic visit to churches and religious houses in 1580, a proposal strenuously resisted by the Venetian government, at least as far as the convents went. It was already hard enough to get young noblewomen to agree to the monastic alternative. After a stringent reform, none would agree, and even the rumor of the visitation had led some to refuse to take the veil. That would be, thought the Senate, the ruin of many families.[37]

Freedom of access to the convents, in addition to making that life more appealing to young patrician women, produced another benefit, a particularly interesting one. The papal nuncio residing in Venice described it in a letter to the papal secretary of state: "I see that in the acquisition of political office in this Republic, relatives and friends are important; everyone capitalizes on the nuns who can send for their fathers and brothers and other relations and by favoring that one or this one can significantly help or hinder [political careers]. And for this reason even the most powerful Senators strive to gratify the convents." [38] Broglio, as the continuous Venetian political maneuvering was called, could not do without its monastic component. Patrician women in this case, even confined, were not without considerable political influence.

To some, such as Arcangela Tarabotti, this freedom, this influence, was woefully insufficient, although it was in the relative liberty of a Venetian convent that she could make the most outspoken statement of feminism in the Venetian seventeenth century. Arcangela Tarabotti had been a nun at the Convent of St. Anna since she was sixteen years old. She was not a patrician lady, yet she spoke for all Venetian women. In a book entitled *Paternal Tyranny* or *Simplicity Deceived,* she castigated Venetian fathers for forcing their daughters into what she described, in another work, as the "monastic inferno." [39] Their tyranny was rooted in avarice and in their own lascivious appetites for expensive illicit pleasure. It was prompted by their preference for male children, who would themselves dissipate their wealth and by an egotistical desire to marry one daughter well rather than several more modestly. It was a tyranny aided and abetted by the government whose reputation for liberty was a farce since it freed its Jews and incarcerated its daughters, burying them alive. Women were not only forced to be nuns by clever deceits—for the religious profession had to be voluntary—but they were deceitfully deprived of that education which might make them lawyers and doctors and governors, which would render them able to defend themselves against the guile of men. They were deprived of an education that would bring out their natural superiority. For women were superior to men. Eve had been superior to Adam. She came from his rib; he came from the mud. She ate the apple for love of learning; he just gobbled it down. Yet women, with all their abilities, were denied by men any role in religion, philosophy, science, the arts or letters.[40]

There were, in fact, few women luminaries in the seventeenth century. Whether that was due to a general "spiritual mortification," as it has been described, or to the influence of conservative Spanish custom, there were no salons over which a patroness presided, no female patronage of art or poetry, no feminine writers who compared with those of the Italian Cinquecento.[41] An intellectual woman was viewed with suspicion. "It is a miracle," wrote a seventeenth-century doctor, "if a woman in wishing to overcome her sex and in giving herself to learning and the languages, does not stain her soul with vice and filthy abominations." [42] The maxim that "an eloquent woman is never chaste" was common currency from the fifteenth century on.[43]

What, then, could a woman do if she was drawn to the life of the mind, considered a masculine preserve, but detach herself from society, taking refuge in personal or institutional sanctuary, embracing a protective and even defiant chastity? [44] There was no independent role for her unless she wished to risk her reputation, and few did. Between marriage, with its impositions, and the con-

vent, with its impositions, there was no middle ground unless to
live at home unmarried, a choice fraught *cum rubore et periculo,*
"with shame and danger." [45]

That is what makes the achievement of Elena Lucrezia Cornaro
Piscopia both remarkable and instructive. She was born in 1646
into an exceedingly rich and important Venetian noble family, the
Cornaro, whose relations with the kings of Cyprus had procured
them Cypriot estates known as Episkopi—thus the Italian title of
Piscopia.[46] Her mother was a plebeian of Brescian origin whose
provenance so discredited the family that only an enormous sum of
money allowed her sons to enter the nobility.[47] Elena herself may
well have sensed some obligation to restore the family's prestige.
There had also been a political scandal some years before her birth,
involving a Cornaro from another branch, and this shame rested on
the entire clan.[48] Elena Cornaro was cognizant of her birth and her
nobility, of her obligation to her name. In that sense, she was a true
Venetian lady.

In another, however, she was not. From her earliest years, she
denied her femininity. Barely free of her swaddling clothes, she
turned with a vengeance on those tokens of womanhood which
might have bound her to the limitations of her sex, as well as
tempted her young spirit to sensuality, to that *lusso,* that love of
luxury to which so many young women were thought to succumb.
After her death in 1684, an orator for the Academy of the Infecondi
at Rome, one of the several academies that had invited Elena to
membership, gave a funeral oration in which he described the
lady's childhood as if he himself had witnessed it. He assured his
audience that what might seem to them a rhetorical excess was the
simplest and purest truth:

Come with me into the home of the child Elena, and ask those
who waited upon her in her tender years. You will hear with
amazement how she was no sooner dressed in feminine garb
and left free than—within a short time—all her quarters would
be strewn with her garments . . . so that they seemed a battle-
field on which lay the remnants of the massacre of luxury. . . .
Ribbons untied, hair-pieces unfastened, broken mirrors, cas-

kets emptied, strewn pearls, torn veils, scattered ornaments, the whole arsenal of beauty sacked and destroyed! [49]

To the admiring orator, it seemed that Elena had rooted from her feminine nature the very shadow of desire, knowing how easily, he remarked, a woman can pass from purity to attractiveness, from attractiveness to caprice, from caprice to ostentation, from ostentation to *lusso*, from *lusso* to *libertà*, from *libertà* to *licenza*.[50] Even as a child, Elena Cornaro would have no truck with luxury, liberty, or license. Her contemporaries saw it as a form of sanctity. We may see it as revealingly exaggerated behavior, an effort to rid herself of a restrictive stereotype. In any event, the sumptuary temptations were not hers. This young woman would not be a woman—not in its secular sense.

Nor could she be a nun, as she may have wanted. She had vowed herself to chastity at an early age, and when, later, her ambitious father pressed her to accept the marital suit of a German prince, she chose rather to formalize her vow by becoming a Benedictine oblate.[51] During her remaining life she wore that monastic habit under her patrician garb. Her parents had no choice but to accept her commitment. On her part, while she had not agreed to the well-endowed marriage her parents hoped for her, as a loyal Cornaro she would not thwart her father's social ambition, and, almost as a penance, she allowed him to exploit her prodigious learning.[52]

That prodigality of genius was apparent from the age of seven on. It was discovered by her parish priest, and from that time forward, she was tutored (for women could not attend school) in the ancient and modern languages, in all the liberal arts and the higher disciplines of dialectic, philosophy, and theology. She demonstrated her skill in learned debates, held before distinguished audiences in her father's *palazzo*. On one such occasion in May 1677, the entire Collegio (one of the highest organs of the Venetian government) and most of the Senate were in attendance, rejoicing and consoled, said a contemporary description, that Venetian womanhood could boast such an example. After that same debate, her proud father requested her to sing, which she did, in six languages, with "virtue, joy, and modesty." And those who heard her were astounded, the description continues, and took it for certain that she would receive her doctorate, the following November, at the University of Padua.[53] Indeed, on November 18, 1677, the Riformatori dello Studio di Padova, the Venetian magistrates in charge of the university wrote the rectors of Padua that the ceremony by which the noble lady Elena Lucrezia Cornaro would receive the doctorate in sacred theology should be held in a sufficiently large room, perhaps the public library, because a great crowd could be expected to attend.[54]

It was at that point that the ecclesiastical authorities intervened. The news had reached Gregorio Barbarigo, himself a Venetian nobleman, who was bishop of Padua, ex officio chancellor of the university, and a cardinal in Rome. When he heard that preparations for the examination and awarding of the degree in theology had gone forward, he was shocked, and he halted the proceedings. "I never understood," he wrote, "that the doctorate would be in theology." [55] The *laurea*, the doctor's degree, gave the right to teach. But St. Paul had stated that "a woman must be a learner, listening quietly and with due submission. I do not permit a woman to be a teacher, nor must a woman domineer over man; she should be quiet." To make Elena a doctor, wrote the cardinal, would be to produce a comedy; Padua would be the laughing stock of the learned community. Elena's father would not be deterred. He was insolent and adamant and, as a Venetian procurator, powerful politically. He threatened to seek the support of the most famous academies of Europe. "Let him write," said the cardinal, "because when these pronounce what should be done, I must do it willingly, willingly, most willingly, for I shall then have nothing to lose." [56] For months that winter the letters went back and forth between Venice and Rome, until finally a compromise was reached. Elena Cornaro would receive her degree, but the discipline of philosophy was substituted for that of theology. Some still objected and called it *pazzia*, folly, to give a doctorate of any sort to a woman.[57] Nevertheless, the ceremony went forward, attended by the predicted crowds and amid huge excitement. So learned a woman was a miracle, one might also say a freak.

No wonder she faltered before the final event. "Questo io non posso, perchè in fine sono una zitella." Indeed, she was only a maiden. Neither married woman nor nun, she found herself in a role hitherto unknown and undefined, a role she had not herself created and one she did not develop, to any great extent. She never went on to teach, for Venetian nobility could not hold chairs in the Paduan university. Nor did she, in the six years of life remaining to her, write extensively. Her chief contribution was a collection of Venetian poems in praise of a particularly popular Jesuit preacher, to which she added her own verse in Latin, Greek, Spanish, French, and Hebrew, a virtuoso effort in what appears to be an unimportant cause. She corresponded; she received important guests who came to sample and admire her erudition; she participated in the debates of those academies who had admitted her. Several of her preserved orations are interesting for the political loyalty to Venice that they show. But altogether, her *opera* are negligible, her literary accomplishment small, her deeds more interesting for their charity than for their intellectuality. Her self-assessment is perhaps best summarized in her statement that "the highest ornament of woman is silence. They are made only to stay at home, not to go abroad."[58] Molmenti would have concurred.

Yet her life belied her limitations. In spite of her demurrals, she had played a heroic part. She had hoped, as she wrote some years earlier, to rescue the family name from "ruin and oblivion." That she had done, by aptitudes that rendered her, in the contemporary idiom, superior to her sex.[59] And she had created a precedent, a lady whose endowment could not be measured in ducats, whose ornaments, although invisible, were widely admired, and whose abilities had now received a public academic sanction. (See Plate 6.) It was an impressive achievement.[60]

She was unusual. Yet she owed something to a society that for all the constraints imposed on women, still accorded them some privileges and some power. The discreet shadows and becoming silence that marked the earlier history of Venetian women have yielded to our new insights a lady possessing her own economic advantage, flaunting with flounce and furbelow her feminine presence or insisting on the privilege of freedom from the constraints of costume, a lady whose family connections were always significant, who would politick in her parlor or in the *parlatorio* of her convent, a lady who, here and there, argued her natural superiority. Elena

Lucretia Cornaro Piscopia was an exceptional woman; she was also a thoroughly Venetian exceptional woman.

Notes

1. A scholarly biography, *Elena Lucrezia Cornaro Piscopia 1646-1684*, has recently been written by Francesco Ludovico Maschietto and published in Padua (1978). The earlier work of Nicola Fusco, *Elena Lucrezia Cornaro Piscopia 1646-1684* (Pittsburgh, 1975), is useful mainly for its bibliography, collected by Maria Tonzig. Informative but not entirely accurate are Angelo de Santi's series of articles entitled "Elena Lucrezia Cornaro Piscopia (1646-1684): Nuove Ricerche," in *Civiltà cattolica*, ser. 17, 4 (1898): 172-86, 421-40, 678-89; vol. 5 (1899): 176-93, 433-47.

2. "Era tale in queste funtioni il suo patimento, che tutto il sangue le correva in volto, et essendo per altro candida come la neve variava di colore in guisa, che pareva punta dalle vespe, onde alla madre, che la confortava perchè superasse la verecondia, rispondeva: 'questa io non posso, perchè in fine sono una zitella.' " P. Massimiliano Deza, *Vita di Helena Lucretia Cornaro Piscopia* (Venice, 1686), p. 42. Deza's biography is the earliest, followed by the Latin biography of Benedetto Bacchini, "Actorum Helenae Cornarae . . . Florilegium," included in his publication of her writings, *Helenae Lucretiae Piscopiae opera quae quidem haberi potuerunt* (Parma, 1688), and the Italian life of Antonio Lupis, *L'eroina veneta ovvero la vita di Elena Lucrezia Cornaro Piscopia* (Venice, 1689). See Maschietto, pp. xv-xvii, for evaluations of these earlier works.

3. "Nei paesi e nei tempi in cui l'uomo spiega tutta la sua energia, la donna non ha, per lo più, azione efficace sui pubblici eventi. L'ombra silenziosa e discreta che avvolge la vita femminile ne accresce le attrattive; poichè la donna ci appare più bella e più cara quando non tenta di competere con l'uomo, quando non s'immischia nei negozi civili e passa i giorni in oscura pace, simbolo soave di virtù domestica. Così nell'antica età forte e gloriosa di Venezia, non ha importanza alcuna nella vita pubblica la donna, anzi resta ignorata fra tanto ardore di lotte, tanta gloria di vittorie, tanto fervore di traffici. Quando poi succedono i tempi, nei quali lo splendore e lo sfarzo nascondono i germi della decadenza, la donna veneziana appare in tutto il fulgore della bellezza e del lusso, tra la pompa delle pubbliche feste, o nelle sale illuminate da lampadari di Murano, dalle pareti ricoperte di arazzi o adorne dei dipinti di Tiziano, di Paolo, del Tintoretto." Pompeo Molmenti, "Galanterie e salotti veneziani," *Nuovo Antologia*, ser. 4, 109 (January-February 1904): 193-216. See also Mol-

menti's introduction to his book on *La Dogaressa di Venezia* (Turin, 1884), pp. v-vii, for similar sentiments. Molmenti's great work, first published in 1880 and most recently issued in three volumes (Trieste, 1973), is *La Storia di Venezia nella Vita Privata*, hereafter cited as *Vita Privata*.

4. Among the important recent contributions to the study of Venetian women have been the following: Stanley Chojnacki, "Patrician Women in Early Renaissance Venice," *Studies in the Renaissance* 21 (1974): 176-203, "Dowries and Kinsmen in Early Renaissance Venice," *Journal of Interdisciplinary History* 5 (Spring 1975): 571-600 and "La posizione della Donna à Venezia nel Cinquecento," unpublished paper read in Venice, 1976; James Davis, *A Venetian Family and Its Fortune, 1500-1900* (Philadelphia, 1975); Margaret L. King, "Thwarted Ambitions: Six Learned Women of the Italian Renaissance," *Soundings, an Interdisciplinary Journal* 59 (1976): 280-304; "The Religious Retreat of Isotta Nogarola: Sexism and Its Consequences in the 15th Century," *Signs* 3 (Summer 1978): 807-22; and "Book-Lined Cells: Women and Humanism in the Early Italian Renaissance," the essay included earlier in this volume. Also useful is the much older work of Bartolomeo Cecchetti, "La donna nel Medio Evo à Venezia," *Archivio Veneto*, a. XVI (1885), t. XXXI, pt. 1, pp. 33-69; pt. 2, pp. 305-45. My concern in this essay is essentially with patrician women.

5. Davis p. 91.

6. Ibid., p. 62; Maschietto, p. 32. See, e.g., the useful and informative genealogies of Marco Barbaro, "Arbori de' Patritii Veneti," a seventeenth-century manuscript in the Archivio di Stato of Venice, or the nineteenth-century Pompeo Litta, *Famiglie celebri italiane* (Milan, 1819-98).

7. A law of 1420 had established a ceiling of 1,600 ducats for a marriage between patricians, although a plebeian wife was allowed to bring a dowry of 2,000 ducats to her marriage with a patrician husband (G. Bistort, *Il Magistrato alle Pompe nella Republica di Venezia* [Bologna, 1912], p. 108). A century later, the permitted sum had doubled (G. Priuli, *I Diarii*, ed. R. Cessi, *Rerum Italicarum Scriptores*[Citta di Castello, 1912-14] t. XXIV, pt. 3, vol. 2, p. 392) and actual dowries reached 16,000 ducats (Bistort, p. 111). By the middle of the sixteenth century, certain dowries amounted to 25,000 ducats (Brian Pullan, "The Occupations and Investments of the Venetian Nobility in the Middle and Late Sixteenth Century" in *Renaissance Venice*, ed. J. R. Hale [London, 1973], p. 389). By the eighteenth century, dowries might run as high as 60,000 ducats (Molmenti, *Vita Privata*, 3: 372).

8. "Li padri et altri che hanno cura di maritar figliuole o altre Donne . . . si danno ad accumular danari per poter dar le dote eccessive, e la gioventù nostra non si dà più al negociar in la Città nè alla navigatione, nè ad altra

laudevole industria, ponendo ogni loro speranza in ditte eccessive dote."
Correttori delle Leggi, B. 27, Stampa Rampazetto (N. 26) as cited in
Bistort, pp. 111-12.

9. Davis, pp. 107-8. Over a period of two centuries and nineteen marriages, the family netted 123,177 ducats.

10. Reinhold C. Mueller, "The Procurators of San Marco in the Thirteenth and Fourteenth Centuries: A Study of the Office as a Financial and
Trust Institution," *Studi Veneziani* 13 (1971): 175-76; Davis, p. 89.

11. Chojnacki, "Dowries," pp. 586-87, where the relevant Venetian statutes are cited. See also Edgcumbe Staley, *The Dogaressas of Venice* (London, 1910), p. 98. The importance of dowries to the Bollani family in the
sixteenth century has been well demonstrated by Christopher Cairns in his
Domenico Bollani (Nieukoop, 1976), ch. 1 on "Origins and Family." Man-
lio Bellomo, in his *La condizione giuridica della donna in Italia* (Turin,
1970), raises some interesting questions as to fictional dowries and the
uncertainties of actual payment.

12. Davis, p. 110. For marriage as a bonding of two families see the
passage from Francesco Sansovino's *Venetia città nobilissima et singolare*
(Venice, 1581), p. 149: "poichè per l'ordine del governo son uniti insieme
perpetuamente, come se tutti fossero d'una stessa famiglia." (Cited in Jacopo Morelli, *Della solennità e pompe nuziali già usate presso li Veneziani*
[Venice, 1793], p. 55).

13. See Marino Sanudo's classic statement of this ideal in his *Cronachetta* (Venice, 1880), p. 16: "Questi habitanti attendevano a far merca-
dantie con loro barchette, a li liti vicini portando sal et pesse; non erano
superbi, nè stimavano riccheza, benchè ricchi fussero, ma pietà et inno-
centia; non vestivano ornatamente, nè cercavano honore, ma, contenti et
lieti, per ben dil comun intravano al governo; non era differentia alcuna."

14. On the sumptuary laws of Venice see Bistort, passim: Molmenti,
Vita Privata, vol. 2, chaps. 7 and 9, or in the English translation (by
Horatio F. Brown) entitled *Venice: The Golden Age* (Chicago, 1907), pt. 2,
vol. 2, chap. 13; Margaret Newett, "The Sumptuary Laws of Venice in the
Fourteenth and Fifteenth Centuries," in *Historical Essays by Members of
the Owens College, Manchester*, ed. T. F. Tout and James Tait (London,
1902), pp. 245-78; Rita Casagrande, *La cortigiane veneziana nel '500*
(Milan, 1968), p. 52. Marco Ferro provides a brief survey of the sumptuary
laws and their rationale in his *Dizionario del diritto comune e veneto* (Venice, 1778-81) (v. "Lusso" in vol. 14, p. 55).

15. Bistort, p. 26.

16. The magistracy of the "Provveditori sopra le pompe" was established on March 13, 1512. For the official document, see Senate, *Terra*, reg.

18, fols. 27-30 (modern numeration), May 8, 1512, in the Archivio di Stato of Venice. Sanudo, in his *Cronachetta,* p. 150, calls this an "officio odioso," a judgment still echoed in the seventeenth century by Gian Francesco Loredano: "Vuole V.E. ch'io vada Inquisitore in Terra ferma contro le Pompe, e non per guadagnarmi riputatione. Al ritorno tutti i rei saranno assoluti, ed io innocente condannato. La pompa è un peccato d'onore, che avendo fatta la penitenza con la borsa, ricusa ogni altro castigo. Si ricordi che quest'Inquisitione non è stata giamai praticata da alcuno; ed uno solo eletto già alcuni anni, volle più tosto farsi monaco, ch'esporsi all'odio comun" *(Lettere,* pt. 2, pp. 170-71, as cited by Emilio Zanette, *Suor Arcangela, monaca del Seicento veneziano* [Venice, 1960], p. 261).

17. Sanudo, *Chronachetta,* p. 34.

18. Newett, pp. 251, 276.

19. Bistort, pp. 33-35.

20. Ibid., pp. 70-71; Cecchetti, "La Donna," p. 42.

21. Chojnacki, "La posizione della Donna." I am indebted to Professor Chojnacki for sharing this interesting hypothesis with me.

22. "Sono adunque le donne honorate con l'uso de gli ornamenti, i quali avanzano di gran lunga quelli de gli huomini, come si può vedere, e è cosa meravigliosa il vedere nella nostra Città la moglie di un calzolaio, o di un beccaio, overo di un fachino vestita di seta con catene d'oro al collo, con perle, e annella di buona valuta in dito, accompagnata da un paio di donne, che la sostentano da ambo i lati, lequali le danno mano; e poi all'incontro vedere il marito tagliar la carne tutto lordato di sangue di bue, e male in arnese, ò carico, come un'Asino da soma vestito di tela, della qual si fanno i sacchi, à prima vista pare una deformità da fare stupire ogn'uno, il vedere la moglie vestita da gentildonna, e il marito da huomo vilissimo, che sovente pare il suo servo, ò fachino di casa; ma chi poi bene ciò considera, lo ritrova ragionevole; perche è necessario, che la donna, ancorche sia vile, e minima, sia di tali vestimenti ornata per le sue eccellenze, e dignità naturali, e che il Maschio come servo, e Asinello, nato per servir lei, meno adorno se ne stia." Lucretia Marinella, *La Nobiltà et L'Eccellenza della Donne co' Diffetti, e Mancamenti di gli Huomini* (Venice, 1621), pp. 35-37. On the "Querelle des Femmes," see G. B. Marchesi, "Le polemiche sul sesso femminile nei secoli XVI e XVII," *Giornale Storico della Letteratura Italiana* 25 (1895): 362-69, and Zanette, *Suor Arcangela,* chap. 6: "La polemica femminista."

23. Zanette, *Suor Arcangela,* p. 23.

24. John Evelyn, *The Diary of John Evelyn,* ed. E. S. de Beer (Oxford, 1955), 2: 447. See also Fynes Moryson, *An Itinerary Containing His Ten Years Travell* (Glasgow, 1908), 4: 220, on what he calls "choppines": "For

this attire the women of Venice are proverbially said to be, Grande di legni, Grosse di straci, rosse di bettito, bianche di calcina: that is tall with wood, fat with ragges, red with painting, and white with chalke."

25. Alexandre Toussaint de Limojon, sieur de Saint-Didier, *La Ville e la république de Venise* (Paris, 1685), p. 303.

26. Ibid., p. 297. See also Thomas Coryat's description, based on a trip he made to Venice in 1608: "For the Gentlemen do even coope up their wives alwaies within the walles of their houses . . . so that you shall very seldome see a Venetian Gentleman's wife but either at the solemnization of a great marriage, or at the Christening of a Jew, or late in the evening rowing in a Gondola." *Coryat's Crudities* (New York, 1905), 1: 403.

27. Zanette, *Suor Arcangela*, pp. 141-42.

28. "Avvisi notabili del mundo," Biblioteca Nazionale Marciana in Venice, Ital. cl. VII, cod. 1229 (=8886), eighteenth century, fol. 256: "e le donne sue hebbero somo dispiacere godendo della quiete di Venetia et della delitia e sicurta sua con grandissimo gusto."

29. Cf. Marinella, pp. 40-41.

30. In 1568 Giacomo Bollani left 600 ducats in his will to any of his daughters who might enter convents after his death and a dowry of 5,000 ducats to any who might marry (Cairns, p. 10). One nun's dowry in 1620 amounted to 1,000 ducats. See Zanette, *Suor Arcangela*, pp. 21, 28-30, and 114 for a nun's disclaimer of any further rights to her patrimony. Pompeo Molmenti refers to the payment of an annual life pension of 60 ducats for a "donna agiata" who became a nun (*La Dogaressa*, p. 149).

31. Priuli speaks of fifteen convents in Venice, Torcello, and Mazorbo in which "la mondanità" had so penetrated that "se judichava fusse proceduto in grande parte la ruina del Statto Veneto" (4: 115). Cf. Giuliani Innocenzo, *Genesi e primo secolo di vita del Magistrato sopra Monasteri* (Padua, 1963), p. 12.

32. Saint-Didier, p. 319.

33. Priuli refers to "monasterij dele monache conventuale . . . che se chiamavanno monasterij apertti, quali herano publici bordelli et publice meretrice." The Senate's reforming legislation was ineffective, and "le monache fazevanno pegio che per avanti et uscivanno deli monasterij per bene luxuriare, et poi ritornavanno, come a loro piazevanno, et heranno nobille venete et de dignissimo parentado, tamen publice meretrice, et non hera alto remedio che bruxare li monasterij predicti insieme cum le monache per salute del Stato Veneto" (4: 115). Cf. Pio Paschini, "I monasteri femminili in Italia nel Cinquecento," *Italia Sacra* 2 (1960): 46-47.

34. Ibid., p. 57; Zanette, *Suor Arcangela*, pp. 48, 180.

35. "Les plus galantes ne sont jamais sans des fleures qu'elles attachent

devant elles, ou qu'elles mettent dans leur sein; il faut avouer qu'on ne peut rien voir de plus agréable" (p. 325).

36. Zanette, *Suor Arcangela,* pp. 35-37. Patriarch Giovanni Tiepolo (1619-31) wrote to the doge and Senate of Venice, explaining his action: "riflettando in me stesso come esse siano nobili, allevate e nodrite con somma delicatezza et rispetto, che se fossero d'altro sesso ad esse toccarebbe il comandare e governare il Mondo," ("Monache della città e diocese di Venezia," Biblioteca Museo Correr in Venice, MS Cicogna 2570, p. 303).

37. Paschini, p. 58. The papal nuncio in Venice reported the Senate's concern: "che riformandosi i Monasterij de Monache e riducendosi a maggior strettezza le figliole de' nobili che prima anco vi entravano mal voluntieri doppo la riforma non vi vorrebbono entrare in modo alcuno, et vien detto che già se ne vede l'effetto d'alcune che ricusano arditamente di monacarsi doppo il romore di questa visita. Il che dicono sarebbe causa della rovina di molte famiglie per l'eccessive doti che usano dar i nobili alle figliuole che si maritano." There was another sort of ruin possible for those young women whose dowries were not sufficient to gain them worthy husbands, poignantly described by Giovanni Francesco Loredano in a letter to a girl unwilling to take the veil: "E nata nobile, di dignissimi parenti, ma non avendo dote uguale alla nascita, bisogna o che degradi dalla sua condizione o che avventuri agl'incommodi della povertà. Il macchiare la nobiltà con soggietti inferiori, è incontrare lo sprezzo universale. L'unirsi a povere fortune è un accomunar le miserie, che vuol dir moltiplicarle. Riescono sempre infelici quei matrimoni che sono disuguali nella nascita ed uguali nella povertà. Il monastero è un ricovero di tutte l'ingiurie del destino." *(Lettere* [Bologna, 1647], pp. 201-2, as cited in Emilio Zanette, "Una monaca femminista del Seicento," *Atti del Reale Istituto Veneto di Scienze, Lettere ed Arti* 102 [1942-43]: pt. 2, pp. 489-90.)

38. Paschini, p. 57 (letter from Bolognetti, September 10, 1580): "Vedo che nell'ottenere i gradi et le dignità di questà Republica, importando le parentele et amicitie quasi il tutto si fa grandissimo capitale delle Monache, le quali con mandarsi a chiamare patri et fratelli et altri parenti et pregargli a favore di questo et di quello possono giovare et nuocer assai. Et per questo anco i Senatori principalissimi premono molto in gratificare i monasterij di Monache; da questo se seguita che il prohibir l'adito et colloquio delle Monache a parenti e cosa difficilissima."

39. Emilio Zanette's book on Arcangela Tarabotti presents a thorough description and analysis of this literary nun. Her *Tirannia paterna,* written in her earlier convent years, was later revised and published in the winter of her death (1651-52) with the new title of *La semplicità ingannata.*

40. Zanette, *Suor Arcangela*, pp. 92-93, 105, 223-24.

41. Benedetto Croce, *Nuovi saggi sulla letteratura italiana del seicento* (Bari, 1931), p. 154. See chap. 13, "Donne letterate nel seicento." Cf. Maschietto, p. 79, n. 8, and p. 167.

42. "Si debba a miracolo recare s'alcuna femmina volendo superare il sesso, data alle dottrine e alle lingue, non macchia l'anima di vitij e di sporche abominationi." Eureta Misoscolo [Francesco Pona], *La Lucerna* (Venice, 1628), p. 18.

43. King, "The Religious Retreat of Isotta Nogarola," p. 809. The maxim "nullam eloquentem esse castam" appears in an anonymous invective against Isotta Nogarola and her family.

44. Margaret King discusses this detachment in her essay, "Book-Lined Cells: Women and Humanism in the Early Italian Renaissance," in this collection.

45. Bistort, p. 107.

46. George F. Hill, *A History of Cyprus* (Cambridge, 1948), 1: 269; 2: 328, n. 1; 3: passim. On the Cornaro family, see Maschietto, pp. 3-16. Giambattista Cornaro, Elena's father, was a man of considerable learning himself and achieved political distinction, eventually purchasing a procuratorship in 1645. He was described as "uomo di gran spirito, e testa, et abilità singolare, e come tale da tutti considerato," Biblioteca Museo Correr in Venice, MS Cicogna 1213 (=86), "Origine delle famiglie aggregate alla nobiltà veneta per offerte assieme con le suppliche." See also the contemporary description of him as "il più verboso huomo. . . . Ha una facondia . . . di censura," in "La Copella Politica, overo esame fatto dal Zecchiere statisra etc." (1675), Biblioteca Museo Correr, MS Gradenigo 15.

47. See Maschietto, pp. 23-32 and 37 for the story of the liaison between Zanetta Bonis and Giambattista Cornaro. Five illegitimate children were born of this union, including Elena, before her parents married in 1654. The two sons were admitted to the nobility (which was also extended to the daughters) in 1665, after four supplications and the final offer of 105,-000 ducats. These are all recorded in the eighteenth-century MS Cicogna 1213 (=86), fols. 196v-205v. The charge in this manuscript that Zanetta was originally"dele più infime Cortiggiane" (fol. 23v) is, according to Maschietto, unwarranted.

48. Andrea Da Mosto, in his work on *I Dogi di Venezia* (Milan, n.d.), offers the following information in connection with Doge Giovanni Corner I (1625-29): "Per lavare l'onta derivante a tutta la famiglia in seguito alla condanna a morte per intelligenza con la Spagna di un Girolamo di Giacomo appartenente ad un ramo meno provveduto, avventuta nel 1659,

le casate principali arrivarono ad offrire ben cento mila ducati, senza però riuscire nel loro intento" (p. 441). Elena Cornaro is apparently referring to this in a letter written to her father from Padua in 1680: "Ego studii laetitia aeris salubritate, atque diligenti cura medicorum satis viribus utor, quare in spem sum in posterum posse me navare operam studiis et Domus nostrae nomen ab interitu vindicare" (Bacchini, p. 156).

49. This funeral oration was given by "Signor Michele Brugueres, detto il Ribattuto" and printed in *Le pompe funebri celebrate da' signori accademici infecondi di Roma per la morte dell' illustrissima Signora Elena Lucrezia Cornaro Piscopia, accademica detta l'inalterabile* (Padua, 1686), pp. 13-24: "Entrate meco nel domestico tectto d'Elena ancor fanciulla, interrogate chi la serviva in quei più teneri anni, e sentirete non senza vostro stupore che appena adornata de gli arredi feminili se mai la lasciavano in libertà era tale lo sdegno, che concepiva in vederseli attorno, che ne ritrovavano poco dopo tutte seminate le Camere, e vi parrà di vedere senza che io ve lo rappresenti coi colori dell' arte un Campo di battaglia, dove siano rimaste le reliquie di una sanguinosa strage del Lusso. . . . Nastri disciolti, chiome svelte, Specchi infranti, qui scrigni vuoti, perle sparse, laceri veli, e disipati Ornamenti, e tutti a terra saccheggiati, e sconvolti gli arsenali della Bellezza. Sembrerà questa a qualcuno di voi un' Iperbole di rettorico ingrandimento, e pure è nudo racconto di schiettissima verità."

50. Ibid.: "si che sembrava in lei estinta, non regolata, quella naturale inclinazione del Sesso, di comparire con ornamenti dicevoli alla dignità de' Natali, essendo che con troppa facilità si passi sovente a poco a poco della nettezza all'avvenenza, dall'avvenenza alla bizzaria, dalla bizzaria alla pompa, dalla pompa al lusso, dal lusso alla libertà, dalla libertà alla licenza."

51. Bacchini, pp. 247, 249, 251. See Maschietto, pp. 171-93, on Elena's spirituality. An oblate was a layman living in close connection with a monastery or convent but who did not take full religious vows.

52. Deza, pp. 40-41; Bacchini, p. 250.

53. On Elena's teachers and studies, see Maschietto, pp. 75-101.

54. De Santi, 5: 176.

55. Ibid., pp. 176-78: "Quando il Signor Procuratore Cornaro mi scrisse per il Dottoramento di sua figlia, mai intesi che fosse di Teologia. Lo credevo di Filosophia. . . . Adesso non siamo più nel caso supposto: non potendomi imaginare che una Donna volesse insegnar Teologia" (January 22, 1678). St. Paul's statement is in 1 Tim. 2: 11-13.

56. "Ma il Signor Procuratore dice di voler scrivere alle Accademie più famose di Europa contro di me. Scriva: perchè, quando queste dicono che

si deva fare, io lo farò volontieri, volontieri, volontierissimo, perchè io non ci perdo niente" (Sebastiano Serena, S. *Gregorio Barbarigo e la vita spirituale e culturale nel suo Seminario di Padova* [Padua, 1963], 1: 215-16).

57. De Santi, 5:181. On Elena's doctorate, see Maschietto pp. 105-30.

58. "L'ornamento, che rende gratiose le Donne, e famosissime da per tutto, è il silenzio; ne sono fatte, che per istar' in casa, non per andar vagando" (Bacchini, p. 184). See de Santi, 4: 435-38, on her book in praise of the Jesuit preacher. An earlier work, a translation of a devotional text from the Spanish version, went through five editions. It is possible that the value of her writings would be greater had so many not been destroyed by her command (Maschietto, pp. 153-54).

59. A contemporary writer and designer of engravings had this to say about her: "Recasi [ed: resasi] dunque superiore al sesso sino da principii della sua gioventù." *La virtù in giocco, overo dame patritie di Venetia famose per nascita, per lettere, per armi, per costumi, stampato da Giovanni Parè libraro all'insegna della Fortuna* (Venice, 1682), p. 186. The words of her cenotaph contain a similar rejection of her femininity: "In ea praeter sexum, nihil muliebre / Sub delicatis Puellae membris robustum animum servans" *(Pompe funebri,* p. 187). One biographer, Bacchini, wrote that she had an "ingenium supra sexum ad maxima natum" (p. 244) and another, Lupis, that it was entirely fitting that Venice, which had built an empire upon the fragile waters, should give birth to a soul who had overcome the weakness of her sex (p. 4).

60. There was considerable concern at Padua that Elena's precedent not be too easily invoked, as the following directive from the Riformatori to the rectors of Padua bears witness: "VV.EE si compiacerrano far intendere alli Presidenti de Colleggi et altri Professori, che occorresse, che non debbano admetere alla Laurea dottorale Femine dí qual si sia conditione, ne meno far passi che attendino a questo fine, senza previa nottitia et assenso del Magistrato nostro." February 7, 1679, in Busta 75 of the "Lettere de' Riformatori dello studio di Padova," Archivio di Stato of Venice. A French professor of medicine at Padua had sought a similar honor for his own daughter, an endeavor vigorously and successfully opposed by Giambattista Cornaro. Indeed, Elena Cornaro's precedent was not followed at the University of Padua for at least seventy years thereafter.

CHAPTER 8

Gender and Genre: Women As Historical Writers, 1400-1820

Natalie Zemon Davis *

When George Ballard published in 1752 his *Memoirs of Several Ladies of Great Britain who have been celebrated for their Writings*, there was only one lady included who could be considered a historian, namely the duchess of Newcastle, with her *Life . . . of the . . . Noble . . . William Cavendish*. In another ten years or so, the first volume of Catharine Macaulay's *History of England* would have appeared, but even that does not raise the number very high. The biographical dictionaries of French literary women compiled in the eighteenth century do yield more historical publications than in England, but they were still much surpassed by stories, romances, and poems from the female pen.[1] All of this makes no difference to me, however, for I do not write to "illustrate" woman, as the early feminists used to say, or to extol her skills against her detractors. I

* I am grateful to the Humanities Research Council of the University of California, Berkeley; the Committee on Research in the Humanities and Social Sciences of Princeton University; and the Institute for Advanced Study for assistance toward the research and preparation of this essay. Of the many friends and colleagues who have offered suggestions and criticisms of this work, I especially want to thank Lionel Gossman and Orest Ranum.

will not even ask whether a woman could have produced Gibbon's *Decline and Fall of the Roman Empire* (though I cannot resist noting that in her day Catharine Macaulay was thought by some to be as good a historian as Hume). My goal is more modest. I want to consider what prompted a few women in the fifteenth through the eighteenth centuries to do research and writing on the past or on the history of their own time. What were the subjects of female historians? Did they have a distinctive voice or not?And how was their work viewed by contemporaries? Such an inquiry may help us understand some of the limits of female learning in the early modern period, as well as the challenges faced by anyone not called to political responsibility who wants to write about it nonetheless.

Let us begin by asking what is needed for a person to write history. And I would say that a person, or a learned woman, needs more than Virginia Woolf's room of her own and £500 a year. She needs first of all some access to materials about her subject, written, printed, or oral; and she needs enough public life to be able to go and ask people questions or to observe intrigue, conflict, and debate. She might need to travel to find manuscripts or to see monuments, ruins, and inscriptions. Now, this was not always so easy to arrange. A woman was not likely to find herself chancellor of the Florentine Republic, as were the historians Leonardo Bruni and Niccolò Machiavelli; not likely to be Florentine ambassador to Spain or Governor of Modena, as was Francesco Guicciardini; not likely to be keeper of the king's archives or councillor in the Parlement of Paris, as were Pierre Pithou and Etienne Pasquier in sixteenth-century France. She might have printed chronicles and histories near at hand, especially if she were the daughter or wife of a lawyer; but the great collections in the monastic libraries and in university libraries would ordinarily be closed to her. The female historian would have to fashion her subject accordingly.

Second, the historian needs access to the genres of historical writing, to the rules for ordering and expressing historical material. Even the most innovative usually begin with some familiarity with the accepted modes of historical discourse. Some of these could be acquired easily enough from historical texts likely to be in the library of any learned person. But women were not always taught composition and were even advised by so liberal a pedagogue as the fifteenth-century humanist Bruni not to learn the rhetorical devices used in certain kinds of historical writing.[2] By the late seventeenth century, to be sure, Archbishop Fénelon was advising wellborn mothers to expose their daughters to "the history of France . . . and of other neighboring countries," for this would "elevate their minds and stimulate them to noble thoughts." A few of the boarding schools for wealthy girls in France and England began to include history in their advanced classes, basing its study at least on vernacular texts, if not the Latin ones used in the grammar schools and Jesuit colleges for boys.[3] By the mid-eighteenth century, popular history books were being advertised in the new periodicals for women. The *Ladies' Magazine* ran a *History of England by Question and Answer* as a two-year serial in 1749-50, and Eliza Haywood, editor of the *Female Spectator,* recommended *Bailey's Dictionary* for ladies who wanted not too much information about one period, but "a general notion of all." "There never was a place," she said, "a person, nor an action of any note from the creation down to the time of its being published but what [*Bailey's Dictionary*] gives a general account of [it]." Among the books excerpted or advertised by the women editors of the *Journal des Dames* in the 1760s were *Histoire des Tartares, Histoire générale de Hongrie* and a *Histoire des Amazones.*[4] These books varied in quality and of course in their usefulness as models for serious historical writing. The question is, Could they compete with the kind of training Gibbon had with his tutor? With repeated translation of texts from Latin and French, and systematic reading of Latin philosophers and historians, "studied [as Gibbon said] to imbibe the spirit most useful to my own"?[5]

To return then to the needs of our would-be historian, I would say third, and especially important, she needs a sense of connection, through some activity or deep concern of her own, with the areas of public life then considered suitable for historical writing— namely, the political and the religious. And furthermore she wants to have an audience who will take seriously her publications on these topics. All the major historians of the late fifteenth and the sixteenth century had this "connectedness" with the issues of public life—whether they were Florentine secretaries trying to set off their city-state from imperial traditions and from Rome, French lawyers trying to find the medieval roots of a distinctive national constitution, or Protestant reformers trying to find their precursors among the medieval heretics. Even when writing from exile, they once had been close to the workings of political power. Consider the case of Francesco Guicciardini. A lawyer, descendant of a family that had long served the Florentine state, and holder himself of several important offices, Guicciardini wrote first a family chronicle, intended, as he said, to exalt the city and perpetuate the glory of the family; then a *History of Florence,* for which his family's experience could be a major source; and subsequently in the 1530s a widely read *History of Italy,* in which (as one recent commentator has observed), he could assess his own political deeds "as a small part of the general failure of Italian statesmanship." [6]

In contrast, women had few political responsibilities in the early modern period, either as citizens or as subjects. In France, for instance, a propertied widow, as head of a household, might be expected to pay taxes or produce a man for the urban militia, but she was not any longer called to village or civic assemblies; a noblewoman with a fief might be convoked to meetings of the provincial Estates, but they rarely came, sending bailiffs in their stead. (Perhaps they agreed with Madame de Sévigné, who said of the Estates of Brittany in 1671, "the [meeting] won't be long. There's only the asking what the king wants. No one says a word.") [7] So long as this was the case—and it was so in France throughout the whole *ancien régime*—so long as queens were the only women with authority to declare on political matters, and public utterance on policy by other women was sanctioned only when they fell into an ecstatic trance or had visions of angels—and this was ordinarily so at least till the mid-seventeenth century—why, so long will you find the relation of women to the classical subjects of historical inquiry somewhat tenuous. A female mystic might write her autobiography; a lady maneuvering in politics from the court or salon might write her memoirs; a female grain rioter did not write anything at all.

Until the eighteenth century, then, the learned woman interested in the past was led most often to write about the world she knew—say, the history of her family or of her circle at court or of her religious order—a world that might have a temporal rhythm of its own, different from those of kings and revolutions, but a world about which her statements had some authority. As the seventeenth-century duchess of Newcastle was to say in her biography of her husband, I write "a particular history," which is "the most secure, because it goes not out of its own circle, but turns on its own axis, and for the most part keeps within the circumference of truth." [8]

What we will see here is the expansion of that circumference of truth, the regularizing by the late eighteenth century of the learned woman's relations with the various aspects of the historian's craft: with its sources, style, and subjects, if not wholly with its audience. One could begin the story with the eleventh-century Byzantine princess Anna Comnena,[9] but since her historical work was not known in the west until the early seventeenth century, we will start with Christine de Pisan. Apart from this extraordinary figure, who wrote in the era before printing, the process of women's familiarizing themselves to historical writing was a gradual one. And I will offer the following arguments about it: what brought learned women into the so-called mainstream of historical writing was some strong connection or concern with the politics of their time, but what they contributed to the rivulets of historical writing was not without value and had some effect on the later direction of historical inquiry.

Christine de Pisan's unusual career in the late fourteenth and the early fifteenth century illustrates concretely the circumstances that could move a woman to write history. She was brought from Bologna to the French court by her father, who was physician, astrologer, and important councillor to Charles V. Though her mother thought girls should spin, her father thought them none the worse for letters and gave her a good vernacular education in Italian and French and the rudiments of Latin learning. Widowed young from her marriage to a royal secretary, Christine decided not to remarry, as most women would have done in her day, but instead to find a way to support her children and her widowed mother by herself. To console herself from the lawsuits that assailed her inheritance, she began to study.

> I betook myself to history—to the history of former times, from the beginning of the world; the history of the Hebrews, the Assyrians, and other principal seigneuries, proceeding to the Romans, the French . . . and others.

She then went on to read philosophy and poetry, and finally to write herself. (See Plate 2.) [10]

The corpus she produced was astonishing in size and range: lyric poetry, courtly romance, moral tales, literary criticism, instruction for knights, instruction for women, and then a set of tracts on important public matters—pleas for the end of schism in the church, and for the end of immorality at the court, and especially for peace among the warring factions in France. And she was listened to. Her manuscripts, dedicated to important personages, male and female, brought fat purses in return, and they were quickly copied for aristocratic libraries in France, Burgundy, and Italy. This was partly because of the importance her late father had once held at court and partly because she wrote with imagination and intelligence. But also she was introducing successfully into France certain of the literary roles developed by her Italian countrymen, Dante, Petrarch, and Boccaccio, and adapting them to the style of her sex. Specifically, she was instructing those around her, not as the holder of a university degree and not as a religious or a prophet (not with the legitimation of St. Catherine of Siena, who died when Christine was in her teens, or of Joan of Arc, whom the elderly Christine saluted in her last poem). Rather, Christine was a learned poet and writer, and as such, became a critic of society, political life, and morality. If she sometimes referred to herself as "a woman in the shadow of ignorance," she hastened to add, "but endowed by God's gift and nature's . . . in the love of study." If she sometimes referred to herself as "a poor creature, a little ignorant woman," she also announced, "now I am truly a man." The chancellor of the University of Paris dubbed her "distinguished woman, manly female" *(insignis femina, virilis femina).*[11]

Thus, in early 1404, when Philip II, duke of Burgundy, wanted to commission an official history of the reign of his late brother, Charles V of France, he asked Christine de Pisan, then in mid-career. It was not a light choice, for Philip was making a bid for political power as well as perpetuating the memory and example of the late king. The "manly female" went to work, so she informs her readers, sifting through many existing chronicles, racking her memory for everything her father had told her and for her own girlhood reminiscences of Charles V, and interviewing a goodly number of former royal servants.[12]

The resulting *Livre des Fais et bonnes meurs de sage Roy Charles V* was a reputable piece of late medieval chivalric history. Ordered around the themes of "courage," "chevalerie," and "sagesse" rather than following a strict narrative, reliable in its facts if not always in its dates, Christine's text gave adequate treatment to Charles's economic and financial policies and very full treatment to his military prowess, his generosity, his interest in books and knowledge, his justice toward widows, and his piety. Written in praise of Charles V, Christine's story looks back to the moral biography of Joinville's St. Louis—an appropriate voice, perhaps, for a woman—rather than expressing the hard-boiled realism of the *Chroniques* by her contemporary Froissart. And however much Christine was purveying to the French certain Italian styles of literary action and debate, her book breathes nothing of contemporary developments in Florentine historiography. To be sure, the republican and rhetorical values of the city-state would hardly have suited her courtly story of the French king.

If Christine's *Deeds of Charles V* was not innovative in regard to genre, it certainly brought something new into her own life. It was her first major work in prose, and she used it to experiment with a vigorous, rhythmic, and concrete style. After writing the history, her political voice in tracts such as the *Livre du corps de policie* became even more direct, independent, and passionate. Perhaps, too, it urged her to think afresh about an aspect of her literary career that she found disquieting. Though poets praised her as a "Muse eloquent among the nine," she had some opponents who treated her with patronizing condescension, or even claimed that monks and clerks had forged her work. To silence such critics of women's potential, Christine wrote her *Cité des Dames* in 1405. Her scheme she borrowed from Boccaccio's *De claris mulieribus*, but added dialogues with Dames Justice, Reason, and Righteousness that reflected on the significance of her illustrious ladies from history and myth. Thus, it could be shown, say, that women were able to fight battles well, even though they were now happy to leave that recklessness to men, and that they had "suffycyent understandynge . . . to lerne the lawes" and "naturall wytte . . . [for] polycye and . . . governance," even if God had not ordained women to the office of justice. The *Cité des Dames* is not a history of women, but it shows Christine doing some rudimentary thinking about the position of women at different periods.[13]

Christine de Pisan was to be a model for literary women in the next 150 years, but not for female political historians. Though her *City of Ladies* and several other books were printed in the late fifteenth and early sixteenth centuries, the *Life of Charles V* remained in manuscript, to be consulted by a few learned specialists in the seventeenth century, and to have its first printed edition only in 1743.[14] In any case, the concatenation of circumstances that surrounded Christine's turning to history—political connections with courts that included important female personalities, outstanding talent in an enterprising woman of unusual and uprooted background, the availability to the literary person of a new kind of critical stance toward society—these do not seem to have recurred. When Queen Elizabeth had Cecil commission a historian for her reign, no female was entrusted with that task. Meanwhile, the political life of the Italian republics and northern cities gave learned women less *direct* access to the conflicts of public life than did the courts, and they seem to have participated not at all in the composition of the urban histories so important in the fifteenth and sixteenth centuries. Similarly, law and legal research were central to the new humanist historiography in Renaissance France, and women were cut off completely from this kind of training.[15]

On the other hand, there were two areas of historical inquiry in the sixteenth and seventeenth centuries that some women felt "went not out of their own circle, but turned on their own axis." One was small-scale religious history. Women were not supposed to speak in church, as Paul had said, but nuns could at least write, as an exemplar for others, of an admired mother superior and of their own order. Already in the tenth and eleventh centuries they had produced such works,[16] and the innovations of the Catholic Reformation inspired many more among the nuns of the Visitation, of Port Royal, and the Ursulines. Though ostensibly directed only toward their sister religious, these chronicles were usually printed and had an influence beyond the walls of convents.[17]

Protestant women did not write this kind of history, of course, and they left it to John Fox and Jean Crespin to celebrate the blood of female martyrs. The Swiss Reformation did provoke one little religious-political history, however—*La guerre et deslivrance de la ville de Genesve. Fidèlement faicte et composée par ung Marchant demourant en icelle,* published anonymously in that city in 1536. Its author was Marie Dentière, onetime abbess of Tournai, who left her cloister, married a Protestant pastor, and became deeply involved in efforts to reform Geneva in the 1530s, including haranguing the Poor Clares about how they shall marry. Her *Deslivrance* is an ardent piece, in which the Lord helps the city over a period of decades to rid itself of its Catholic and Savoyard pharaohs. Interestingly enough, one of the Genevan Poor Clares whom Marie failed to free from her virginity—a Sister Jeanne de Jussie—wrote her own report of these upheavals. It is a detailed and dramatic account of local religious and political change, as seen out of a convent grill and heard from friendly and hostile visitors to the nunnery. The Catholic chronicler told of the actions of women on both sides, even among "the heretical dogs"; but Marie Dentière could not read about how she was described—"a faded wrinkled ex-abbess"—for Jussie's history was printed only many years after both women had died.[18]

A second genre to which women contributed in the sixteenth and seventeenth centuries was that of family history. Literate men had begun to record the story of their families and patrimonies in the fourteenth century; but whereas in Italy this responsibility seems to have remained in male hands, in France and England it was sometimes taken over by wives or widows. The families involved ranged from lesser nobles to prosperous tradespeople, and the inquiry about the past ordinarily pushed back only to grandparents. Almost never intended for publication, they were written for sons or for other children, who might then carry them on in subsequent generations.[19]

The subject of the family history was in principle the same no matter who wrote it: births, marriage, deaths, the education and careers of husbands and sons, quarrels and alliances, moves, advancements, sometimes catastrophes. In fact, there was considerable variation in coverage, style, and organization. The ones by men, for instance, tended to order their material around the stages of a career; the ones by women tended to order their material around the stages of the life cycle. In both cases, however, the point of the history was to celebrate the fortunes of families headed by males; even when widows were in charge, they described themselves as acting to fulfill the husband's intentions.

Now, if the political connections of the husband were important, a family history could intersect with public events, as we saw earlier with the Guicciardini. Under these circumstances, the family chronicle, even in the hands of a mere woman, could expand itself into a form of political history. Let us examine two such cases and see how this occurs.

Charlotte Arbaleste was a Huguenot noblewoman of unusual independence, who disobeyed her mother rather than be disloyal to God's church. She was so articulate that her future husband, who cared for intelligence in a woman, decided to marry her the minute she opened her mouth (or so she said). His name was Philippe du Plessis de Mornay, one of the great religious polemicists and political figures of the late sixteenth century. Charlotte was completely caught up in his work in France and abroad for the Reformed cause, sometimes helped him check references for his writings or found him a printer, but more often was kept at home by her pregnancies and ill health. She was informed of his doings by oral accounts; by frequent letters to her, often in code; and by an archive she established by dispatches and letters.

These were the sources for her book.[20] She started writing in 1595, as her son was about to leave home for the first time, "to see the world, learn the manners of men and the state of nations." She began with an account of both of their families that took her back some seventy years in time and climaxed it with their separate and terrifying escapes from the Saint Bartholomew's Day Massacres in Paris in 1572. Once she and Philippe meet and are married three years later, though she mentions her deliveries or her conflicts with local pastors and the like, the story is her husband's, of his "service to God." A long work—the printed version brought out by Guizot's daughter in the mid-nineteenth century covers some five hundred pages—it has clarity, forcefulness, and movement. The narrative of political and military events is full (and indeed, is of considerable use to scholars today), but the voice of the independent political historian is not heard in these memoirs. King Henri IV's long hesitations before returning to Catholicism, Philippe's fruitless efforts to dissuade him, and his subsequent willingness to see the king to secure what advantages he could for the Reformed church—all of this is told just as Philippe saw it. The wife records, lends her voice to her husband, and does not take hold of the material on her own; does not describe character or offer speculations as to cause and motive. Trained in mathematics and painting and by her own account not "learned," Charlotte was using no historical works as models. But style she had; she simply chose to write in a passive mode.

For what scholars thought of her book she would not have cared. She aspired to teach only her son Philippe; here was a souvenir of his parents and of their service to God. She hoped he would always have an image of his father before his eyes and carry on that holy work. And when the son Philippe died young in battle in 1605, she abruptly stopped the book she had been composing for over ten years. "It was undertaken," she said, "only to describe to him our pilgrimage in this life." [21]

Over in England, some fifty-five years later, Margaret Lucas had no children. She did have literary talent (see Plate 5); any number of published plays, poems, opinions, and fancies; enough self-consciousness to undertake an autobiographical essay on her own "birth, breeding and life"; [22] and enormous devotion to her husband, William Cavendish, the duke of Newcastle. Cavendish was a much rewarded servitor of King Charles I, his lieutenant in Nottinghamshire and his general against the parliamentary troops in the Civil War. The Commonwealth years he spent with her in exile on the continent, mourning his monarch and his lost estates, and

offering political advice to Charles II on how he might once again
be "not only an absolute king, but pope within [his] own dominions." [23] Margaret's life of her husband—she calls him "My Lord"
throughout—is a richly documented, if partisan description of Newcastle's career, his efforts to regain his vast estates after the Restora-
tion, his literary friendships with men like Hobbes, his character
and opinions. It is in no sense a history of the Revolution, which she
refers to in passing as "an infatuation of the kingdom to oppose and
pull down their gracious King"; but it is a coherent and consciously
fashioned portrait of the political, economic, and cultural life of an
aristocrat during those years.

What is most interesting for our purposes about the *Life*, however, is the fact that Margaret published it in 1667 to declare, not
to family, but to "after ages" the "truth [of Newcastle's] endeav-
ours for the service of . . . King and . . . country" and that she
included a preface in which she speculated on historical writing
and her own relation to it. The chief sorts of histories, she said,
were three: general history, of the ways and customs of the known
parts of the world, useful for merchants and travelers and composed by the same; national history, best written by statesmen, and
often political in content, "pernicious," because it stimulated conflict between factions and countries; and finally particular history,
or a kind of heroic biography, best written by the prime actors or
spectators of these actions, like herself. In such history she need not
"preach on the beginning of the world nor [make] long observations upon the several sorts of government."

> Nor is it inconsistent with my being a woman to write of wars,
> that was neither between Medes and Persians, Greeks and Tro-
> jans, Christians and Turks, but among my own countrymen,
> whose customs and inclinations, and most of the persons that
> held any considerable place in the armies was well known to
> me.

Particular history was—to present her quote again—"the most secure; because it goes not out of its own circle, but turns on its own
axis, and for the most part keeps within the circumference of
truth."

Margaret was defensive about her heroic history, as Christine had been somewhat long before her, for readers had maintained that a man had really authored her previous publications. So she stated exactly who her witnesses were and "challenged anyone (although I be a woman) to contradict anything I have set down or prove it to be otherwise than truth." She admitted that she had not learned the rules for the "method and style of histories." But no matter. If she were not learned scholar, yet she had been a student from her childhood. If she had no elegant style, yet she would write her history "in a natural plain style, without Latin sentences, moral instructions, politic designs, feigned orations or envious and malicious exclamations." The modesty topos and the appeal to the plain style could be used by male writers as well—as in Marvell's "naked narrative" of 1677, *An Account of the Growth of Popery and Arbitrary Government*—but they have special bite in the mouth of a woman.[24]

The duchess' published book had its influence. More than one woman tried to imitate it, such as Lucy Hutchinson, the Puritan wife of Col. John Hutchinson,[25] and it surely suggested that females could become familiar to historical composition. In the next decades, family history continued as a popular genre and undoubtedly had some significance in the formation of historical consciousness among learned women. And the linkage between family and politics continued to be important for women: both our eighteenth-century historians, Catharine Macaulay and Germaine de Staël, were first pulled into political activity by their kin and then went on to come to grips themselves with the national and general histories that Margaret Lucas Cavendish had eschewed.

Other changes had occurred as well, which made historical research or reflection a more natural activity for the learned female, even while raising new questions about the goals and audience of historical inquiry. Especially in France in the seventeenth century, the boundaries between the novel, the story, history, and the memoir had become fluid, and aristocratic women had contributed actively to the process. Madame de Lafayette had had a stunning success in putting history wholly to the service of literary art and psychological romance in her *Princesse de Clèves;* had given shape

to the memoirs told her by Henriette of France, exiled widow of
Charles I, who thought her life would make "une jolie histoire";
and then had written, though left unpublished, an impersonal narrative of the political and military life of the court in 1688-89.
Mademoiselle de Montpensier, daughter of Gaston d'Orléans, had
begun her memoirs not long after the Fronde des Princes had cata-
pulted her at age twenty-four into political and military adventure
against her cousin, the king. Composing them over decades, she
had written sometimes "only for myself" and sometimes for others,
"who might read of the wrongs done to me and have compassion" (they were published twenty-five years after her death). Remembered events mixed with reconstructed conversations; court
intrigue, ceremony, and heroic action, with the discovery of particular and intimate feelings. So her entry into Orléans in 1652,
carried in triumph among the cries "Vive le roi, les princes! et
point de Mazarin" (Long live the king! Long live the princes! Out
with Mazarin!), led her to exclaim in her text:

> I do not know whether I was seated in [the wooden seat] or on
> its arms, so beside myself with joy was I; everyone kissed my
> hands, and I was overcome with laughter to see myself in such
> a pleasant situation.[26]

By the eighteenth century, the salon had flowered into an institution in which well-mannered men and women could converse
together about philosophical and political matters, as well as historical subjects, both fanciful and serious. Especially in England,
political pamphleteering by a few literary women, such as the Tory
Mary de la Rivière Manley, had become a reality. The female press
had developed in both countries, as we have seen, and was encouraging a taste among women for edifying popular historical writings.
Wealthy or wellborn Englishwomen, like Lady Mary Wortley
Montagu, were traveling, and their observations of the political,
social, and economic customs of the people they had visited were
being published.[27]

Learned and literary women in France also were publishing a
variety of historical works. From the prolific pen of one Marguerite
de Lussan in the 1730s to 1760s came not only *Anecdotes de la cour*

de François I and *Annales galantes de la cour de Henri II* in the romantic vein but also a set of readable, if unoriginal popular histories based on existing chronicles: a nine-volume *Histoire et Règne de Charles VI*, four volumes on *La Révolution du Royaume de Naples dans les années 1647 et 1648*, and several others. (See Plate 7.) A Madame Retau-Dufresne published a *Histoire de la ville de Cherbourg* in 1760, possibly the first publication by a woman in the field of local antiquarian history. Her pen directed by "le génie patriotique" in the wake of the recent English attack on the city, she had consulted old chronicles and charters and had taken "the most exacting precautions to acquire certainty about the facts." The polymath Charlotte Thiroux d'Arconville, wife of an important French jurist, published in 1774 a firmly written *Vie de Marie de Médicis*, based on wide-ranging research, including manuscripts in the Bibliothèque Royale, "precious monuments" as she said, "for those who wish to study history." Finally, in 1792, Marie-Charlotte de Lezardiere brought out four volumes of documentary "Proofs" about French law and political institutions from the Gauls through the ninth century.[28] This, then, is the cultural context for the work of our last two writers of history.

In 1763, some one hundred years after the duchess of Newcastle had dedicated her *Life* to his sacred majesty Charles II, Catharine Sawbridge Macaulay published the first volume of her *History of England*. It was dedicated to the cause of those who had executed Charles I, to liberty and virtue, and to just resistance to tyranny.[29]

The Sawbridges were a well-off Kentish family, with banking and trade connections in London. Catharine's father was a staunch Whig, hostile to aristocratic titles and pretention. He put her early to reading the annals of Roman and Greek republics, and this, she said, excited the natural love of freedom in her breast. Barred by her sex from the English universities, she thought she would not have learned much there anyway. "The study of history is little cultivated in these seminaries," she claimed, "and not at all the fundamental principles of the English constitution." (The only exception was Blackstone's new courses on the history of common law.)[30] She did marry a Dr. Macaulay, a physician and male midwife, who admired and encouraged her and seems not to have dom-

inated over her at all. While her brother John Sawbridge went on
to defend radical Whig principles in Parliament and as a London
alderman, she went on to do so with her pen: She believed in wider
suffrage, shorter parliaments, decentralized government, freedom
of the press, and good education for women as for any rational
being. All of this she argued in numerous treatises and pamphlets,[31]
taking on the formidable Edmund Burke more than once; and all of
this informed the spirit with which she wrote the eight volumes of
her *History of England from the Accession of James I to the end of
the reign of Charles II.*

When her first volume appeared, she was still anticipating "the
invidious censures which may ensue from striking into a path of
literature rarely trodden by her sex," still hoping "the defects of a
female historian" would be outweighed by "her integrity and industry." She very soon lost any feeling of strangeness about her
vocation and began to pontificate about the criteria required of the
true historian and to upbraid David Hume for the faults of what she
considered his Tory version of English history.[32] For about fifteen
years, as her volumes appeared one by one, her reputation was
extraordinary. (See Plate 8.) An admirer in her circle of radical
Whigs commissioned a statue of her as Dame Thucydides; her
fellow historian Joseph Priestley talked of her performance as
"masterful." Horace Walpole, who had dismissed the duchess of
Newcastle as a "fertile pedant," said that Macaulay had written
"the most sensible, unaffected and best history we yet have." *The
European Magazine,* a Whig review, said her work was composed
"in a style strong, nervous, and eloquent, untinctured with the
weakness of the female pen, breathing sentiments the most manly,
generous and patriotic." Even Hume took her seriously.[33]

And yet despite all this, the reputation of a Dame Thucydides
was precarious. Her republican views and political sallies angered
part of her public, and they were happy to fasten on her "scandalous" second marriage to a man half her age to discredit her.
Though she continued to be an inspiration for Mary Wollstone-
craft, and Madame Roland in France, and, indeed, continued to
have readers, the *European Magazine* commented in 1783, "Her
marriage has totally extinguished all curiosity about her opinions.
Perhaps there never was an instance, where the personal conduct

of the author so much influenced the public opinion of their writings." [34]

Was her history worth reading? She certainly lived up to her own important criteria. The historian's business, she said, was first "to digest voluminous collections." This she did, much more than David Hume, working on Civil War pamphlets, manuscripts in the British Museum, and recently published parliamentary debates and memoirs. She experimented with stylistic devices over the years, trying by volume VI to weave the erudition of her footnotes into the text, because she had heard "that long notes were tedious and disagreeable to the reader." [35] Then she composed a new work, *The History of England from the Revolution to the Present Time* (1778), "In a Series of Letters to a Friend," namely to the Reverend Doctor Thomas Wilson rector of St. Stephen's in London, who shared her ideals of patriotism and liberty. Here was a built-in critical audience, whose responses she would relate at the beginning of a fresh letter, thanking him for "paying me many elegant compliments on the unaffected stile of my narrative, which, you assure me, conveys to you a very full idea of the temper of parties and the humor of the times." He agrees with her, she reports, that the conduct of the "partisans of liberty" in the late seventeenth century was "reprehensible" for doing so little "to limit the power of the elected monarch"; he supports her view that since descriptions of battles are "in general the dullest part of an historical narrative [she] should in the future be as short on this subject as the matter will permit." He is so fond of "her characters" that she will allow herself to depart from her rule not "to draw a very just and accurate description of the principal persons near to the present times." [36] Oliver Goldsmith had already applied the epistolary form to his *History of England in a Series of Letters from a Nobleman to his Son* in 1764, but Mrs. Macaulay used the device with more imagination than he.

She also thought the historian must be "impartial" in interpreting his or her facts. This did not mean withholding judgment on the past. Like many historians before her, she frankly stated that the purpose of history was "to instruct the reader on morals, religion, policy and good government." Thus, it was her duty to defend the interest of the commons of England and to distinguish between the

liberty-loving Commonwealth men on the one hand and their enemies, the despotic Stuarts and the usurping tyrant Cromwell on
the other. "Impartiality" meant ignoring "party spirit," refusing to
twist facts so as to accord with the views of the party in power. It
was for his alleged partisanship that she rebuked Hume, otherwise
considering him a man of genius. Not that he was a toady, but that
"He entertained prejudices inimical to that candour which must
have placed him at the head of all our historians." [37]

The result was that Macaulay characterized her heroes and vil-
lains with more vehement "impartiality" than one might wish.
Where Hume and others had sullied, she would cleanse. She did try
to nuance her portraits a little: for instance, Cromwell's heart was
selfish and corrupt, but his military ability was "a splendid part of
his character." On the whole, one learns much from Mrs. Macaulay
about events, less about purposes other than those that emerge
from the flawed characters of political leaders or the varying loyalties, "the whims and errors" of the multitude.[38]

Mrs. Macaulay's reputation spread to Paris, where she was fêted
and her works translated into French in the early years of the Revolution; and to the new republic of the United States, where she
visited President Washington and frequented the circle of Mercy
Otis Warren in Milton, Massachusetts. The reputation of her much
younger contemporary, Madame de Staël (see Plate 9), extended
from the United States, where she had many friends and even investments, to Russia, where she traveled in triumph at the same
time that her enemy Napoleon embarked upon his losing battle
there. The daughter of Jacques Necker, wealthy Swiss banker and
several times director general of finance for Louis XVI, Anne-
Louise-Germaine Necker passed her girlhood amid the political
and philosophical argumentation of her mother's salon. As a young
adult she saw her father first as the hero of the Third Estate in the
early months of the French Revolution, and then saw him super-
seded and forced into exile as the Revolution moved to the left.
Here began her own long political career, carried on alternately
from Paris and from exile in Switzerland. She worked on her own,
through her writings, and through her friends and lovers (she and
her husband, a Swedish diplomat, were cheerfully unfaithful to
each other). Always she defended with ardor what she saw as "lib-

erty"—that is, moderation and reasonableness—first against the artificial and hierarchical society and arbitrary government of the Old Regime; then against the uncivilized and vulgar excesses of the Jacobins; and then against the new tyrant Napoleon. Though preferring constitutional monarchy, she did not oppose republican government in itself, so long as it succeeded in stimulating morality and decorum.[39]

The extent to which political and cultural engagement had moved Madame de Staël beyond the old limits of "family history" and the memoir is well illustrated by her *Considérations sur les principaux événemens de la révolution françoise.* Written in 1816 toward the end of her life and published posthumously in 1818, the work had been intended as a justification of her father. Through an examination of his political actions and writings, she would show that he had understood rightly the interests of the French people. Indeed, if the king had just followed Necker's advice and made the proper concessions in June 1789, the Revolution would never have occurred at all. But Madame de Staël the historical writer could not limit herself to her father; to her own dangerous escape from the republican crowds in Paris in 1792; or to the narrative, feelings, and political commentary of her own *Dix Années d'exil.* Her subject conducted her naturally to an examination of the fundamental political and social causes of the French Revolution, to contrasts between English and French institutions, to an examination of the major turnings of the Revolution through the demise of the tyrant Napoleon.[40]

Her work on the French Revolution is clearly very different from Macaulay's history of the English Revolution. The *Considérations* are an analysis by a widely read actor, while the solid pages of Mrs. Macaulay are lacking in any serious speculation about underlying causes. Madame de Staël is the first of our women historians to write the "philosophical history" that so delighted the eighteenth century. Indifferent to research and to masses of detail, one reflected on the stages of historical progress, on the effect of climatic and especially political and social institutions on literary culture and national character. Certain of her theories are well known and were very influential in her own time—such as her contrast between the rationalist, witty, sensuous culture of the Latin South and the emotional, melancholy, impractical culture of the German North.[41]

Her views on the place of learned women in different political societies, however, are more striking and have a bearing on the tale we are following here. For Madame de Staël there is no longer any problem at all of the learned woman's estrangement from her subject. She can be a historian or any other kind of writer she wishes. But she is still in a strained relation with her audience. In part it was the fault of the women, the timidity of even the most distinguished of them in the face of malevolent criticism. "Il y a toujours un peu de coquetterie dans les services que rendent les femmes," she had said, "puisqu'elles cherchent ainsi à se faire aimer" (There's always a little coquetry in the services performed by women, for they seek thereby to make themselves loved). Though she claimed that once her own works were printed she no longer bothered herself about how they were doing, she was in fact sensitive to the furor caused by her writing. In part it was the fault of the audience. In monarchies, the woman of great talent must fear ridicule. There the etiquette of place is so firmly established that if anyone steps out to do something extraordinary, he needs an excuse, like duty. Men find excuses easily enough, de Staël went on, concealing their desire for applause behind the appearance of noble and virtuous passions. A woman cannot, and if she writes, it is just assumed that she wants to show off. The public knows it can do without her, withholds its approval, and impresses on her with harshness her dependence.

The duchess of Newcastle would have understood this, dubbed "Mad Madge" as she was by those who mocked her for love of glory. Catharine Macaulay would have understood too.

In a republic, in principle, men and women should be able to share philosophy and literature. In fact, things were little better. Since the Revolution—Madame de Staël was writing this in 1800— men had reduced women to the most absurd mediocrity, addressing them in the crudest of language and trying to limit the sphere of their thought. The minute a woman did anything "distinguished," the public was warned against her. Of course a superior man terrified the public too, but at least he had a *career* ahead of him to which he could put his talents and by which he could ultimately acquire power and make the jealous fear him. But a learned woman was not called to a career: all she could do was offer the public the new ideas and elevated sentiments it did not want to hear. Learned men, astonished to have female rivals, responded to them with hate.[42]

At any rate, during the next 150 years it became possible for women historians to have careers of a sort, as the market for popular histories and school textbooks widened; as historical teaching, research, and writing were professionalized; and the universities were even opened to women. But the important contribution of women to historical scholarship in these years and the problematic nature of their relationship to the historical profession is beyond the scope of this essay.

It is time now for us to draw some conclusions. From Christine de Pisan to Madame de Staël, we have seen some women try their hand at varied genres of historical writing, from the domestic history to the national history, from the biography and memoir to philosophical history. They found ways to use certain manuscript collections despite their sex, but evidently did not have the kind of entrée or resources to make possible the great scholarly editions of the male religious orders, such as the Maurists. (The Ursulines, for instance, may have been too caught up in the practical tasks of teaching girls to imagine such an erudite enterprise for themselves, and their houses would have had much smaller libraries than the old Benedictine foundations.) The time span of the female historical writers stretched back more than three hundred years, though, Mademoiselle de Lezardiere apart, few of them ventured into ancient history or early Christian history, which had their learned male historians. (Female scholarship on the classical world or on early antiquities was of a literary or philosophical kind: Anne Lefevre Dacier translating and commenting on Greek poetry and Greek and Latin comedy; Elizabeth Elstob preparing a grammar of Anglo-Saxon, the "Mother-Tongue" of the English; and Elizabeth Carter, translating and commenting on Epictetus.[43] Perhaps, as the duchess of Newcastle said, it still seemed somehow "inconsistent with . . . being a woman to write of wars . . . between Medes and Persians, Greeks and Trojans.")

The "circumference of truth" of the learned women was ex-

panded, so I have suggested, especially through their establishing
strong connection with political events, which male historians had
as a matter of course because of their vocation, training, duties, or
offices. If the political stance of the females differed, we have heard
one common note in the voice of the three major figures, Christine
de Pisan, Catharine Macaulay, and Madame de Staël—a note of
passion, almost tinged with prophecy, as they plead for peace or
impartiality or liberty or justice. Male historians could also speak
for their values with ardor; but the women seem to regard themselves as special truth-tellers, even when they worry that their facts
will not be believed.[44]

It would be a mistake, however, to assess the achievement of
these early female historical writers only in terms of some hierarchy of genres, in which general or national history is at the top
and particular history is at the bottom. Particular history has some
of the advantages that Margaret Lucas claimed for it: it can be
densely textured, persuasive, and in its concreteness and intimacy
full of surprises about how the past was actually experienced. The
temporal rhythms that emerge from domestic life or the life of
small units are sometimes very much in tension with those that
govern the rise and fall of monarchs and parties. So, too, conflicts
and solidarities, across or between classes and generations, can
often be properly understood only when examined up close in the
small circle. The kind of historical consciousness evidenced in the
"particular histories" by women and men in the early modern period is one of the paths leading to the genre of social history.

However diverse in their historical interests and style, the writers we have looked at here had one point in their orbit where they
all slowed down to reflect. All of them were conscious of the relation of their sex to their work; and all of them somehow took up
women as subject—whether in their self-presentation to their readers in words or pictures (it was rare for a female historical writer to
conceal her identity before the end of the eighteenth century) or in
writing tracts on the education of females or in including and commenting on women in the historical record.[45] Indeed, I do so myself
in this essay. I suspect, as did Virginia Woolf before me, that gen-
der and genre will continue to have some linkage for a while; that
for a while Cities of Ladies will still be constructed, from which

women can assure an orbit not too restricted, a revolution not too slow, and an ever widening circumference of truth.

Notes

1. George Ballard, *Memoirs of British Ladies who have been celebrated for their Writings or Skill in the Learned Languages, Arts or Sciences* (Oxford, 1752), pp. 299-306. He also mentioned the unpublished family history of Anne Clifford, Countess of Pembroke, "a most critical researcher into her own life . . . [and] a diligent enquirer into the lives, fortunes and characters of many of her ancestors" (p. 314). L'Abbé Joseph de La Porte, *Histoire littéraire des femmes françoises* (Paris, 1769). Louise de Keralio, *Collection des meilleurs ouvrages français composés par des femmes* (Paris, 1786-88).

2. A. Labarre, *Le livre dans la vie amiénoise du seizième siècle* (Paris, 1971), pp. 226-30; H. J. Martin, *Livre, pouvoirs et société à Paris au XVIIe siècle (1598-1701)* (Paris, 1969), pp. 197-206, 840-48. Leonardo Bruni, "Concerning the Study of Literature, A Letter to . . . Baptista Malatesta," in W. H. Woodward, *Vittorino da Feltre and Other Humanist Educators* (1897; repr. N.Y., 1963), p. 126: "Rhetoric in all its forms—public discussion, forensic argument, logical fence and the like—lies absolutely outside the province of woman." He did think women should read history books, however, "to understand the origins of our own history" (p. 128).

3. *Fénelon on Education*, trans. H. C. Barnard (Cambridge, 1966), p. 86. Lawrence Stone, *The Family, Sex and Marriage in England, 1500-1800* (New York, 1977), pp. 353-54. L. Abensour, *La femme et le féminisme en France avant la Révolution* (Paris, 1923), pp. 43-45.

4. B. M. Stearns, "Early English Periodicals for Ladies, 1700-1760," *Publications of the Modern Language Association* 48 (1933): 38-60. Evelyne Sullerot, *Histoire de la presse féminine en France des origines à 1848* (Paris, 1966), pp. 29-30.

5. Edward Gibbon, *Memoirs of My Life*, ed. G. A. Bonnard (London, 1966), pp. 72-76.

6. Mark Phillips, *Francesco Guicciardini: The Historian's Craft* (Toronto, 1977), p. 120; and more generally, Felix Gilbert, *Machiavelli and Guicciardini. Politics and History in Sixteenth-Century Florence* (Princeton, 1965), and John Pocock, "England," in Orest Ranum, ed., *National Consciousness, History and Political Culture in Early-Modern Europe* (Baltimore, 1975), chap. 4.

7. Abensour, *La femme et le féminisme*, pp. 324-40. Marie de Rabutin-

Chantal Sévigné, *Lettres*, ed. Gérard-Gailly, 3 vols. (Paris, 1953-57), 1, no. 138, letter to her daughter of August 5, 1671.

8. Margaret Lucas, Duchess of Newcastle, *The Life of William Cavendish Duke of Newcastle*, ed. C. H. Firth, 2d ed. (London, n.d. [1914]), p. xl.

9. The first edition of Anna Comnena's history was published in Greek in 1610 by David Hoeschel, who had found the first eight books in Munich: *Alexiados Libri VIII. De Rebus a Patre Gestis Scripti* (Augsburg, 1610).

10. Among several studies on Christine de Pisan, see Mathilde Laigle, *Le Livre des Trois Vertus de Christine de Pisan* (Paris, 1912); Marie-Joseph Pinet, *Christine de Pisan, 1364-1430. Etude biographique et littéraire* (Paris, 1927); C. C. Willard, "The Manuscript Tradition of the Livre des Trois Vertus and Christine de Pizan's Audience," *Journal of the History of Ideas* 27 (1966): 433-44; and Suzanne Solente, "Christine de Pisan," in *Histoire littéraire de la France*, published by the Académie des Inscriptions et Belles-Lettres (Paris, 1824-   ), 40: 335-422 (includes full bibliography). Christine de Pisan, *Lavision-Christine*, ed. M. L. Towner (Washington, 1932), p. 163.

11. Christine de Pisan, *Le livre des fais et bonnes meurs du sage roy Charles V*, ed. S. Solente, 2 vols. (Paris: Société de l'Histoire de France, 1936-40), p. 5; Pinet, *Christine*, pp. 99, 273. See also the range in her self-presentation in her epistolary debate with Jean de Montreuil and Pierre and Gontier Col over the *Roman de la Rose:* from "femme ignorant d'entendement et de sentiment legier" to "ta bienvueillant amie de science, Christine de Pizan" (C. F. Ward, "The Epistles on the Romance of the Rose and Other Documents in the Debate." Ph.D. dissertation, University of Chicago, 1911). E. Nys, *Christine de Pisan et ses principales oeuvres* (Brussels, 1914), p. 75.

12. Christine de Pisan, *Charles V*, 1: 7-10, and the excellent introduction to this text by Suzanne Solente, pp. xxvi-ciii. Christine had recently presented to Duke Philip her *Livre de la mutacion de Fortune*, a long philosophical and moral poem, which includes some material on ancient empires.

13. I have benefited from discussions with Jeffrey Richards about Christine's prose style. Eustache Deschamps, "Ballade MCCXLII: Réponse à une epitre de Christine de Pisan," *Oeuvres complètes*, 6 (Paris, 1889). Alfred Coville, *Gontier et Pierre Col et l'humanisme en France au temps de Charles VI* (Paris, 1934), pp. 202-4. Christine de Pisan, *Lavision*, p. 143; *The Cyte of Ladyes*, trans. Bryan Ansley (London, 1521), fols. Ff i-Ff ii, Ff iv^v-Ii iv^v.

14. *Vie de Charles V dit le Sage, Roy de France, Ecrite par Christine de*

Pisan, Dame qui vivoit de son tems in M. l'Abbé Lebeuf, *Dissertations sur l'histoire ecclésiastique et civile de Paris* (Paris, 1743), 3. Lebeuf used a fifteenth-century manuscript, which had been part of the library of Mazarin and was then acquired by the Royal Library under Colbert (Sol-ente, "Christine," p. 380, who also lists other manuscripts).

15. Donald Kelley, *The Foundations of Modern Historical Scholarship: Language, Law and History in The French Renaissance* (New York, 1970).

16. Examples of this work by medieval nuns: Hroswitha's history of her abbey at Gandersheim, *Primordia Coenobii Gandeshemenis* (before 968) and the life of Adelaide (late tenth century), first abbess of Willich, by Bertha, nun of Willich in the first half of the eleventh century.

17. Françoise-Madeleine de Chaugy (1611-80), *Mémoires sur la Vie et les Vertus de Sainte Jeanne-Françoise Frémyot de Chantal, Fondatrice de l'Ordre de la Visitation Sainte-Marie*, ed. T. Boulangé (Paris, 1843); *Les vies de VIII venerable veuves, religieuses de l'Ordre de la Visitation Ste Marie* (Annecy, 1659); *Les vies de sept religieuses de l'Ordre de Visitation* (Annecy, 1659). Chaugy has been the subject of a biography by E. Lecouturier, *Françoise-Madeleine de Chaugy et la tradition Salésienne au 17e siècle* (Paris, 1933). *Chroniques de l'ordre des Ursulines recueillies pour l'usage des religieuses du même ordre, par la M.D.P.U.* [la Mère de Pom-mereu Ursuline] (Paris, 1673); *Journal des illustres religieuses de l'ordre de Sainte-Ursule . . . tiré des chroniques de l'ordre et des mémoires de leur vie, composé par un religieuse du même ordre au monastère de Bourg-en-Bresse* (Bourg-en-Bresse, 1684-90). See Mère Marie de Chantal Gueudré, *Histoire de l'Ordre des Ursulines en France*, 1 (Paris, 1957).

Angélique de Saint Jean Arnauld d'Andilly (1624-84), comp., *Mémoires pour servir à l'histoire de Port Royal et à la vie de la Reverende Mere Marie Angelique de Sainte Magdeleine Arnauld* (Utrecht, 1742.)

18. *La guerre et deslivrance de la ville de Genesve. Fidèlement faicte et composée par ung Marchant demourant en icelle* (n.p., n.d. [Geneva, 1536]), reprinted by A. Rilliet in *Mémoires et documents publiées par la Société d'histoire et d'archéologie de Genève* 20 (1881): 309-84. *Le Levain du Calvinisme ou commencement de l'heresie de Genève. Faict par Rever-ende Soeur Ieanne de Iussie, lors Religieuse à Saincte Claire de Genève, et apres sa sortie Abbesse au Couvent d'Anyssi* (Chambéry, 1611), repr. by A. C. Grivel (Geneva, 1865). In England, one Anne Dowiche, wife of a minis-ter of Devon, published *The French Historie. That is; a lamentable Dis-course of three of the chiefe, and most famous bloodie broiles that have happened in France for the Gospell of Iesus Christ* (London, 1589). Based on French sources, this is a description in verse of the events on the rue Saint Jacques, the execution of Anne de Bourg, and the massacres at Paris

on St. Bartholomew's day. I am grateful to Barbara Rosen for this reference.

19. For background and bibliography on the genre of family history, see N. Z. Davis, "Ghosts, Kin and Progeny: Some Features of Family Life in Early Modern France," in Alice Rossi et al., eds., *The Family* (New York, 1978), pp. 96-100.

20. Charlotte Arbaleste (d. 1606), *Mémoires de Madame de Mornay*, ed. for the Société de l'histoire de France by Madame Henriette de Witt, née Guizot, 2 vols. (Paris, 1858-59). The memoirs had partial posthumous editions in the seventeenth century under the title *Mémoires de messire Philippe de Mornay, seigneur du Plessis-Marly, baron de la Forest sur Sèvre* from 1624 on.

21. *Mémoires de Madame de Mornay*, 1: 1-4; 2: 111.

22. *A True Relation of my Birth, Breeding and Life*, by Margaret, Duchess of Newcastle, first published as Book XI of her *Nature's Pictures* (1656); repr. by C. H. Firth along with her *Life of William Cavendish* (n. 8, above), pp. 149-78. For further information on the duchess, see Firth's Preface pp. xxv-xxxii; Joyce Horner, *The English Women Novelists and their Connection with the Feminist Movement*, in *Smith College Studies in Modern Languages* 11 (Northampton, Mass., 1929-30); and Douglas Grant, *Margaret the First, A biography of Margaret Cavendish, Duchess of Newcastle, 1623-1673* (London, 1957).

23. Newcastle's advice to the king, from "a little book wherein he delivered his opinion concerning the government of his dominions" (Firth, Preface to *Life of William Cavendish*, pp. xxii-xxiii).

24. Lucas, *Life of William Cavendish*, pp. *xxxv-xlv*. The work was first published under the title *The Life of the thrice Noble, High and Puissant Prince William Cavendishe, Duke, Marquess, and Earl of Newcastle . . . Written by the thrice Noble, Illustrious, and Excellent Princess, Margaret, Duchess of Newcastle, his wife* (London, 1667). A second edition was printed in 1675, and a Latin translation appeared in 1668. Lawrence Stone points out that the duchess was "demonstrably untrustworthy in her use of figures" and exaggerated the amount spent by her husband on entertaining his sovereign (*The Crisis of the Aristocracy* [Oxford, 1965], p. 453).

Annabel M. Patterson, *Marvell and the Civic Crown* (Princeton, 1978), pp. 221-29.

25. *Memoirs of the Life of Colonel Hutchinson by his widow Lucy*, ed. C. H. Firth (London, 1906). The work was first printed in 1806, edited by J. Hutchinson, and is worthy of study in its own right.

26. On all of this material, see the excellent study of Marie-Thérèse Hipp, *Mythes et réalités. Enquête sur le roman et les mémoires (1660-1700)*

(Paris, 1976), esp. pp. 58-67, 132-94, 227-47, 263-73, 450-72. Lennard J. Davis is writing a book on the fluid boundaries between factual and fictional narrative in seventeenth- and eighteenth-century English prose; it appears that aristocratic women contributed less actively to this process than in France. Madame de Lafayette, *Histoire de Madame Henriette d'Angleterre, Premiere Femme de Philippe de France* (1st printed ed., 1720; Amsterdam, 1742), Preface; *Mémoires de la Cour de France pour les années 1688 & 1689* (Amsterdam, 1742). See also R. Francillon, *L'oeuvre romanesque de Madame de Lafayette* (Paris, 1973), pp. 117-27. *Mémoires de Mademoiselle de Montpensier* (1st printed ed., incomplete, 1718; first complete ed., 1728), in Petitot, ed., *Collection des mémoires relatifs à l'histoire de France*, 40-43 (Paris, 1824-25): "Il est vrai que dix-sept années de discontinuation de tout ce qui s'est passé pendant cette interruption peut m'avoir ôté le souvenir de beaucoup d'affaires. Comme je n'écris que pour moi, l'exactitude m'en paroît moins nécessaire" (42: 418); "J'écris ceci avec complaisance pour moi-même; je veux que ceux qui liront les maux que l'on m'a faits et que j'ai soufferts en aient compassion" (42: 120); the entry into Orléans (41: 179-80).

27. Gwendolyn B. Needham, "Mary de la Rivière Manley, Tory Defender," *Huntington Library Quarterly* 12 (1948-49): 253-88. Lady Mary Wortley Montagu (1689-1762), *Letters of the Right Honorable Lady M . . . y W . . . y M . . . e: written during her travels in Europe, Asia and Africa (London, 1763); The Genuine Copy of a Letter Written from Constantinople by an English Lady* (London, 1719). Lady Mary was also a political essayist. Celia Fiennes (1662-1741) prepared her travel accounts for publication, but they were not printed until 1888, long after her death.

28. Marguerite de Lussan (1682-1758), *Anecdotes de la Cour de Philippe Auguste* (1733); *Anecdotes de la Cour de François Ier* (1748); *Annales galantes de la Cour de Henri II* (1749); *Histoire et Règne de Charles VI* (Paris, 1753); *Histoire et règne de Louis XI* (Paris, 1755); *Histoire de la Revolution du Royaume de Naples, Dans les Années 1647 & 1648* (Paris, 1757); and other works. *Histoire de la ville de Cherbourg et de ses Antiquités, Qui découvre des Faits très-importans sur l'Histoire de Normandie; Par Madame Retau Dufresne* (Paris, 1760), Preface. [Marie Geneviève Charlotte d'Arlus, 1720-1805, wife of Lazare Thiroux d'Arconville], *Vie de Marie de Médicis, princesse de Toscane, Reine de France et de Navarre* (Paris, 1774), Preface. Madame d'Arconville also published a *Vie du Cardinal d'Ossat* (1771), and *Histoire de François II, roi de France* (1783), as well as several scientific works and novels. Marie-Charlotte-Pauline-Robert de Lezardiere (1754-1835), *Théorie des loix politiques de la monarchie françoise*, 4 vols. (Paris, 1792). (I am grateful to Donald Kelley for calling this work to my

attention.) Mlle de Lezardiere used as her sources the printed collections in her father's chateau in Poitou and those of his friends, such as Malesherbes, who became her patron and saw the first edition of her book through the press. The posthumous 1844 edition of the *Théorie* included materials from the ninth to the fourteenth centuries, though much of her documentation had been lost when the family chateau was burned during the Revolution.

29. Catharine Sawbridge Macaulay, *The History of England from the Accession of James I to that of the Brunswick Line*, 8 vols. (London, 1763-83). On Catharine Sawbridge Macaulay (1731-91), see Lucy Martin Donnelly, "The Celebrated Mrs. Macaulay," *William and Mary Quarterly* 6, 3d ser. (1949): 173-207; Bridget and Christopher Hill, "Catharine Macaulay and the Seventeenth Century," *Welsh History Review* 3, no. 4 (1967): 381-402; Lynne E. Withey, "Catharine Macaulay and the Uses of History: Ancient Rights, Perfectionism, and Propaganda," *Journal of British Studies* (Fall 1976): 59-83.

30. Macaulay, *History of England*, 1: vii, xiv.

31. For instance, *Loose Remarks on Certain Positions to be found in Mr. Hobbes Philosophical Rudiments of Government and Society. With a Short Sketch of a Democratical Form of Government in a Letter to Signior Paoli* (London, 1767); *An Address to the People of England, Scotland, and Ireland, on the Present Important Crisis of Affairs by Catharine Macaulay* (Bath and London, 1775), an attack on oppressive British policy toward the American colonies; *Observations on the Reflections of the Right Hon. Edmund Burke on the Revolution in France, in a Letter to the Right Hon. Earl of Stanhope* (London, 1790), a defense of the aspirations, if not the executions, of the French Revolution; *Letters on Education with Observations on Religious and Metaphysical Subjects by Catharine Macaulay Graham* (London, 1790).

32. Macaulay, *History*, 1: x-xviii, 6, Preface, dated January 1781 (Hume had died in 1776).

33. Dictionary of National Biography, 11: 407-9. "Account of the Life and Writings of Mrs. Catharine Macaulay Graham," *The European Magazine* (November 1783): 330-32, including long quotations from Hume's published letter to her of March 29, 1764.

34. Ibid., p. 332.

35. *History*, 1: x; 6, advertissement. Before vol. 6, her notes included both brief references to sources and dates in the margins and long, interesting footnotes, expanding on the text, listing parliamentary acts, adding sources, and the like. From vol. 6 on, there are only the brief marginal notations. On the significance of footnotes for creating tension with the

historical text, or introducing other voices into it, see Stephen Bann, "A Cycle in Historical Discourse: Barante, Thierry, Michelet," *Twentieth Century Studies* 3 (May 1970): 110-30; Lionel Gossman, *Augustin Thierry and Liberal Historiography* (History and Theory. Studies in the Philosophy of History, Beiheft 15, no. 4 [Middletown, Conn., 1976]), esp. pp. 45-55.

36. *The History of England from the Revolution to the Present Time in a Series of Letters to a Friend* by Catharine Macaulay (Bath and London, 1778), pp. 30, 181, 270. Dr. Wilson was very troubled by her marriage to William Graham later that same year, and removed the statue of her as "History," which he had placed in St. Stephen's.

37. *History of England from the Accession of James I*, 1, Introduction; 6, Preface: 499. In a recent work Leo Braudy talks of Hume's "narrative detachment" and of his intense dislike of the work of "party-historians" (*Narrative Form in History and Fiction: Hume, Fielding and Gibbon* [Princeton, 1970], pp. 36-37).

38. *History of England from the Accession of James I*, 5: 214 ff. *History of England from the Revolution*, pp. 216-17. Bridget and Christopher Hill stress, however, the value of her description of the social origins of the Revolution. "It is derived from Clarendon, but she makes her own sense of it" ("Macaulay," p. 392).

39. Among the large amount of biographical and critical writing on Madame de Staël, there is a standard biography by J. Christopher Herold, *Mistress to an Age: A Life of Madame de Staël* (Indianapolis, 1958), and a fascinating book by her close relative and dear friend Madame Albertine Necker de Saussure, *Notice sur le caractère et les écrits de Madame de Staël* (Paris, 1820). See also Madame de Staël's own *Dix Années d'Exil*, covering the period roughly from 1800 to 1804, 1810 to 1812, and published posthumously by her son in 1821 (modern ed. by Simone Balayé [Paris, 1966]).

40. *Considérations sur les principaux événemens de la révolution françoise ouvrage posthume . . . publié par m. le duc de Broglie et m. le baron de Staël*, 3 vols. (Paris, 1818). *Considerations on the principal Events of the French Revolution. Posthumous work of the Baroness de Staël . . . translated from the Original Manuscript*, 3 vols. (London, 1818).

41. As in her *De l'Allemagne* (1810).

42. Necker de Saussure, *Notice*, pp. xciv, cccli, cccxxi. Madame de Staël, *De la littérature considerée dans ses rapports avec les institutions sociales*, 2 vols., 2d ed. (Paris, 1800), vol. 2, chap. 4, pp. 141-59: "Des femmes qui cultivent les lettres." Madame de Staël's *Considérations sur . . . la Révolution françoise* was taken seriously enough by two male critics that it was immediately answered, which suggests that if she were "hated as a rival,"

she was also respected: *Examen critique de l'ouvrage posthume de Madame la Baronne de Staël, ayant pour titre: Considérations . . . par J. Ch. Bailleul, ancien Député* (Paris, 1818); *Observations sur l'ouvrage de Madame la Baronne de Staël, ayant pour titre: Considérations . . . Par M. de Bonald* (Paris, 1818).

43. Anne Lefevre Dacier (1654-1720), *Comédie de Plaute, traduite en François, avec Des Remarques et un Examen* (Paris, 1683); *Comedies Grecques d'Aristophane. Traduites en François, Avec des Notes Critiques* (1692); *Les poesies d'Anacreon et de Sapho, traduits de Grec en François, Avec des Remarques* (1699); *Les Comedies de Terence, traduites en François par Madame Dacier. Avec des Remarques,* 3d ed. (1700). Elizabeth Elstob (1683-1756), *An English-Saxon Homily on the Birth-Day of St. Gregory . . . Translated into Modern English, with Notes* (1709); *The Rudiments of Grammar for the English-Saxon Tongue* (1715)—"the language we speak is our Mother-Tongue; And who so proper to play the Criticks in this as the Females." Elizabeth Carter (1717-1806), *All the Works of Epictetus, which are now Extant . . . translated from the Original Greek* (1758); Catharine Sawbridge is among the list of subscribers to this work.

44. I have considered the role of the female as "truth-teller" in festive and popular life in my essay "Women on Top," *Society and Culture in Early Modern France* (Stanford, 1975), chap. 5.

45. Marie Dentière presented herself as a "merchant" in the title of her *Deslivrance . . . de Genesve,* but in 1536 this was a book that could have got its author burned. Madame Thiroux d'Arconville did not put the author's name on the title page of her *Vie de Marie de Médicis* in 1774, nor did Mlle de Lezardiere in her *Théorie des lois politiques* of 1792, a dangerous year for such a book. Apart from these cases, the women historians insist on their identity, even to including author portraits. This is in contrast with the practice of Marie de Flavigny, comtesse d'Agoult (1805-76), who wrote her interesting *Histoire de la Révolution de 1848* and other works under the name Daniel Stern. It would be interesting to see what effect, if any, this assumed identity had on the historian's voice.

In addition to the work of Christine de Pisan on the training of women (*Le livre des trois vertus*), Catharine Sawbridge Macaulay also wrote on female education. Her treatment of females in her historical text varied from harsh words for the strong-willed Queen Elizabeth and the weak-willed Queen Anne to praise for the women petitioners to the House of Commons in 1641 (*History of England from the Accession,* 1: 2, and 3: 198, *History of England from the Revolution,* pp. 84, 185-86).

Index